"The First Day of the Week" Scripture or Tradition?

REVEALING FATHER'S CALENDAR
AND HIS DIVINE APPOINTMENTS

Mark R. Heston
Foreword by Obadyahu ben Yosef

outskirts
press

"The First Day of the Week" Scripture or Tradition?
Revealing Father's Calendar and His Divine Appointments
All Rights Reserved.
Copyright © 2017 Mark R. Heston
First Edition, 2007
v7.0

The opinions expressed in this manuscript are solely the opinions of the author and do not represent the opinions or thoughts of the publisher. The author has represented and warranted full ownership and/or legal right to publish all the materials in this book.

This book may not be reproduced, transmitted, or stored in whole or in part by any means, including graphic, electronic, or mechanical without the express written consent of the publisher except in the case of brief quotations embodied in critical articles and reviews.

Outskirts Press, Inc.
http://www.outskirtspress.com

ISBN: 978-1-4787-7307-8

Cover Photo © 2017 thinkstockphotos.com. All rights reserved - used with permission.

Outskirts Press and the "OP" logo are trademarks belonging to Outskirts Press, Inc.

PRINTED IN THE UNITED STATES OF AMERICA

DEDICATION

This treatise is dedicated to all Berean students willing to investigate the ancient languages beyond the modern constraints, and proclaim the verifiable truth regardless of social or physical consequences, when so led by the holy Spirit.

"In past generations He allowed all the nations
to walk in their own way; yet
He did not leave Himself without witness …"

Acts 14:16,17

"For nothing is hidden, except to be revealed;
nor has anything been secret,
but that it should come to light."

Mark 4:22

Table Of Contents

Foreword i
Preface v
Acknowledgements vii
Explanation Of Terms ix
Commonly Used Abbreviations xi
"The First Day Of The Week" Scripture Or Tradition? xiii
    Introduction

Chapter 1 ~ *The First Day Is After The Seventh Day* 1
    Two Greek Words 3
    What's Greek For "Week" 4
    "To The Jew First, Then To The Greek" 4
    A Transliteration 5
    The Temple Restored 6

Chapter 2 ~ *Nothing New Under The Sun* 11
    Sabbatone / Sabbaton 13
    Verses In Question 14
    Question Authority 16
    Change Definitions To Establish Traditions 18

Chapter 3 ~ *Mark Your Calendar* 23
    Perfect Timing 25
    Justification By Calendar 32
    Fact, Fiction, Or Fraud 36

Chapter 4 ~ *Presto Chango* 43
    Tradition Magicians 45
    The Tragic Magic 47
    "Mia," "Mia" On The Wall 48
    The First "First Day Of The Week" 49

Chapter 5 ~ *Lost In The Translation* 53
    Multinational Transliterations 55
    The Institution Of Substitution 56
    Objections Overruled 59
    Black Sabbath 63
    Interlinear Comparison 64

Chapter 6 ~ *The Third From The Fourth* 67
    "Let God Be True, But Every Man A Liar" 69
    "The Third Day" 70
    The Sign Of Jonah 72
    Inclusive Reckoning 74
    Pope Dope 78

Chapter 7 ~ *Right On Time* 79
    Extra-Biblical Extras 81
    Re-Pentecost 84
    At One-Ment 87
    Blue Moon 88
    The Twilight Zone 90

Chapter 8 ~ *Word Surgery* 93
    The Shell Game 95
    "Precept Upon Precept; Line Upon Line" 95
    "Not By Bread Alone, But By Every Word" 99
    "The First Shall Be Last; And The Last Shall Be First" 106
    "On The Time Appointed" 108

Chapter 9 ~ *Two-Edged Sword* 117
    "Faithful Is He That Calleth You" 119
    "For The Time Is At Hand" 122
    The Warning 125
    Other 7th Day Sabbath Events In The OT 128

Chapter 10 ~ *His Way Is Perfect* 133
    "Thy Word Is Truth" 135
    "In The Fullness Of Time" 141
    Blood Moon 152

Figure 1. – 364 Calendar As Given Back To Moses In Exodus 12 157

Figure 2. – The First Year Of Creation - The First Year And The Eighth Year 158

Figure 3. – The Seventh Year 159

Appendices 161
    Appendix A: Evaluation Of The Term "New Moon" 163
        Verse Studies 169
    Appendix B: Sabbasi / Sabbasin = Feast Of Weeks 173
    Appendix C: As To The First Adam, So To The Last 175
        Now For The "Rest" Of The Story 187
    Appendix D: Preparation/ Sabbaton/ Preparation/ 7th Day Sabbatone 192
        Literal Translations --In Mt, Mk, Lk, And Jn. 193
    Appendix E: The Time & Season Of Our Savior's Birth To Secure
        The Sabbatical Year 194
    Appendix F: Seven Forms Of The Greek "Sabbaton" - G#*4521* [G#*4315*] ... 197
    Appendix G: Is King James Your King? 198
    Appendix H: Embriological Celebration 209

References
    Bibles: 213
    Concordances: 214
    Dictionaries & Commentaries: 214
    Other References: 215

Index 217

Personal Notes 231

Foreword

"Then Jesus said to those Jews who believed Him, 'If you abide in My word, you are My disciples indeed, and you shall know the truth, and the truth shall make you free.'

They answered Him, 'We are Abraham's descendants, and have never been in bondage to anyone. How can you say, You will be made free?'

Jesus answered them, 'Most assuredly, I say to you, whoever commits sin is a slave of sin, and a slave does not abide in the house forever, but a son abides forever. Therefore, if the Son makes you free, you shall be free indeed" (John 8:31-36, KJV).

"But, he that doeth truth cometh to the light, that his deeds may be made manifest, that they are in God" (John 3:21, KJV).

"Jesus answered, 'I am the way, the truth, and the life. No one comes to the Father except through me'" (John 14:6, KJV).

In years past, during the 1960's and 1970's, there was a Christian college program called "Search for Truth" wherein the student was to learn and come to the knowledge of the "Truth." Yet, for the genuine Truth-seeker their questions would still echo the words that Pilate put to Jesus, **"What is Truth?"** (John 18:38). This treatise by Dr. Mark Heston, entitled "The First Day of the Week, Scripture or Tradition? – Revealing Father's Calendar and His Divine Appointments," has brought forth great enlightenment in the restoration of hidden understandings on the 7th day Sabbath and the feast sabbaths with the true solar calendar prophesied by Enoch, used by Noah, Abraham, Yitshac (Isaac), and Ya'acov (Jacob), which was given back to Moshe (Moses), and followed by all the prophets and kings in the Old Testament.

Mark Heston has done some remarkable language research regarding this question of the Sabbaths and their relationship to the solar 364-day calendar, as an intercalated 360-day calendar of Scripture, outlined in the book of Enoch, and extolled in the book of Jubilees, with a pattern matching dates in our present day Bible translations. Truth beyond what even Samuele Bacchiocchi declared in his book "From Sabbath to Sunday" (1977, A Historical Investigation of the Rise of Sunday Observance in Early Christianity, Rome, Italy: The Pontifical Gregorian University Press). This work that was entrusted to Dr. Heston to describe should be distributed to every sincere student of the Word that the Truth of all the Sabbaths be as it was, and meant to be in these last days. The paganized substitutions and their false dogmas that have twisted the Holy Scriptures to morph into traditional translations for so long, will succumb to this scrutiny of Scriptural sleuthing. Alas, these are not without persecution. Authenticity is generally rebuked before the coveted traditions, and the bearer thereof is typically discredited to more easily ostracize.

This was the case with Mark Heston in his attempt to share these truths with several Sabbath-keeping groups as these grounded, Scripturally-based concepts went counter to certain traditions. Over the years, a few opportunities were given to Mark to present his findings, and today a remnant of true-calendar believers continues to expand; as even most who have known Mark would describe him as a sincere student, a meticulous researcher, and a passionate gifted teacher. As Paul the apostle wrote to Timothy, Mark Heston has heeded the admonition to present himself:

> ***"To God as one approved, a worker who does not need to be ashamed and who correctly handles the word of truth… Nevertheless, God's solid foundation stands firm sealed with this inscription: '[Yahuweh] knows those who are his,' and everyone who confesses the name of [Yahushua] must turn away from wickedness" (2 Timothy 2:15, 19, NIV).***

In respect to the above statement, I highly recommend every one of the following pages to you the reader. Search out the gems of "Truth" herein with fear and trembling, listening to the voice of God our Savior, as Dr. Heston unscrambles the ***truth of the*** *sabbaths* and ***the 7th day Sabbath,*** and presents YHVH's true calendar of perfect Sevens (364 days) in disparity to the Jew's inconsistent lunar calendar only found to be taught in the Talmud. There is a conspiracy to ***change times and laws,*** (Dan 7:25), but the false ***pen of the scribes*** (translators) ***are in vain*** (Jer 8:8), and becomes evident as the true feast sabbaths begin to unfold, to expose the pagan dogma behind the counterfeit days of worship.

All blessings to you dear reader from our everlasting Father, and may this increase your Holy Faith as you study this Biblical exposition.

Elder Obadyahu ben-Yosef

March 8, 2016

Preface

After some 15 years as a born-again Christian, there was a nagging concept that began to frustrate me, as earlier searches for an answer came to no avail. This concept was the only sign our Savior gave to the Pharisees that the Son of Man would be "three days and three nights in the heart of the earth" (Mt 12:40). The conventional belief that this phrase was congruent with the Friday crucifixion and Sunday Resurrection did not rest well with me, and I was bidden more strongly to look deeper.

The explanation given by one church that our Savior started the three days and three nights in the garden of Gethsemane, with the agonizing weight of the world's sin and His "sweat was as it were great drops of blood falling down to the ground" (Lk 22:44) the day before His crucifixion did not sufficiently resonate with my more recent Bible studies. The "great drops of blood," conjectured to initiate His being "in the heart of the earth," was especially highlighted as a false theory when I came to understand that for the Jew, to be officially declared dead, one had to be dead for "three days and three nights" (1 Sam 30:12, etc.). If our Savior was taken off the cross and placed in the grave on Friday afternoon, and supposedly resurrected just before the morning of "the first *day* of the week," then at best we only have two days and two nights, and the Savior of the world would not have had an official resurrection by His own standards.

I had heard of a Wednesday crucifixion to Saturday afternoon resurrection model from a couple of different sources, but each Saturday afternoon resurrection, on both accounts, were inferred to be exactly 72 hours simply because our Savior said "three days and three nights" (Mt 12:40), without any consideration to the ancient use of inclusive reckoning. Both groups mention that the empty tomb was not found by the disciples until the morning of the "first *day* of the week," which makes for too long a time from the "great earthquake" (Mt 28:2) for them to so determine. After sufficient cognition was given to these teachings, I wound up throwing my hands in the air, praying to Father one last time to bring me to the truth on this problem, and I then proceeded to other doctrinal studies that were summoning my attention.

Nearly eleven months later, in May of 2002, I was at a home church meeting where a lay-scholar by the name of Curtis McDonald had been invited to address our small gathering in Redding, California. This very unassuming gentleman proposed a Biblical scenario to the three-days-and-three-nights I had never heard of before; yet once he clarified a couple of elements for me, the other pieces of the puzzle I had previously determined fell into place and made perfect sense.

His presentation was in conjunction with an introduction to what I came to recognize as the one Bible-based calendar that in turn clarified the date and time of our Savior's prophecy in the Hebrew Old Testament, and verified this punctuality in the Greek New Testament; as opposed to the passive reliance upon mainstream translations. He also showed how these numbered days of the week had compatible significance to the meaning of the numbers for the Hebrew, and I saw their time-matching events of the day synchronize; making this time-piece worthy of further investigation.

I wound up studying with this rather insightful believer and his pleasant wife in their Sacramento home quite a number of times as he mentored me on these truths, and acquainted me with other like believers. Many a Sabbath day was spent searching the Scriptures together, each of us learning from the other, and over many months our small Sacramento group began to cement several of these, now, immoveable stones of truth that are found in this paper.

It was the intent of this writer, who by the awe-inspired fascination with the beautiful consistency of our Heavenly Father, to express these gleaned gems and ancillary principles in significant detail for the serious student.

May the reader be attended with the added measure of faith as these explanations are comprehended and may His Divine Spirit fill your heart to so reflect His glory in unapologetic worship back to our Heavenly Father and contribute to your soul preparation for these coming last days.

Acknowledgements

The holy Spirit initiated this work through the insistent encouragement of James "Ya'acov" Russell, whose passion for truth as a fellow layman has always invigorated my spirit and bolstered my faith.

Special appreciation to Curtis McDonald, who first introduced me to several of these concepts, and whose quiet, rational, and patient approach caused me to give them some consideration; to his sweet wife Teresa, a vibrant example of discipleship and hospitality in action.

To Ken Davidson, my friend and mutual nature-lover, a Buddhist Monk whose intellect and exegetical skills helped to bring this paper to a deeper level in these ancient languages, and who now teaches his followers the real truth of the seventh-day Sabbath.

To Fritz Alseth and Charles "Bud" Compton for their untiring collaboration in validating the etymology of this study, and for their analysis of the Dead Sea Scrolls calendar in conjunction with the prophetic account of the Passion week.

To Devon Tassen, founder and leader of a Messianic assembly, for his broad knowledge of the Scriptures, his objective insight, and willingness to consider all available resources broached upon the Hebrew language.

To Lew White, for helping modern Ephraim with the 3rd Angel's Message and for listening to his readers with each new edition of his book.

To Ray Foucher, for validating the Hebrew in Leviticus 23 and quoting commentary for a second witness.

To Larry Ing, for his enthusiasm in contributing many hours of editing and evangelizing the two earlier editions.

To Obadyahu ben-Yosef, for his reliance upon YHVH in taking hold of His true calendar, even after many years as a traditional Messianic leader, and for acting upon the Divine urge to set up our first website.

And to the many other brothers and sisters in the remnant faith who read the earlier editions and have expressed their gratitude for having the scales fall from their eyes to see the awesome depth of harmony and consistency come from our Heavenly Father's Word.

Explanation Of Terms

"**God**" is used solely for its common recognition in the English for the Almighty Creator, being aware of this transliteration from pagan sources, yet used as a title as opposed to a name, and is tolerated by this writer in text format for the sake of the majority of readers.

[(Recognize that some names of pagan elohim's are included in Scripture, but likely not read aloud (Nu 22:41; 1 Sa 5:5; Ez 8:14; Ex 23:13)].

"**Our Savior**" "**Messiah**" "**Advocate**": Titles are used as opposed to the traditional name "J-e-s-u-s" which comes from questionable Latin sources, transliterated into most languages across the globe. The use of the true name, without adequate deliberation, may jade some seekers, and even some name followers; so the true Name, as understood by this writer, was chosen not to be included. For those willing to study such a topic, *Fossilized Customs* (see Bibliography) is a good place to start. For those more seasoned, *What Is His Name?*, by J.C. Green, New Beginnings Pub., Waynesville, N.C. (1995).

"**YHVH**" is the English consonant equivalent of the Hebrew letters for the true Name of the Supreme Sovereign, Creator of the Universe, our Heavenly Father. This is referred to in the Greek as the "Tetragrammaton," meaning "four letters," for the early Greek manuscripts of even the Gospels and the Epistles, when they were transposed from their original Hebrew to Greek, they retained the four Hebrew letters of the Father's Name, יהוה. (In some ancient Hebrew scrolls, even in paleo-Hebrew script.)

Some quotes are found in the text with **bolding**, and/or <u>underlining</u>, (parenthetical inclusions), or CAPITALIZATION that is/are supplied intentionally by the writer that the reader might more easily identify the point expressed, usually accompanied with: "(*Emphasis supplied*)."

Note that there are some grammatical and contextual differences between the actual spelling of the word catalogued in the concordance and that which is found in the interlinear copies of manuscripts, denoting specifics to the literary intent.

Commonly Used Abbreviations

(Acronyms listed in alphabetical order)

(CLNT) Concordant Literal New Testament,
(CVOT) Concordant Version Old Testament,
(HCSB) Holman Christian Standard Bible,
(HTT) Honest Truth Translation,
(IB) Interlinear Bible,
(JB) Jerusalem Bible,
(KJV) King James Version,
(LAP) Lamsa's Aramaic Peshitta,
(*lit.*) Literal translation utilizing IB Hebrew or Greek words
(NAS) New American Standard,
(NRP) New Race of People,
(YLT) Young's Literal Translation

BCE	Before the Christian Era	CE	Christian Era
DSS	Dead Sea Scrolls	Eng.	Summary in English
FF	First Fruits	NT	New Testament
OT	Old Testament	SI	Strong's Index
UB	Unleavened Bread	USNO	US Naval Observatory
X	Number of occurrences		

Strong's Abbreviations -

comp. = comparison
i.e. = *id est*, that is
e.g. = *exempli gratia*, for example
prim. = primitive
var. = variation
+ = (*addition*) a word in connection with the one in consideration
( ) = (*parenthesis*) denotes a word given in conjunction
[ ] = denotes the number of times a word is found in the Manuscript

uncert. der. = uncertain derivation
phys. = physical (-ly)
mor. = moral (-ly)
prop. = properly
cer. = ceremonial (-ly)
x = (*multiplication*) rendering that results with language idiom
denom. = denominative (-ly)
fig. = figurative (-ly)
lit. = literal (-ly)

Note: The Hebrew index numbers are in standard format, (i.e. H# 1234) and the Greek index numbers are in italics (i.e. G# *1234*).

"The First Day Of The Week" Scripture or Tradition?

Revealing Father's Calendar and His Divine Appointments

Introduction

Paul wrote to the Thessalonians, "…when ye received the word of God…ye received *it* not *as* the word of men, but as it is in truth, the word of God," (1 Th 2:13). Regrettably, the Word of God can become the words of men, simply by a few mistranslations. If there is anything Satan would try to falsify, it would be the greatest events in all of history for the distortion of foundational Biblical doctrine, to thwart the plan of salvation.

Our Messiah came to fulfill the original writings of the law and the prophets, right to the letter (Mt 5:17,18), that His disciples might gain "the full assurance of understanding, to the acknowledgement of the mystery of God" (Col 1:26; 2:2,3), glory in the Truth (Rom 9:23,24), and rejoice greatly over those who walk in Truth for the Truth's sake (2 Jn 1-4). For if something is made perfect, then nothing can be added to it to make it better, and nothing can be taken from it if it is to remain that way (Dt 4:2; Mt 5:18; Rev 22:18,19). Although man may attempt to add or remove for his own blindness, or conformity, our Father is without shadow of turning (James 1:17), and does not change (Mal 3:6), simply because His ways are perfect from the beginning (Ps 18:30, 19:7; 2 Sa 22:31).

As expected, after the days of the early disciples there came the suppression of Truth, later, versions of Truth, and today, confusion of Truth. One might think that with all the research and discoveries over the years, producing volumes of references, theologians would be more united in their understanding today. Then again, there has always been the laying aside of the commandments to hold the traditions of men (Mk 7:8).

Yet, as a witness, our Father has maintained down through the ages, a self-learned remnant; who have been unleavened, willing to lay aside every weight (Heb12:1), who have sacrificed positions of honor within their church and community to satisfy a true hunger and thirst for all that is righteous (Mt 5:6). Trusting in God rather than man (Ac 5:29), enduring persecutions and counting all things but loss for the excellency of the knowledge of our Savior Messiah (Ph 3:8); knowing that our Father had purposely hid things from "*the* wise (sophisticated) and prudent (cunning), revealing them unto 'babes'" [Gk#*3516*], or those less formally trained (Mt 11:25; 21:16; Lk 10:21).

Therefore, as prayerful and humble workmen that need not to be ashamed, let each one of us rightly divide the Word of Truth (2 Ti 2:15). Not that prophecy of the scripture is of any private interpretation (2 Pt 1:20), but by two or three witnesses (verse by verse) shall every word be established, that we might prove our own selves in the faith (2 Col 13:1,5); earnestly contending for that faith which was once delivered unto the saints (Jude 3); to assure our hearts before God (1 Jn 3:19).

For if we believe that the Spirit of Truth will guide us into all truth (Jn 16:13), then, in asking, we should prove all things, including our preconceived notions, and hold fast to that which is good (1 Th 5:21); even if it means to challenge the very translation of certain texts from Bibles we have learned to trust. This is why multiple Bibles, concordances, and other ancillary resources have been facilitated here to properly solve these few equations. As the resultant material set forth in the following pages is very in-depth with the attempt to root out all areas of concern regarding these topics; every rock and pebble is turned over to leave no doubt as to their consistent outcome. The approach to the information is done sequentially; in most areas defining the dots and then connecting them, so that the concepts might begin to take shape toward the latter chapters.

To make a more simplified presentation would not do appropriate justice to these Words of our Savior and His disciples. There are particular Words shrouded in tradition to their own distorted adulteration that without the extensive detailed analysis would cause some to perceive it as just another weightless argument.

The reader who is intent on understanding is encouraged to have one or two Bibles handy, and a concordance if possible, when reading this study as many passages and their various words are cited to verify the presented points. Because each of us, as a body of priests (Rev 5:10), need to show ourselves approved unto God (2 Ti 2:15); it would be best to read this book in segments, not reading more than a chapter at one time, unless you are more than familiar with some of the information. Do not be discouraged if you find you have to review some sections two or three times, for this is a concentrated work and paradigm shifts require the tedious job of intricate dissection and patience.

May the sincere student prayerfully enter into this research, and allow the Almighty to help them glean, from the ancient writings of Scripture, the true meaning of these Heavenly Words, that they might be better prepared to receive a greater out-pouring of His Spirit at His scheduled time.

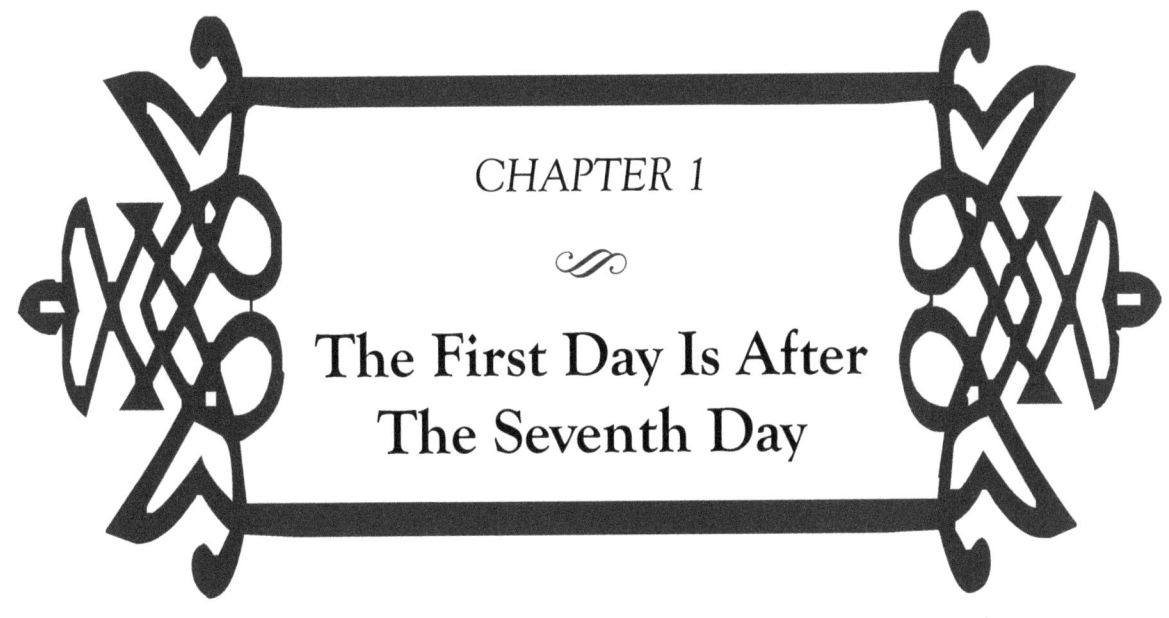

CHAPTER 1

The First Day Is After The Seventh Day

Two Greek Words

This phrase, "the first *day* of the week," is found only in the New Testament (NT). The Greek index of any concordance reveals essentially two words for this phrase: "**μια σαββατον**" (Strong's *#3391* and *#4521*) [mia sabbaton], or "**εισ σαββατον**" (*#1520*) (*#4521*) [heis sabbaton], depending upon the manuscripts origin. "Mia" is understood to be the feminine form of "heis," and "heis," is primarily found in translation as the Greek cardinal number "one." "Mia" is consistently seen in our phrase "the first *day* of the week," in any concordance for the King James Version (KJV). "Heis" is typically seen in "the first *day* of the week" in alternate Bible concordances, such as those for the NIV or NASV, and the newest Strong's called the Strongest Strong's. All the other editions of Strong's are based on the KJV, and have "heis" listed in other verses as "a prim. numeral." The Strongest Strong's index lists the interpretations by the number of times they are found. The following table will help us see the first inconsistency (*Emphasis supplied*).

Earlier STRONG'S	STRONGEST STRONG'S
G#*3391* **Mia** a (certain), + agree, **first**, one, x other.	G#*3391* **Mia** one, single, [no itemization]
G#*1520* **Heis** a prim. numeral; *one*: a (-n, -ny, certain), + abundantly, man, one (another), only, other, some.	G#*1520* **Heis** one, single; one [289], a [13], **first** [8], some [6], the other(s) [6], certain [5], any [2], an [2], man [2], another [1], only [1], . . .

Notice that **Heis** is not translated "first" in the earlier Strong's, and **Mia** is not translated "first" in the Strongest Strong's. Is "first" truly a proper translation of these two related words, or are the translators obliged to their publishers, so as not to rock the boat of tradition? Note, that in comparing James Strong's concordance to the more recent one with his name on it (Strongest Strong's), there are different Greek manuscripts utilized. Only James Strong based his analysis on the KJV, which has a single line of manuscript.

What's Greek for "Week"

The Greek word for "*day* of," and sometimes "*day* of the" are found conjuncting "mia" and "sabbaton," and are not in contention here; with "*day*" supplied in the KJV to give the grammatical correctness in our language, (*italics* in the KJV denote added words in English). Ordinarily, the Greek word for "first" is "πρωτοσ"(protos G#*4413*), and the word for "week," as found in a Greek dictionary, can be either "εβδομασ"(hebdomas), or "εβδομαδα" (hebdomada), meaning "of seven" and "given by seven;" but neither (hebdomas) nor (hebdomada) are found listed in any Bible index because they cannot be found in any NT manuscripts. However, the word "εβδομαδα" (hebdomada) is found in ancient Greek literature, contemporary with the NT writing. The meaning of "sabbaton," as defined by early 20th century Greek-to-English dictionaries, is typically "Sabbath," with no other meaning listed. Yet all the major contemporary <u>Bible</u> dictionaries have translated this word as either "sabbath," or "week." Have both words "mia" and "sabbaton" been adulterated in Bible translation?

"To the Jew first, then to the Greek"

All the various Strong's indices (New Strong's, Expanded Strong's, etc.), that relate to the KJV, inform us that the King James translators rendered the Greek *sabbaton* (#*4521*) as "sabbath(s) [59X]," and "week [9X]." However, the earlier Strong's reveals that this word *sabbaton* is "of Hebrew origin [#7676]," meaning it came from, or had its roots in Hebrew. The Hebrew word #7676 is "שבת" (Shabbat, *shab-bawth*)[Hebrew is read from right to left]. Similar to the Greek pronunciation, it is defined in Strong's to be "the seventh day of the week… as a day of rest and worship," with nothing in the Hebrew index to indicate its use or relation to *week*. Even more similar to the Greek is the related Hebrew word #7677 "שבתון" (shabbatone, *shab-baw-thone*), which means "holy day," or "rest." Neither definition makes any reference to seven consecutive days to comprise a week.

Since #7676 is defined specifically as a seventh-day of rest, with no mention of its use as a holy feast day; and #7677 is defined as a holy rest day, with no indication listed to mean simply a seventh-day of rest; we could read contextually all the Old Testament (OT) *shabbats* and *shabbatones* by locating them with our concordance, just to verify, and we would find that *shabbat* does indeed refer solely to the weekly seventh-day Sabbath, and *shabbatone* specifically to resting, and the holy ceremonial feasts. Here is a summation of all the Hebrew *Shabbats* and *shabbaton/es* found in the OT Scriptures, utilizing a Strong's concordance; substantiated with the use of a Young's concordance as a second witness.

#7676 - "*shab-bawth*" - "sabbath" **70**x's + "sabbath<u>s</u>" **34**x's = **104** *shabbat(s)*

#7677 - "*shab-baw-thon*" - "sabbath" **3**x's + "rest" **8**x's = **11** *shabbaton/e*

When #7677 is "rest" it always accompanies a #7676 and is "shabbatone," when not joined with a #7676 it is "sabbath," pronounced "shabbaton," the difference of a vowel point in modern Hebrew, denoting a "feast" sabbath. These three (3) "shabbaton" are all found in Leviticus 23, each specifically a feast not meant to fall on a 7th day Sabbath. These 3 are the feast of Trumpets, and the first and last days of Tabernacles, as holy convocations (Lev 23:24,39,39). This distinction in proper Hebrew will help us further validate our Greek.

In the NT, there are seven (7) forms of the Greek *sabbaton* (*#4521*) (see "Interlinear Comparison," p. 65 and Appendix F). Interestingly enough, some are more phonetically similar to the Hebrew forms of *shabbat* and some to *shabbaton/e*. For instance, two of the seven Greek forms relate particularly to Hebrew feast days, and, as might be suspected, are linguistically identical to their Hebrew counterpart, *shabbaton/e*-- in the Greek, *sabbaton* and *sabbatone*. Considering the fact that the ancient Greeks had no "sh" sound; by "Hebrew origin," the seven Greek forms of *#4521* should actually be classified as "transliterations" from the Hebrew, as opposed to these forms having some unassociated etymology.

A Transliteration

To transliterate (L. *trans* - carry across, *littera* - letter of the alphabet) is to carry a word into another language phonetically, using the corresponding characters of even a different alphabet to represent the same or similar sound. In so doing, this same word continues to retain all its inherent meanings from the previous language; no meaning is added, and nothing is taken away; literally carrying the word across into a new language.

Consequently, the base forms of *sabbat* and *sabbatone* should both be listed numerically in the Greek NT index as they are in the Hebrew OT index; *sabbat* only for the seventh-day Sabbath, and *sabbaton/e* for rest and the holy feast sabbath. This would certainly eliminate some of the confusion, as presently both the seventh-day Sabbath and the feast day sabbath are lumped together and simply translated "sabbath(s)" in both the Old and New Testament. This difference in the Greek is noted more plainly in the Young's Concordance, but without definitions, leaving the reader to make the observation.

The Temple Restored

The fact that there is no distinction made between the feast sabbaths and the seventh-day Sabbath in either the translations, or the more commonly used Strong's Greek index, with no definition even in Young's derivations; relates to the reluctance of the ruling authorities to allow the Word of God translated into the common languages; yet our Father has caused them to leave a trail of evidence.

Their use of the term "versions" should alert us as a clue to what they want you to believe; while so many mainstream denominations limit themselves to these versions and propagate shallow lesson studies accordingly; in some cases playing lip-service to many Christ-centered truths while discouraging, even demonizing, any deeper personal investigation of the Word of God beyond their theologian's commentary. If these words of our Savior, "by their fruits you shall know them" (Mt 7:20) are translated correctly, then maybe, knowing their fruits in other vineyards, we ought to be hesitant to fully accept their doctrine and "times and laws" (Dan 7:25) simply as printed - to do so would be to place our faith in the hands of others, when we are encouraged to "rightly divide the word" for ourselves (2 Tim 2:15).

To "rightly divide" means to "dissect correctly" (a single word in the Greek #3718 "ορθοτομεω - orthotomeo") in order to get to the core understanding; and you start by going through the earliest language, making a habit to check the references, and being attentive to any discrepancies. Just as any intricate detailed analysis takes more time, it does reveals more things. With a concordance, like Strong's, it's a matter of looking up a particular Bible word alphabetically, just as you would with a dictionary; then finding the index number, and locating this number in the appropriate index in the back of the book, find their definition, paying attention to the origins, and any relations listed, using the Hebrew Index for OT words, and the Greek Index just behind the Hebrew index, for NT words. (Young's does not offer indices.)

The earlier editions of Strong's, typically printings before 1986, are invaluable for their retention of derivatives and root meanings with related index numbers listed; unlike the later Strong's, or other concordances, that give abbreviated information at best, besides the various words in translation.

The First Day Is After The Seventh Day

Recognizing in the Strong's, on a given index number, after the terms of definition are the English words as they were determined by King James and his translators. Not that most of the words are purposely changed, for by and large the KJV is a reasonably-well translated version of the Bible; certainly in respect to many contemporary versions which have utilized questionable manuscripts, but when it comes to certain words in verses that may relate to "times and laws" where doctrinal points and traditional concepts might be taught, we should be watchman on the wall. This would include the common misconceptions that we will investigate here, that both the Hebrew feasts and the seventh-day convocations were entirely done away with at the cross, begging the proper meaning behind this term "mia" "sabbaton."

Though all the sacrifices down through the ages had prefigured our Savior's crucifixion (Rom 3:23-25), the question might be asked, "Are we to discard these holy days entirely?" True, the veil in the Temple was rent, but the Temple withstood the earthquake. Though in metaphor our Savior talked of His body, "Destroy this temple, and in three days I will raise it up" (Jn 2:19), He had merely removed the wall of separation in the heavenly sanctuary (2 Cor.3:14-16), evidenced in the physical (Lk 23:45), and He became our "High Priest" (Heb. 8:3); and we, His "royal priesthood" (1 Pt. 2:9). As Scripture says, "By His own blood He entered in once into the holy place, having obtained eternal redemption for us" (Heb 9:12); in the "greater and more perfect tabernacle, not made with hands" (vs 11), as a minister of the true tabernacle (Heb 8:2).

For He continues to minister in our behalf (even today) "now to appear in the presence of God for us:"(vs 24), as the "one mediator between God and men" (1 Tim. 2:5). In this dispensation of time, with the glorified Son of the Father as our heavenly High Priest, ministering in the more perfect tabernacle before His Father; "Wherefore He is able also to save them to the uttermost that come unto God by Him, seeing He ever lives to make intercession for them" (Heb. 7:25).

With consideration to the ordinances of the earthly tabernacle made with hands; which was patterned after the heavenly, now elevated to a "more complete covenant, which has been established upon more complete promises" (Heb 8:6 HTT). This pattern included the ministration of the Sabbath, and the feast days, now in the tabernacle made without hands.

There are multiple accounts of the early disciples observing the feasts after our Savior's ascension, mentioned in the book of Acts, and the NT epistles. This is part of the ministerial work of our heavenly High Priest often overlooked.

Ac 2:1-4 - Pentecost outpouring
Ac 12:4,5,12 – "Passing-Over" of Peter on Passover (Easter) (Pascha).
Ac 15:20,21 – Gentiles accepted into fellowship to work toward Baptism, as Moses is preached on the "feast" sabbath
Ac 16:13 – a feast sabbath where prayer was "wont" or customary
Ac 18:4 – a feast sabbath
Ac 20:6 – "<u>unto</u> the days of unleavened bread"
Ac 21:21 – Paul falsely accused doing away with the customs of Moses
(21:26-28) – As custom, Paul took the four Greeks for 7 days of purification
Rom 11:16 – Firstfruits heave (sheave) offering is holy
1 Cor 16:2 – "Upon *a particular 7thday feast,*
…let each one lay by in store
Heb 10:25 – "Not forsaking the 'assembling of <u>ourselves</u> together'" all Hebrew congregations in one place.
Jude 12 - The ungodly "are spots in your feasts of charity, when they feast with you."

Ac 6:14 – Stephen falsely accused of a "change of the customs" of the feasts
Ac 13:13,14 – John to Jerusalem for a feast. Paul to Antioch.
(13:27,42-54) - Gk "Sabbath" used are the feast forms.
16: 21 – Paul and Silas "teach customs" to Roman guards
18:21 – Paul: "I must keep this feast"
20:7 – "upon the 7th day feast Sabbath"
21:24,25 – Paul oversees rites of fellowship for the Gentiles -
Ac 29:9 – "<u>the</u> fast" refers to Day of Atonement

1 Cor 5:8 – "Let us keep the feast"
Col 2:16 – "Let no one ridicule you," in your obligation to a feast
(2:17) – "a shadow of things to come for the body of Christ."
2 Ptr 2:13 - false teachers deceive "while they feast with you."

There are many who would point to the "ordinances" being "nailed to the cross" (Col. 2:14), stating that these ("laws") were "abolished in his flesh" (Eph. 2:15), which has an influence to confirm other mistranslations. These two verses (discussed in the next section), like sandstone bricks in a weak foundation, will crack and crumble the traditional and familiar translations when they come under the objective scrutiny of the ancient languages. For an introduction, let us look at Heb 7:12 as it reads in the KJV: *(Emphasis supplied)*

"For the priesthood being **changed**, there is made of necessity a **change** also of the law" (KJV).

Appearing as if the law is abolished, yet our Father states that He does not change (Mal 3:6). A more accurate rendering of Heb. 7:12 is as follows:

"Because the priesthood has become **wholly established**, (and) by necessity so the law is wrought to **greater affirmation**, …" (HTT).

Quite a contrast from the mainstream translations, as the word "**changed**" in the Greek is:

G#3346 **Metatithemi** - [*meta #3326* beyond, belonging, with + *tithemi #5087*, commitment = **beyond commitment**], i.e. "**wholly established.**"

And the next word, "**change**," is a different word in the Greek:

G#3331 **Metathesis** - [*meta* - with, among + *thesis* – advanced position = **affirmed position**], i.e. "**greater affirmation.**"

In fact, Webster's dictionary defines in English:

"**metathesis** 1. Transposition of letters or sounds, insinuating a deeper meaning in a subject, or a higher key, or distinctive octave in music."

So both *metatithemi* and *metathesis* are not simply "change" as in the elimination of something; *meta*-carpals are belonging with, and more specific in function than the carpals; *meta*-morphosis is into a form of higher expression; *meta*physics, essentially, into the next dimension. In conjunction, *paren*thesis is "the placing of a word or phrase beside another in explanation, as in 'Jim (my son), is here.'", even in the following *paren*thesis (a clause added to give more detail, or greater explanation)!

So if the law had come to *greater affirmation*, maybe the feasts became of greater importance to the early disciples. Remember, our Savior came to "magnify the law, and make *it* honorable" (Isa 42:21).

However, even before King James, during the Dark Ages, many "Christian" leaders measured their success in establishing their interpretations in direct proportion to their keeping the true Words from the people. Not unlike the rabbis in the days of our Savior, for He said, "Do not think that I came to annul the Law, or the Prophets, I did not come to annul, but to perfect." He came to clarify the law, and to establish the prophecies spoken of Him, "Till the heavens and earth pass, in no way shall one iota or one tittle pass away from the Law, until all comes to pass." (*lit.* Mt 5:17, 18); as Paul points out that these feasts "are a shadow of things to come, for the body of Messiah" (Col. 2:17 HTT) [see "Question Authority," p. 17, under the context of **Col 2:14**].

Sabbatone / Sabbaton

Now let us determine which Greek forms of *sabbat / sabbatone* are found in each occurrence of the phrase, "the first *day* of the week." In the Gospels, most of these phrases refer to the time of our Savior's resurrection. Of the [8] "first *day*" phrases, [7] are *sabbatone* and [1] is *sabbatou*, which seems to indicate that possibly 7 of them relate to some holy feast day. To be certain these are referring to feast days, we should analyze all sabbatone(s) and all sabbaton(s) in the NT. All the NT feasts, specifically inferred, and called "sabbath" in the KJV, are either *sabbatone*, or *sabbaton*. These are First Fruits (FF), Unleavened Bread (UB) [Recall FF occurs during the week of UB], and Hanukkah. Here is an interlinear guide listing all the *sabbatone*(s) and *sabbaton*(s):

SABBATONE

Mt 28:1   de **sabbatone**   FF
Mt 28:1   mian **sabbatone**   FF
Mk 16:2   mias **sabbatone**   FF
Lk 4:16   tone **sabbatone** (holy feast?)
  *'as His custom was' as a layman
  reading in a synagogue*
Lk 24:1 mia tone **sabbatone**   FF
Jn 20:1   mia tone **sabbatone**   FF
Jn 20:19 mia tone **sabbatone**   FF
Ac 13:14 tone **sabbatone** (holy feast?)
  *(John went to Jerusalem, vs.13,
  Paul & his company to Antioch)*
Ac 16:13 tone **sabbatone** (holy feast?)
  *(to a riverside where prayer was
  "wont" or "customary")*
Ac 20:7 mia tone **sabbatone**   FF?
  *(Paul breaks bread w/ disciples reasons
  during UB) [lit. vs. 6 <u>unto</u> the days of UB]*
Col 2:16 he **sabbatone** (holy feast) *Let no
  man judge you in "feast" or "holy feast"
  –shadow of things coming*
1 Cor 16:2 main **sabbatone** (holy feast?)
  *According to the "sabbatone" let each
  lay by in store as God has prospered*

SABBATON

Mt 12:5 to **sabbaton** priests profane the *sab-
  baton* and are blameless"
Mk 2:27 to **sabbaton** "the *sabbaton* was made
  for man not man for the *sabbaton*"
Mk 15:42 pro**sabbaton** day before the 1st day
  of UB
Lk 23:54 kai(as) **sabbaton** 1st day UB
Lk 23:56 to men **sabbaton**   1st of UB
Jn 5:9 de **sabbaton** (holy feast Jn 5:1)
Jn 5:10 de **sabbaton** (same feast)
Jn 5:18 to **sabbaton** (same feast)
Jn 9:14 de **sabbaton** heals blind man *(Feast of
  Hanukkah)* with clay
Jn 9:16 to **sabbaton** this man not of God
  (Hanukkah) keeps not *sabbaton*
Ac 13:27 pan **sabbaton** voices of Prophets
  read every *sabbaton*
Ac 13:42 metaxu **sabbaton** Gentiles besought
  the word preached next *sabbaton*
Ac 15:21 pan **sabbaton** Moses preached
  every *sabbaton*
Ac 18:4 pan **sabbaton** Paul persuaded Jews
  & Greeks in synagogue every *sabbaton*

[6] of the [12] *sabbatone(s)* are known FF; [8] of the [14] *sabbaton(s)* are known feasts. After scrutinizing the remainder, it does seem feasible that these two Greek words could easily be transliterations from the Hebrew. For verification, let us take a closer look.

Verses in Question

[Mt 12:5; Mk 2:27] "to (on /the) **sabbaton**"- Two (2) of the *to sabbaton(s)* were known feasts (Jn 5:18; 9:16), as well as *to men* (even the) *sabbaton* (Lk 23:56). Regarding Mt 12:5, remember the 7th day Sabbath is one of the Ten Commandments. The feast days were not part of the Decalogue, thus the priests could *profane* or "work" on the holy feast day and be *blameless*, or without sin. In Mk 2:27, our Savior was correcting the Pharisees, who made both the *shabbat* and the *shabbaton/e* a burden with their traditions (Mt 23:6; Lk 5:29, 30; 14:12-14, Jn 5:1,16). The *feast* days, with their sacrifices and offerings, were for the redemption of man (Lev 1:4; 4:20, 31; 6:7 etc.); which is why our Savior told the Pharisees, "the holy feast day was made for the sake of man, not man for the sake of the holy feast day."(*lit.* Mk 2:27). "The seventh-day is the 'Shabbat' of the Lord thy God" (Ex 20:10; Dt 5:14), and was referred to by our Father as "My Shabbats" (Ex 31:13; Lev 26:2 etc.). Please note that each time the Pharisees accused our Savior of misrepresenting the "sabbath" our Savior was actually fulfilling prophecy from the Torah, not the Talmud (Mt 12:2; Mk 2:24; Lk 6:2; Ac 9:16, etc.), which at the time were oral traditions.

[Acts 13:14] "tone (of the) **sabbatone**" - Three (3) times in a year, all Hebrew men were required to appear before their God in a place of His choosing (Ex 23:17, Dt 16:16). These three were the Feast of UB, (includes Passover and FF), the Feast of Pentecost, and the Feast of Ingathering, or Tabernacles; and it was customary, since the time of David that all men go to Jerusalem (also Jn 5). Prior to David taking the throne, they met in Mizpah. On the feast in Acts 13, John went to Jerusalem, and as Antioch was becoming a center for Christianity, Paul and others had gone there.

[Jn 9:14] "de (and a) **sabbaton**" - The healing of a man blind from birth was accomplished during the feast of Lights or Dedication, called Hanukkah (extends to Jn 10:22 "the feast of the dedication, and it was winter"), and our Savior said, just prior to opening the mans eyes, that He was "the 'Light' of the world." (*Emphasis supplied*)

[**Acts 13:27; 15:21; 18:4**] "pan (every) **sabbaton**" – From Acts 13:13,14, it seems likely the disciples are traveling in preparation for a special convocation, and typically the "voice of the prophets" and especially the writings of Moses were expected to be read as these were the historical accounts on their given feast. "Pan," more accurately means, "all," as in a series of sabbaths, so "every 'sabbaton'" is more precisely "all feast sabbaths" (*lit*.). Moses was not always read every 7th day Sabbath, but certainly on "all" the feast times.

[**Acts 13:42**] "metaxu (next) **sabbaton**" - "metaxu" (#3342) is "between [6x]." In your KJV margin for "the next Sabbath" is *"in the week between,"* or *"in between the week,"* as feast sabbaths generally occur. In Acts 15, as head of the Jerusalem council, James recommends the Gentile believers to abstain from idols, fornication, food strangled, and blood as initial guidelines for fellowship (vs.13-21), and encourages their attendance in a synagogue on any or "all" "sabbat<u>on</u>," to learn more of the ways of Moses, in preparation for baptism. Synagogues were unlike the Temple, as these were under the direction of Jewish laymen, and sacrifices were never offered. Chiefly, they were places for a congregation to conduct readings, exposition, schooling, and some to administering justice. Therefore, these were ideal locations for Gentile believers to gain some understanding of the Torah and the prophets as a foundation of faith, and still maintain regular "Shabbat" attendance there with those who were Messianic and of some Jewish heritage.

[**Lk 4:16**] "tone (of the) **sabbatone**" – The OT portrays that only priests, or the king, were to read the law before all the people (Dt 31:11, Jos 8:35, 2 Ch 34:30, Ne 8:5-8). Since our Savior was to fulfill all that was written about Him (Lk 18:31; 24:44, Jn 15:25), His reading before the people of His hometown that day, early in His ministry, happened on the Day of Atonement feast, always meant to be on Shabbat as a seventh-day feast (more later). On this occasion, He read Isa 61:2 "To preach the acceptable year of the Lord." (Lk 4:19). The Day of Atonement, as a Shabbat, is the appropriate way to start the count to the next year in a sabbatical cycle (Lev 25:9, 10).

[**(Acts 16:13); Col 2:16**] "he (or) **sabbatone**" - Regarding the holy days, their accompanied feasts, and the beginning of months (see Num 28:11-14), they are a shadow of things to come, as they were so ordained under Moses (Col 2:17, Heb 8:5). The 7th day Sabbath was given from the foundation of the world, for all time (Gen 2:2, 3; Isa 66:22, 23), later written on stone by a Divine finger for the mixed multitude there and beyond. The ceremonial days, as commemorative rehearsals in the plan of salvation, were instructions written by inspiration and placed "on the side" of the Ark as a type and shadow (Deut 31:26). The word "wont" (nomizo *#3543*) means "customary," not compulsory, which typically relates to feast days (Lk 2:42; Jn 18:39).

[**1 Cor 16:2**] "mian (the-*singular*) **sabbatone**" - To "lay by in store as God has prospered" is considered a "freewill offering," at the disposition of the giver; as opposed to a tithe which was required as a tenth of one's increase; this calculated the day before a 7th day feast Sabbath. Freewill offerings are "a tribute of thine hand" brought upon a holy feast (Dt 12:6; 16:10, 16, 17). Recognize, "the" (mian) denotes a particular "sabbatone."

Now with one exception for Firstfruits (FF), and two for Unleavened Bread (UB), the entire determined FF's are "sabbatone," and all the determined UB's are "sabbaton." Each of the three exceptions is "sabbatou," known as being very early on the FF in Mk 16:1, 9, and Jn 19:31 (more detail later). In analyzing all the "sabbatou" [10X] contextually, it appears this form was used in reference to all holy convocations, both *sabbat*, and *sabbaton/e* together.

Therefore, it seems confirmatory that the Greek "sabbaton/e" reflect their Hebrew origin #7677, just as the Greek "sabbat" forms do with the Hebrew #7676. Remember, a true transliteration from one language to another adds no definitions in the new language, and takes no meaning away. Again, the reason for the confusion is relevant to the fact that the KJV "sabbath," an English transliteration from the Greek "sabbat," is inappropriately used for the holy feast days as just "sabbath," in both the OT and NT. With no English "sabbaton/e," this universal "sabbath" blurs the lines between the feast day sabbath and the 7th day Sabbath.

Question Authority

As most preachers and scholars teach that the Sabbath and the feasts have been done away with at the cross, they typically cite Eph 2:15 and Col 2:14 in their defense.

"Ephesian's tell us <u>what</u> was done away with at the cross. Enmity against the law. Colossians tells us <u>how</u> it was and is done. The sacrifice of (our Savior) upon the cross. 'And I will put <u>enmity</u> between thee and the woman, and between thy seed and her seed;

it shall bruise thy head, and thou shalt bruise his heel' (Gen 3:15). 'Because the <u>carnal mind</u> is <u>enmity</u> against God: for it is <u>not subject</u> to <u>the law of God</u>, neither indeed can be.' Rom 8:7" [C. McDonald, *Enmity, A Critical Review*, p. 1]. As man is made in the image of God, so the enemy of souls attempts to disassociate the two.

<u>Eph</u> <u>2:15</u> in the KJV reads:

"Having abolished in His flesh the enmity, *even* the law of <u>commandments</u> *contained* in ordinances; ... "

The NRP translation reads:

"Having <u>rendered inactive</u> through His flesh the <u>deep seated hatred against</u> the law and the commandments in binding legal decrees in order to recreate through Himself the two of us into one new race of people, *so making peace.*"

The JB has:

"actually <u>destroy</u>ing in his own person the <u>hostility</u> caused by the rules and decrees of the Law." (*Underlining's supplied*)

Neither the commandments nor ordinances were ever intended to be "abolished," but the "hatred" only. Nowhere in the OT is any Hebrew law ever prophesied to be done away with, or to be changed, but are promised unto "a thousand generations" (1 Chr 16:15-17).

<u>Col</u> <u>2:14</u> in the KJV reads:

"<u>Blotting</u> <u>out</u> the handwriting of <u>ordinances</u> that was against us, which was <u>contrary</u> <u>to</u> *us*, . . . <u>nailing</u> <u>it</u> to his cross."

The NRP has:

"<u>Blotting</u> <u>out</u> what the hand had written of the <u>indictments</u> (<u>sins</u>) <u>against</u> <u>us</u>, which was <u>accorded</u> <u>to</u> <u>us</u>, . . . yet <u>He was nailed</u> to a cross;"

The LAP has:

"And by his commandments he cancelled the written bond of our sins, which stood against us; and he took it out of the way, nailing it to his cross."

These three translations (NRP, JB, and LAP) are quite a bit different from the KJV on these two points. It appears it was just our sins and the guilt that was blotted out and abolished, not the feast or the law; as Paul continues in verses 16 and 17 (*Emphasis supplied*):

"So, do not let anyone condemn you in eating or in drinking (offerings), or in your obligations of a feast day, or of the new *month (service), or of the holy 7th day Sabbath feasts, which are a shadow of things to come for the body of Messiah." Col 2:16, 17 (HTT).

The early disciples did not follow the lunar calendar that the Jews have kept since their Babylonian captivity. All the patriarchs, prophets and kings; our Savior and His disciples determined their feasts using the same calendar God the Father gave us from the beginning; because he does not change (more on that later). But notice in this proper translation of Col. 2:16,17, the feasts are distinct from the weekly 7th day Sabbath, and are considered the pattern (shadow); for the form of "sabbath" used is *sabbatone*; confirming that the sanctuary services, in their proper timing, are still prophetic. *(see Appendix A)

Change Definitions to Establish Traditions

The significance of all the detail in this study is to demonstrate from the ancient languages that our Father stands behind His Words, and that no evidence can be found for a Sunday resurrection (Mt 28:1; Mk 16:9; Lk 24:1; Jn 20:1); for Sunday worship (Ac 20:7), Sunday offerings (1 Cor 16:2), or the doing away with the holy days for holidays, of which, none were ever intended to occur on a Sunday. A critical analysis of the Greek will prove our Savior's fulfillment of all the Hebrew prophesies spoken of Him, right on time, in accordance to the appropriate ceremony, on the proper day of our Father's calendar.

So to move on to the next consideration, let us try and rationalize the KJV translator's apparent explanation of their secondary definition of "sabbaton" in the Strong's (Gk *#4521*): "'week', or 'a *se'nnight*,' (seven nights) i.e. the interval between two Sabbaths."

"Se'nnight" is an old English slang with no relationship to counting the "days" to Sabbath in Greek or Hebrew. Remember the Greek word for "week" is "hebdomada" with no Strong's # because the true Greek word for "week" is not found in the NT, and in Hebrew the word for "week" is #7620 "שבוע" (shabua), with no transliteration between the two languages. Though "shabua" shares the first two Hebrew consonants with "shabbat" and "shabbaton," they are all three distinct fixed periods of time set by the Father.

If you turn to the word "week" in the concordance and read all the NT verses listed, an interesting pattern emerges. You'll find [8] of the [9] have the same phrase "first *day* of the" that precedes the common translated word "week;" conveniently referring to the venerated day of the Sun, strategically placed in these verses to counterfeit the greatest event to have ever occurred on planet earth, and to falsify prophecy, setting a precedent for Sunday worship and Sunday offerings. There is absolutely no difference in this Greek word they chose to call "week," and in other places translate "sabbath;" not by letter, context, or accent mark.

Even their defining term "between two Sabbaths," creates a problem when [6] of the Gospel accounts occur during the one "week" of UB (Lev 23:5-11) and has [3] "sabbaths" in that one week feast. Even with Firstfruits (FF) 7th day Sabbath between two holy feast convocations within seven days, as the FF 7th day Sabbath marks the beginning of the Feast of Weeks, a count of 7th day Sabbaths for seven weeks (Lev 23:15) leading to Pentecost, a week of weeks if you will; but this could not justify *sabbaton/e* as "week." Otherwise, their translation should be "the first *day* of the *feast of* week<u>s</u>."

Neither do any of the "week" words refer to the other feast of the year that lasts one week, - Tabernacles. Some of these hypotheticals may be a bit absurd, but merely as a final blow to this problem, for none of the scholars have a better answer than what is found in Strong's. Of the remaining [2] "first day of the week" accounts outside the Gospels; Acts 20:7 has translated in vs. 6 that UB just ended, and in 1 Cor 16:2, in the previous verse, they talk of the "collection for the saints" translated to the wrong day for what was intended. (More later).

Of interest here is that "saints" in the Greek, is another transliterated word from the Hebrew. The Greek word for "saint(s)" throughout the NT is the word "hagios" (*#40*). This word in the earlier Strong's has the inclusion "comp. 2282." This number, not italicized, refers you to the Hebrew index. Turning to #2282 in the Hebrew index, we find "hag" or "chag" in the earlier Strong's. (see "Faithful is He That Calleth You," p. 120) The transliterated Greek "hagios" (*#40*) [The Greek "h," is transliterated from the Heb "*ch*," a guttural "h" as in "Bach," (for the Greek has no guttural sounds.)] would be a person who keeps the Hebrew "hag," and the meaning of "hag" in Hebrew is listed as "solemn feast day." Therefore, by definition of origin, a "hagios," or "saint," in the NT, is a "feast-keeper," not a holiday follower.

Rulers and educators have learned, before the days of Rome, that if you control ones beliefs, you can manipulate ones thoughts, interests, and subsequent actions to some degree. In fact, "it has been said that whoever controls the calendar, its feast days and its rituals, controls the society" [Eisenman & Wise, *The Dead Sea Scrolls Uncovered*, p.78].

Today, we have elevated formal education to the level of specialization, where we have been conditioned to defer our thinking to the near-deified expert. This mind-set is no different than in the days of Rome when only the "clergy" were allowed to read and the people were kept illiterate, - the Latin word for clergy means "literate." Formidable leaders came to understand that to change the meaning of a word from another language was more convenient, to condition the beliefs and thinking of the people, than to corrupt manuscripts, or burn books.

So to be true to the laws of transliteration, neither *shabbat* nor *shabbatone* are ever used in its own language to mean "week." Consequently, the English "week" was never meant to be both seventh day and seven days. The English terms "sabbatical leave" and "sabbatical year" properly refer only to the seventh year of rest, not seven years of rest. (As "shabua" is not related to "shabbat"/"shabbatone;" so it is in Greek and English.)

Now there are a few Bible versions that do come close to a true translation of "mia sabbatone," such as "the first of the sabbaths" [see <u>Young's Literal Translation</u> (YLT), or <u>Green's Interlinear Bible</u> (IB)]. However, there is no evidence, in this context, that *sabbatone* can be plural ("mia" is specifically "singular," as we shall confirm later). Nor is there any consistency in the Greek index to denote the use of *mia* as "first," as we had shown, and will expand on. As alarmist as this next thought might sound, the translators are subject to their publishers, who are subject to their denomination, who are subject to the state, who are subject to higher earthly powers. As a final analysis of Gk*#4521* "sabbaton," we should look at the two remaining related words:

G#*4315* "**προσαββατον**" "prosabbaton" - "day before the sabbath [1X]"

G#*4520* "**σαββατισμος**" "sabbatismos" - "Sabbath rest, or observance, 'rest' [1X]."

We can see that "*pro*sabbat<u>on</u>" (Mk 15:42) relates more specifically to the day before a holy feast day, proved in its context, and "<u>sabbat</u>*ismos*" (Heb 4:9) refers to the act of resting on a single day; specifically a 7th day Sabbath, which really leaves no room for *#4521* to be translated "week."

CHAPTER 3

Mark Your Calendar

Perfect Timing

Keep in mind, the Gospels tell us that our Savior accomplished all the things prophesied of Himself (Lk 24:44,Mt 5:17), did them decently and in order (1 Cor 14:40); and that He was to anti-typically fulfill all the feast days perfectly (Heb 5:5-10;7:11;9:11), right on time (Ac 7:17,Gal 4:4,2 Th 2:6,1Pt 1:11,Dan 11:35). For these days reflect the same pattern of what God had done, is doing, and will do for His children, all in accordance with the covenant contract made in the OT (Ex 31:13, Col 2:16,17).

Therefore, since <u>all</u> things are according to our Fathers timing (Gen 21:2, Ex 9:5, 14; 23:15, Mk 1:15, Heb 8:5), and He has a reason for everything He does (Ecc 3:1,14,17;8:6), without change (Mal 3:6, Jas 1:17), and with perfection (2 Sa 22:31,33) - then perfect harmony would logically exist between the feasts, and their relation to the very day of the week they fall on. Each commemorative event had occurred as a proper and true appointment – such as the fall of man, the promise of redemption, the earth subdued by water, the everlasting covenant, deliverance from bondage, entrance to the promised land, the dedication of the Temple, the advent of our Savior, the start of His ministry, the timing of His miracles, to the day of His resurrection, and the ministration of His Spirit. Perhaps it is a similar sequence for the last days described in Daniel and Revelation, even to the establishment of the everlasting kingdom.

If this kind of perfection were possible at all, then the resurrection of our Savior had typified the FF timing to the exact day in the week of it's commencement. We will come to see that the children of Israel had rehearsed this event, each year, on the same day of the week, as well as the usual day of the month for centuries since they crossed the Jordan. If so, the calendar of Moses would not only have the same numbered day of the month as the book of Leviticus portrays, but each feast would correspond to the same day of the week, as the Hebrew will solve - to the same day of the week as the original event, celebrated that way consistently, perfectly, each and every year. This would epitomize what the Psalmist declares, "God, His way *is* perfect;" (Ps 18:30) and "Thy way, O God, *is* in the sanctuary:" (Ps 77:13), which essentially means that every "way" about the "sanctuary" is perfect, which should include the timing of the feasts, even to their origin.

This perfect calendar should have the same number of days for each of the four seasons, the same day of the week for each date of the 3 months in each season, while still keeping pace with the solar cycle. This calendar would have salvation significant feasts fall on the only hallowed and sanctified day of the week at the same time every year, and would never have any holy feast fall on a *first day of the week*. Otherwise this would construe credence of worship and certain symbology to the heathen Sun god, who reigns over all the other nations of the world. To maintain this consistency would establish a long-standing testimony before their neighboring countries for generations.

If any of His feasts ever fell on the venerable day of the Sun, then His "way" in the sanctuary could not be perfect. The seventh-day Sabbath is the only day that God had blessed and sanctified (Gen 2:3), and by it, promised sanctification to His people (Ex 31:12-17; Heb 4:1-9). For any holy convocation to fall on the day of the Adversary, would give ground to the enemy and rob us of the promised blessing and sanctification reserved for the 7th day Sabbath, which would include the Divinely-appointed feast days according to their appropriate commemoration – to be perfect, consistent, and predictable, as a Divine appointment should be, and so convey the true plan of salvation, to be the perfect pattern from heaven, for their perfect fulfillment on earth.

Well it just so happens, not too long ago, there was found a Hebrew calendar that fits these requirements; found in clay jars, in a few Middle-eastern desert caves, written on papyri rolls that are called the Dead Sea Scrolls (DSS). The only calendar sanctioned in these many writings, and mentioned extensively, is a 364-day calendar, which is equally divisible by seven; making every numbered day of the month fall on the same day of the week every year. That is 52 perfect weeks, 91 days to each season, with each day of the season having the same numbered day of the week, corresponding to the same numbered day of the month. This pattern repeats every 3 months (the more commonly recognized scrolls from the Dead Sea that refer to this calendar are the Books of Enoch and Jubilees) (see Figure 1 for a proper representation with the day of the week).

Though this calendar has been known by isolated groups to be used by the ancient Essenes, an ostracized sect that resigned themselves to living in the wilderness, it does place all the feasts consistently on the same day of the week for their numbered day of the month every year. This potentially lends a numerical significance to those particular days of the week, which, with the right start of the year, does happen to coincide with a correct gematria – the meaning of numbers to the Hebrew. Here are the meanings of the numbers 1 thru 7 as garnered from Scripture:

ONE - (1) - **unity** or **commencement**
TWO - (2) - **agree** or **disagree**
THREE - (3) - **completeness** or **resurrection**
FOUR - (4) - **earth** or ***(redemption)**
FIVE - (5) - **tabernacles** or **divine favor**
SIX - (6) - **man** or **preparation**
SEVEN - (7) - **spiritual perfection** or **life**

[Bullinger, E.W., *The Companion Bible*, "Appendixes to The Companion Bible," Appendix #10, p. 14] *[Ex 20:5; 22:1; 2 Sam 12:6; Lk 19:8]

In order for a numbered day to have spiritual representation in Scripture, it's contextual meaning would have to be consistent, and so the days of the week in a consistent calendar should match the same pattern. The true Coptic believers in Ethiopia, even today, understand this; for some of these same writings have been a part of their canon all along, as the majority of the saints there observe their feasts by this 364-day calendar.

This calendar always has 12 months only, in accord with Scripture; four (4) of which have one intercalary day (one additional day at the end of each season); that is 2 months of 30 days, and 1 month of 31 days, repeated every spring, summer, fall, and winter. We find in Genesis 7:11 and 8:3, 4, from the beginning of the flood in Noah's day, the following time-frame of the prevailing waters:

17th of the **2nd** month to the 17th of the **7th = 150 days ÷ (7 – 2) = 30 days / month**

The only pre-existing pattern known that has 5 consecutive months of 30 days is a 360-day calendar (12 months of 30 days). With no other indication from Scripture, we can deduce that the time-piece of one year delineated in the days of Noah was the same as that for Adam (Gen 1:14); which happens to be the same in the prophecies for the last days in Daniel and Revelation (1260 days = 42 months = 3-½ years = 360 days per year; Dan 7:25;12:11; Rev 11:2,3; 12:6,14; 13:5). (This is the origin of 360° in a full circle – from the anti-diluvian earth completing a cycle around the sun in so many days – see Figure 2).

Since God is the same yesterday, today and forever (Heb 13:8), and the fact that He does not change (Mal 3:6), is because His ways are perfect from the beginning (Ps 18:30). What He gave us in the beginning is what He intends to give back to us in the end; but because He does not change, He must have the same calendar today – and He does - only as an "intercalated" 360-day calendar (En 75:1). Four (4) days were added at the Flood of Noah because of the sin that brought about the four (4) seasons, one day of intercalation for each season; for we did not have any seasonal changes prior to the Flood.

Each season ends with a 31st day (Enoch 72:14, 20, 25, 31; Priestly Calendar Scroll). This is where the extra day is placed in respect to the 360-day calendar, and as each season is consistent, it should not be too surprising that a day intercalated for each season is always the same day of the week for each season, every year, and happens to be the 4th day of the week (Wednesday), as "4" means "redemption" for the seasons, as there are 4 of them. Keep in mind, the Hebrews only referred to the days of the week by their number, knowing their gematrial meaning, with the 7th day being the only one having a name, Shabbat.

Each season is 13 perfect weeks, each starting the same day of the week, and ending the same day of the week. To keep pace with the solar cycle, several scrolls of Enoch, also being found at the Dead Sea, had described that one week was to be added to the 364-day calendar every sabbatical year (En 10:2,3; 75:1; Ch 72-82 calendar chapters)[Council of Elders, *The Word of YAH, The King's Covenant*, p. 485]. This additional intercalation week, every seven years, would give an overall average of one extra day per year, giving an annual average over the seven years of 365 days. Yet still maintaining the same day of the week for each feast on the same numbered day of the month, year in and year out; as the numbered days of the month picks up where it was on the same day of the week, one week later, and keeping pretty close to the earths cycle about the sun. (see also 2 Chr 30:23)

To account for the remaining ¼ day a year (solar year = 365 ¼), it has been postulated by some scholars, and even some rabbis have made similar comments, that every seventh and possibly tenth sabbatical, the 50th (Jubilee) and 70th year (a Royal generation), the Essenes added two weeks to this calendar, instead of one (see Abegg, Flint, & Ulrich, *The Dead Sea Scrolls Bible*). On the average, this would compare with the actual solar cycle of 365.2422 days, to within seconds per year. As some scientists have submitted work that shows the earth has continued to slow down ever so minutely since the Flood, and this decline may have accelerated more so since the time of Moses; that they may not have had to do even a Jubilee intercalation in their day, as there is no evidence recorded to account for the quarter-day problem.

But all the prophets understood that any prophecy given was in respect to the 360-day year, and that any intercalations were not to be counted prophetically:

"And the leaders of the heads of the thousands, who are placed over the whole creation and over all the stars, have also to do with the **four intercalary days**, being inseparable from their office, according to the reckoning of the year, and these render service on the four days which **are not reckoned in** the reckoning of **the year**." Enoch 75:1 (*Emphasis Supplied*)

All the OT prophets knew of the writings of Enoch, and many a prophet was aware that sin would continue for 6000 years from Adam's fall (2 Ptr 3:8), which would lead into the Sabbatical millennium (Gen 2:17, 5:5; Rev 20:2-8 – [another study]), yet all intercalation was to adjust for the present solar year, that the 360-day model would remain the prophetic year, as it will be reinstated in the new earth. Today, some feast-keepers who follow this 364-day calendar are planning to add the two weeks on the 4th sabbatical (4 x 7 = 28 years); by appropriating one intercalation week after the week of Unleavened Bread (UB), and another intercalation week after the feast of Tabernacles. This would be the most optimal for redeeming the time in these last days ("4" *redemption* x "7" *spiritual life = spiritual life redeemed*).

Suffice it to say, with what we understand of this time measurement, our Father's feasts would never wander in the week as they do with the Babylonian-based lunar calendar, presently used by the rabbis and followed by the majority of Judaism since their captivity (see Figure 2). In comparison to all the known calendars over the ages, this Dead Sea Scroll calendar, as described, happens to be the most precise <u>and</u> consistent calendar known to man. It shows consistency with Scripture, and is being referred to by many more scholars because of this and its unmistakable presence amongst the Dead Sea Scrolls:

> "Adherence to a particular calendar is the thread that runs through hundreds of the Dead Sea Scrolls. More than any other single element, the calendar binds these works together. … No matter who wrote the scrolls or put them in the caves, the manuscripts … all embrace one particular type of solar calendar and its ancillary developments. Therefore, if we want to understand the Dead Sea Scrolls, we must come to terms with their system of measuring time.
>
> "The authors and readers of the scrolls differed from most Jews of their day in the importance they ascribed to the sun. The sun's annual journey

through the heavens was the basis for their calendar. Most Jews, in contrast, embraced a lunar calendar that was the primitive ancestor of the modern Jewish calendar. … The dispute – and it was a bitter dispute to judge from the polemics we read in the scrolls – was really about which heavenly body was more important. Logically, the more important body should rule, should govern sacred time. Would the sun and its cycle govern the festivals of Israel's sacred year, or would the moon have pride of place? The authors of the scrolls cast their vote for the sun." (Wise, Abegg & Cook, (1996). *The Dead Sea Scrolls*, p. 297).

These same scrolls mention that Abraham, Isaac, and Jacob, had kept the same calendar. This calendar the children of Israel had forgotten during their years of servitude to the Egyptians, until it was renewed for them through Moses, just before that last plague, the death of the firstborn, and was confirmed at the foot of Mount Sinai; placing each feast right on time again. This calendar, apparently used by Abraham, seems to be the same one given back to Moses, as is inferred in Ex 12:41 (*Emphasis supplied*):

"And it came to pass at the end of four hundred and thirty years, **even the selfsame day** it came to pass, that all the hosts of יהוה (YHVH) went out from the land of Egypt."

["YHVH," see "Explanation of Terms"] The word "selfsame" here in the Hebrew is "זה עצם" (zeh etsem) (#2088-6106) and means "exactly identical," and preceding the word "day" would refer to the same numbered day of the month, on the same day of the week. In addition, "zeh etsem" is listed 10 other times in the OT with "day;" 5 of these help establish a convincing supposition for a precise and consistent day of the week for each feast rehearsal, as these others should also be translated the "selfsame" day [Ex 12:17, 41; Lev 23:14; Jos 5:11; Eze 40:1].

The reason for the continued adherence to a lunar calendar by the Jews today is for the same reason most of Christianity worships on Sunday – tradition. Tradition is stronger than Truth amongst the majority, usually established by mistranslations, reinforced with misinterpretations, in order to keep the masses in "Babylon." For those actively pursuing the Word to confirm the Truth for themselves; when it comes to "times and laws" (Divine appointments and instruction - Dan 7:25), they need to "rightly divide" even the very individual Words, for the "full assurance of understanding" (Col 2:2).

For those trying to find the True calendar, most are derailed by the mistranslation "new moon" logically thinking, after seeing it in several translations, that it is properly translated. The unconscious assumption being that since this has been the understanding for so many centuries, apparently unchallenged, it must be right. Yet the two Hebrew words commonly referred to here are **"ראש חדש"** (rosh chodesh) (#7218-#2320), and its first occurrence is found twice in Ex 12:2:

> "This month *shall be* the <u>chief</u> of <u>months</u> for you. It *shall be* the <u>first</u> of the <u>months</u> for you." (*Underlined supplied*)

This is where YHVH returns His calendar back to the people, thru Moses, right on time. This same "rosh chodesh" is even translated "beginning of the month" in three (3) other Torah locations (Num 10:10; 28:11, 14), yet outside the Torah in twenty (20) other locations, they translate "chodesh" with "moed" (H#4150 - "appointed time"), with "yom" (H#3117 - "day"), or "hag" (H#2282 – "solemn feast"), to the monthly feast on the first of the month, but in each instance they call it "new moon" (complete study - see Appendix A).

The calendar that Abraham had, which he received from Shem, which Shem had since the days of the flood (Jubilees 6:24-30), which Noah received from Methuselah, who received the prophecy from his father Enoch (En 10:2,3; 74:9,10) are in several other Dead Sea Scrolls (DSS). This intercalated 360-day calendar (364 days), which Exodus implies that Abraham used (Ex 12:41), and Moses restored (Ex 12:2), becomes significant as you correlate all the OT events that list the numbered day of a numbered month. In completing this exercise (covered later), a striking pattern will emerge showing consistent days of the week for consistent events (see "For The Time is at Hand," p. 123).

So the lingering question, "Was this 364-day calendar truly the same one that Moses used, and if so, which day of the week do each of these feasts fall on?" The DSS give us the same pattern found in Leviticus. Due to ordination vows and language interpretation, rabbis and linguists have varying conclusions. Though each might have a different day of the week for a given feast, they all agree that with this calendar each feast has the same day of the week every year (364 ÷ 7 = 52 perfect weeks).

Thankfully, the confusion is quenched by correlating these writings with the Hebrew in the OT. If you were to add up all the *shabbat*(s) (#7676) in your Hebrew index, you would total 104; of the *shabbaton/e*'s (#7677), there are 11. Recognizing *shabbat* as a 7th day Sabbath and *shabbaton/e* as a holy feast, or rest from labor; if one were to contextually search through all 115 accounts, they would make two (2) startling finds with *shabbat*, and three (3) with *shabbaton/e*.

In Leviticus, there is a numbered day of a particular month that is referred to as a *shabbat* (#7676), a 7th day Sabbath (Lev 16:31; 23:32). Both of these verses tell us that the Day of Atonement, the 10th day of the 7th month, is a *shabbat* (two witnesses). The only way to accomplish this each year is with a consistent calendar. Of all the *shabbaton/e*'s (#7677), there are three (3) that are numbered in the same 7th month (Lev 23:24,39), the Feast of Trumpets, the 1st day of the 7th month, and the two holy convocations of the Feast of Tabernacles, the 15th and the 22nd day of the 7th month. With the 10th of the 7th month being a 7th day Sabbath; then the 1st, 15th and the 22nd could not be 7th day Sabbaths, but would each have to be the 5th day of the week (Thursday); interestingly, the day before the preparation of the seventh-day Sabbath ("5" – meaning "tabernacles" and "Divine favor"). Of interest, we find this quote:

> "In Bible times, as it is today, this feast (of Trumpets) is celebrated for two days instead of one. The Talmudic tradition maintains the second day was added during the times of the prophets." *A Family Guide to the Biblical Holidays*, p. 283

That would make for Th-rsday (1), and Fr-day (2), before the 7th day Sabbath every year as the "third day" (see "Third Day" - p. 70) in the 10 days of Awe to the Day of Atonement. Th-rsday happens to be a convenient day for a holy feast convocation, as the following day (Fr-day) allows preparation (even here at Trumpets) before the 7th day convocation. And because Leviticus is a book of bylaws, not accounting any single event, given as instruction to every priest in each generation, then only a consistent calendar would correlate with these verses with the use of *Shabbat* and *shabbaton*.

Justification by Calendar

To justify our case with more witnesses, let us analyze Exodus 16. Starting at the beginning of this chapter, we find in the KJV translation that the first verse is one entire sentence. Another rendering of the Hebrew, including verse 2, could be as follows (*Emphasis supplied*):

> "They pulled out from Elim, and all the congregation of the sons of Israel came into the wilderness of Zin, which is between Elim and Sinai, On the fifteenth day of the second month, after their departing out of the land of Egypt, the whole congregation of the sons of Israel murmured against Moses and Aaron in the wilderness." (*lit.* Exo 16:1, 2)

Could the 15th of the 2nd month be a day of holy congregation? Obviously, in this sentence structure, all of the children of Israel came together that day, and it was on this day YHVH spoke to Moses of the "bread from heaven;" stating how on the sixth day (from that point), His children shall prepare twice as much as they gather daily (vs.4,5). Later in the chapter we read:

> "And it came to pass, **on the sixth day**, they gathered twice as much bread, two Omers for one. And all the leaders of the congregation came and reported to Moses. And he said to them, 'This is what YHVH had said, **Tomorrow** (seventh day) *is* the rest of the holy **Shabbat** to YHVH: bake what you will bake, boil what you will boil, and lay up for yourselves all that is left over, to keep it until morning.' And they laid it up **until morning**, as Moses commanded, and it did not stink and no maggot was in it. And Moses said, 'Eat it today, for **today is** a Shabbat unto YHVH. ...'" (*lit.* Exo 16:22-25) (*Emphasis supplied*).

No manna was to be found Sabbath morning; just as our Savior, the Heavenly Manna, was not found on the Sabbath morning of the Resurrection, as we will confirm. So, the sixth day from when the sons of Israel first received the bread from heaven would have been the 21st, the next day we are told is a "Shabbat," the 22nd; so the day Moses and Aaron first spoke to the congregation about these provisions was also a "Shabbat," the 15th of the 2nd month. Now, if the 22nd day of the 2nd month is the seventh day of the week, and we advance from that point, using the pattern of the Dead Sea Scroll calendar (364-day), to the 10th day of the 7th month, the Day of Atonement; it too would also come out to be the seventh-day of the week, just as Scripture told us in Leviticus! [The reason for the "afflict"ion on that 7th day Sabbath is because the blood-tattered coat of Joseph was delivered to Jacob on this day (Jub 34:12-19). "And this day has been ordained ... that they might cleanse themselves on that day once a year."]

This pattern in the 2nd month in Ex 16:1-2, 22-23 (15th and 22nd) is the same pattern of the numbered days in the month as we find in the 7th month in Lev 23: 24, 39. Since the 2nd month has no declared feasts, it is logical and appropriate to consider right-off that the day of "congregation" (15th of the 2nd)(Ex 16:1) was a Shabbat, witnessed by the next "Shabbat," counted-out seven days later as the 22nd (Ex 16:22-23). (It is interesting that the occasional 2nd month UB – for those previously unclean, or on a journey – is never spoken of as to any convocations that week, as it appears the first and last days of this week would be a 7th day Sabbath – maybe to commemorate another "Passing-over" for His people, receiving the miraculous provision of unleavened manna from YHVH).

Since the 2nd and 7th months have the same pattern of "holy convocations" on the 15th and 22nd, each mentioned as a "sabbath," and the 1st month has the 15th as a holy convocation (Lev 23:6, 8), it is assumed by some Bible students that these are all 7th day Sabbaths, and that these must be consistent with every month. They further reason that, if you count back from the 15th, the 8th and the 1st would also be 7th day Sabbaths as well as the seventh from the 22nd being the 29th, almost a perfect lunar month, from the 1st to the 29th. Therefore, they are thinking the night of the first clearly visible lunar crescent should be the start of the month as a 7th day Sabbath. This is called a "lunar sabbath" model, as the 1st, 8th, 15th, 22nd, and the 29th are considered 7th day Sabbaths for each month. Some even have the last day of their month (30th) being a preparation before the next "7th day Sabbath," the 1st of the next month, for 6 months out of the year; and the other 6 months can end with a double Sabbath weekend (29th to the 1st of the next) anywhere in the week. This gives them the same number of days per year as the lunar calendar-keepers (354), which would cause both of them to have to add a 13th month every 3 years. As the Lunar sabbatarian's 7th day Sabbath changes to a different day of the week every month; the lunar calendar-keeper's feasts change to a different day of the week every year - neither of these practices has any precedence in the Word, nor is there any evidence for a 13th month anywhere in Scripture.

Some lunar sabbatarians take the waning of the last quarter from the 29th to the next visible crescent for the beginning of the next month, which can typically range between 2 or 4 days; which still gives you a week less than seven days at the end of every monthly cycle. With either scenario, your 7th day Sabbath in one month would be on a Monday, Tuesday, or Wednesday the next month, and would change to a Friday, Saturday or Sunday the next month, or to substitute the numbers the 2nd, 3rd, or 4th day of the week in one month, to the 6th, 7th, or 1st on the next. A few of these students might defend their theory with the inclusion of Ez 32:1, 17 for on the 15th of the 12th month a Word of YHVH came to the prophet, and the last day of the feast of Purim, which has the same date (15th of the 12th). They might use as another witness in the same breath Es 9:18, and 2 Chr 29:17 with the sanctification of the Temple starting from the 1st of the 1st month to the 8th. Yet none of these dates are mentioned as a "sabbath" (and back at Es 9:18, the 13th of the 12th is mentioned as a day they "assembled together" to begin the Feast of Purim, the very day that Haman had planned to kill the Jews. - see Figure 1 for that day of the week).

Another problem with the lunar sabbath model is the count of days to Pentecost. In Lev 23:15, 16 we read that a count of "seven sabbaths shall be complete:" for a count of "fifty days," which you cannot do with this lunar Sabbath model, because of the consistency of their consecutive seven day cycles are not long enough, and you would actually have eight Sabbaths with the fiftieth day landing on something other than a 7th day Sabbath. And Leviticus 25, which denotes the same pattern of seven sabbatical years to the Jubilee (as a Pentecost of years) does not give any evidence for a change in seven sevens to the fiftieth year either. The willingness of these students to be open-minded enough to recognize a pattern is honorable, but every study needs to be complete and pass the acid test of both the Hebrew and Greek languages. Having the knowledge that there are two different words for "sabbath" in Hebrew with a consistent calendar, solves this problem.

Any argument that a Shabbat is also a shabbaton is simply dismissed with Lev 23:15, where 7 "Shabbats" are complete to make 50 days. If "Shabbat" and "shabbaton" are interchangeable, there would be eight Shabbats to include the last day of UB, but it states only 7 Shabbats in 50 days.

So, with the knowledge of a consistent calendar; starting the year with the right day of the week would be critical. If you start with the wrong day of the week, all your week days to the numbered days of the month would be off. The way to solve this is with a proper analysis of the Hebrew language in Leviticus chapters 23 and 16. As was mentioned earlier, these chapters depict the Day of Atonement (10th of the 7th month) on a 7th day "Shabbat" (Lev 23:32; 16:31), and consequently, all the other numbered days of the months mentioned in Scripture, with their stated activity, should all corroborate to their given position in respect to the 10th of the 7th month being a 7th day Sabbath. (see p. 128 – Other 7th day Sabbath events in the OT)

The Day of Atonement, intentionally prescribed to be on a Shabbat, would typify the complete resolution from sin, of perfect rest and at-one-ment with our Maker, on His only hallowed and sanctified day. So, if indeed all the feast days were meant to be consistent to the same day of the week every year; is it without discrepancy that the day of the week Scripture reveals for the Firstfruits (or first omer) that prefigured the resurrection, - was really on a Shabbat? This prophetic ritual was kept on the right day of the week each year during the time of the patriarchs, prophets, and kings; all before the Babylonian captivity. Our Savior had fulfilled it on the right day of the week by coming back to life as the true FF offering (1 Cor 15:20,23; Col 1:18; Rev 1:5).

This sanctuary service of the First Omer was foretold to be kept by the children of Israel shortly after they were to enter the promise land (Lev 23:10), and they came into the land precisely 40 years after the re-initiation of the ordinance of Passover back in Egypt (Jos 4:19; Ex 12:2, 3). That first FF Omer offering would have been the morning of the next "Shabbat," which was, and is, 3 days after Passover (Jos 5:10-12). As the fulfillment of the FF Omer was our Savior's resurrection, the Gospels actually tell us this was also 3 days after Passover. Could it be that all the feasts were truly meant to be on the same day of the week every year? With the fulfillment of First Omer right on time, it was meant for every successive generation to also see our Father's perfect timing regarding prophecy and the feasts; that all could glory in the One, who knows the end from the beginning and reveals everything in between (Jn 15:15), with prophetic punctuality (Am 3:7).

Fact, Fiction, or Fraud

Now we have set the framework to move further into Leviticus 23 to determine which day of the week was truly transcribed for this FirstFruit Omer. Reading from the KJV in Lev 23:10, 11, Moses himself is Divinely addressed:

> "Speak unto the children of Israel, and say unto them, When ye be come into the land which I give unto you, and shall reap the harvest thereof, then ye shall bring a sheaf of the <u>firstfruits</u> of your harvest unto the priest: And he shall wave the sheaf before the Lord, to be accepted for you: on the <u>morrow after the sabbath</u> the priest shall wave it."

Now it would seem to make sense, if the FF offering was indeed on the "morrow after the Sabbath," its fulfillment in the NT would be on "the first day of the week." By simply verifying the OT prophecy with the NT fulfillment, this should settle the question.

In reality, comparing the two ancient languages, nothing could be further from the truth. The original writing has two words for the KJV phrase "morrow after the Sabbath," as there are three in the counterpart phrase "first *day* of the week." The two Hebrew words in Lev 23:11 in the Interlinear Bible (IB) are: ממהרת השבת (#7676) and (#4283), (with the preposition and article at the beginning of each) "mee mohorawth ha Shabbat" or "from morrow the 7th day Sabbath."

Notice the similarity of the Hebrew "mohorawth" to the English "morrow." Typically, "morrow" is not used in contemporary English, and for many the first thought that comes to mind is "tomorrow." Though we could find the definition of "morrow" in any dictionary, it would be best to consult an Oxford dictionary, which traces the etymology of a given word and lists the chronological meanings of words in their time periods.

From at least the time of Chaucer (c.1386), and well beyond the time of Longfellow's poetry (1847), "morrow" meant "morning." The usual salutation of the day in the time of King James was "good morrow;" and "on the morrow" meant "in the morning" (Oxford English Dict., Vol. 6, p. 678). So in reading "morrow after the Sabbath," we should think "*morning* after the Sabbath," specifically the service and its fulfillment to be in the morning - now let us look a little closer. According to Strong's H#4283, the KJV translators translated this word: (*Emphasis supplied*)

"mohorawth: morrow [26X], **morrow after [3X]**, next day [2X], next [1X]."

Since there is no difference in vowel points found between these Hebrew words in their perspective passages, why couldn't we call all these "morrow shabbat," "next shabbat," or even "next day (morning) Shabbat?" We know it cannot be the next feast sabbath, otherwise the Hebrew word at Lev 23:11 would be "shabbaton." (FF Omer was not considered a separate "feast" within UB until after our Savior typified it in the NT). We can see the difference here is that little word "after." Should it be "morning of the 7th day Sabbath," or "morning <u>after</u> the 7th day Sabbath?" Maybe we should look up the word "after" in our Strong's and check out Lev 23:11.

Low and behold there is no number listed there! All we find is: " * " (an asterisk), and the more recent concordance, the Strongest Strong's, shows, "NIH," which means "Not In Hebrew." Referring to the IB translation of Lev 23:11, the phrase actually reads in the direct translation, and in the margin: "...on the morrow of the sabbath," which means, "...on the 'morning' of the Sabbath." It is interesting that King James is not being consistent here in not italicizing this *supplied* word "after." Could it be because it is one of those "times and laws" verses? The IB has "mee mohorawth ha Shabbat" "from (next) morning the Sabbath," which is the morning of the 7th day Sabbath, from which one was to begin the count of 7 Shabbats leading to the feast of Firstfruits, or Pentecost.

Stranger still, back to our place in Strong's, "after" is missing in the next two listings, Lev 23:15, and 16. If we turn to those verses we find these missing "after"s are also translated with the same words "morrow after the Sabbath," insinuating Sunday two more times in the feast chapter, which accounts for all the "morrow after"s listed in translation, "[3X]!" Would it not be somewhat suspect that each one of the "[3X]" are translated "the morrow after the sabbath" in most translations? If the word "after" was intended, there would be a אהר (#310), or at least some additional prefix preceding the Hebrew word. Looking back again in the IB, there is no other letter, prefix, suffix, or word in any of the three cases. This is conclusive evidence of conspiratorial mistranslations to intimate a Sunday prophecy in the OT in order to portray its fulfillment in the NT, which would then presuppose dissolution of the Ten Commandments, confer a "new" covenant, and a few more consequent mistranslations (Col 2:14, Eph 2:15, Heb 7:12, etc.). Now let us consider the YLT on these verses:

" ... on the morrow of the sabbath doth the priest wave it."
(Lev 23:11 YLT)

"And ye have numbered to you from the morrow of the sabbath, from the day of your bringing in the sheaf of the wave-offering: they are seven perfect sabbaths;" (Lev 23:15 YLT)

"unto the morrow of the seventh sabbath ye do number fifty days ..."
(Lev 23:16 YLT)

As the FF Omer starts the Feast of Weeks on a 7th day Sabbath, counting "seven perfect sabbaths" to the true Pentecost, this will still give you "fifty days," inclusively, referring to the 7th day Sabbath morning, not Sunday (Lev 23: 9-16); otherwise it would not be "seven perfect sabbaths." To spell it out – if you start your count at a certain hour on the FF Omer Shabbat (with a portion of that Shabbat already expended), and count seven weeks to the exact hour of the next Shabbat (to include the early morning hours missing from the first Shabbat), to so include the latter portion of the first Shabbat with the first part of the last Shabbat, at the appropriate offering on the same hour, this gives you 50 days exactly by inclusive reckoning for 7 perfect Shabbats.

To verify this, we see the 50 days of Pentecost are laid out in the same fashion as the 50 years of Jubilee. Lev 25:8-10 lays this out as the trumpet of the Jubilee is sounded on the Day of Atonement (10th of the 7th) in the middle of the 49th year to hallow the 50th year to the same date (10th of the 7th) of the next year. So the Feast of Weeks are counted the same way as the weeks of years are counted, from the middle of the first Sabbath to the middle of the last. Could it be that our Savior really meant for the Firstfruits Omer to be waved before the Father on a *shabbat morning*, so that He, on the exact same day of the year, might be waved before His Father in the resurrection? (see also Appendix D)

He was "the bread of the firstfruits" (Lev 23:20), as the unleavened "bread from heaven" (Jn 6:32-35, 48-58), exchanged to be the new showbread, or Bread of the Presence, in the sanctuary every *shabbat morning* (Ex 29:34, Lev 24:7-9). [Lev 24:8 (IB), has "every Sabbath "yom" ('ביום'" - H#3117-"yom," having a bet "ב" preceding the "yom" יום, or "light"- together means "into light") i.e. "every Shabbat morning."]. This symbolized the true FF resurrection every week; as the earthly Tabernacle activities patterned those of the Heavenly one (Ex 25:9).

This analysis makes more sense when you consider that every Sabbath morning the Levites ceremoniously replaced this week-old Unleavened Bread (UB) with freshly sanctified UB, within the holy place of the Tabernacle as the foreshadowing type. The disciples "broke bread" and worshiped the glorified, or risen Savior, at this same time, who's Spirit was present with them (anti-type). The priests would then eat the week-old shewbread, in the holy place (type) every Sabbath. The disciples, having received His symbolic body in a "renewed" Passover service just prior to His crucifixion, continued this in remembrance of Him (1 Cor 11:24) every Passover thereafter. In the week of UB, all Israel was to have the blood over the lintel, and on their doorpost, being free of leaven for 3 days and 3 nights, just before the day of the First Omer, just as our Savior so "magnified" (Isa 42:21).

"The First Day of the Week" Scripture or Tradition?

The reason for no "servile" (i.e. employment) work on Pentecost Sabbath (Lev 23:21; Num 28:26) is for all the sanctified activity of the people having to bring two loaves of leavened bread, preparing all the animals for the burnt offerings per house, along with their meal and drink offerings, and the sin and peace offerings for that day. Notice also that the first and last day of unleavened bread, both as "holy convocations," specifically state "no 'servile' work" (Lev 23:7, 8), even though there is no specific activity, and no sacrifices explicitly prescribed for the people. This is because neither of these two days were ever meant to be on a 7th day Sabbath. With the lunar calendar you could easily have either of these two days fall on a 7th day Sabbath in any given year, which is suppose to require no work at all; yet with the consistent 364-day calendar, these two "no servile work" days were always the same two mid-week days every year, never falling on a 7th day Shabbat.

The first day of UB is always the 5th day of the week [Thursday – (Passover preparation being Wednesday)], and the last day of UB, always the 4th day of the week (Wednesday). The reason the 5th day of the week is the holy convocation for most of the feasts, which includes the beginning of the year, (1st of the 1st month – the true *Rosh HaShannah*), is based upon a particular event that typified the meaning in gematria - "5" = "tabernacles," or "Divine favor." The reason why the children of Israel approach the "tabernacle" (sanctuary) for "Divine favor" on this day for the feasts is because this is the day of the week that sin first occurred (Jub 3:17 – then see Fig. 1, 2, and Appendix D).

Regarding the communion service, this was actually a renewal of the Passover customs by our Savior in the form of a soon-coming promise for a renewed covenant; that mankind might receive His resurrected body and accept His blood for the remission of sins (Mt 26; 26-28; Mk 14:22-24; Lk 22:17-20).

As the 12 unleavened cakes on the showbread table represented the 12 tribes, there were 12 pieces of unleavened bread, one for each disciple. The blood of the Lamb, in type, became the *blood* of the Vine (Jn 15:1,5) that was "poured out for many" (IB), as opposed to "shed for many"(KJV)(Mt 26:28) for the priest was not suppose to "drink" the blood, as the pagans did, but "receive" the blood and "pour" it "out" onto the ground as it represented sin (Lev 17:10; Num 23:23,24; etc.). The blood of the vine, representing the sins of the world, were likely "poured out" into a basin to be poured on the ground later as the other grape juice they "drank" became the symbol of redemption, not blood. For our Savior said, "I tell you, from this moment, I will not drink of the fruit of the vine until that day when I drink it <u>in a new way</u> in My Father's kingdom with you." Mt 26:29 (HCSB) (*Emphasis supplied*).

Tradition dies hard, and truth is always persecuted. These were no different in the days of the KJV translators. Though man may choose to be blind, or worse, choose to blind other men, our Heavenly Fathers ways are always perfect (Mt 5:48, 1 Cor 2:7, 2Tim 3:17). Regrettably, the KJV Bible was declared by royal decree to be the only Bible for England's pulpits, and all other versions were outlawed for public readings under the name of unity. Consequently, resistance developed, then came sanctions, then persecutions, followed by rebellion, culminating in the British Civil War by 1642 (see Appendix G).

In this growing disharmony, a group of the persecuted risked their lives to gain religious freedom by braving the Atlantic Ocean for the New World. We know them today as the Pilgrims of the soon to be Massachusetts Bay Colony, and they carried with them contraband called the Geneva Bible.

The Geneva Bible was an English translation that came out of Geneva, Switzerland; some years after many English Bible scholars escaped the persecutions of Queen "Bloody" Mary in the mid 1500's. Though few today would ever get the opportunity to evaluate an original Geneva, or Tyndale, or Wycliffe Bible, as opposed to edited copies, but certainly this problem of cloaking the Sabbath resurrection for a Sunday one was part of Constantine's agenda, and the multiple counsels through those early centuries. Thus, this "tradition" may have preceded even these translations; but contrary to most historical records, many Puritan congregations were Sabbath-keeping (see *The English Connection*, by Bryan W. Ball, ISBN: 0227678443). Oddly enough, the KJV was not part of the early American colony for over 70 years.

CHAPTER 4

Presto Chango

Tradition Magicians

The leaders of the KJV translation project were directors and professors of linguistic studies in their perspective colleges, whose translation work was government certified. Moreover, with all these interpretations and definitions supposedly confirmed by the country's best minds, the Church of England hoped to encourage other writers, publishers, and religious leaders to establish these teachings and traditions in British society. This gradually oppressive influence had its affect even in America. Though well after the Colonies wilderness experience, an attempt to rationalize tradition can be seen by reading a few consecutive definitions in the first edition of Noah Webster's American Dictionary, printed by Hezekiah Howe at S. Converse Publishing in New York City (1828):

> "SABBATH: ...originally the 7th day of the week, the day on which God rested from the work of creation; and this day is still observed by the Jews and some Christians, as the Sabbath. But the Christian church very early begun and still continue to observe the first day of the week, in commemoration of the resurrection of Christ on that day, ... Hence it is often called the *Lord's day*. The heathen nations in the north of Europe dedicated this day to the *sun* and hence **their Christian descendants** continue to call the day *Sunday*. But in the United States, Christians have to a great extent discarded the heathen name, and have adopted the Jewish name *Sabbath*... ."

(**Bolding** *supplied*)

Just prior to this definition we read:

"SABBATARIAN: One who observes the seventh day of the week as the Sabbath, instead of the first. Pertaining to those who keep Saturday as the Sabbath. A sect of Baptists are called *Sabbatarian's*. They maintain that the Jewish Sabbath has not been abrogated.

"SABBATARIANISM: The tenets of Sabbatarian's"

Based upon this definition of "Sabbath," you would expect a true Sabbath-keeper, or "Sabbatarian," to include a Sunday or first-day worshipper, if indeed Sabbath was also to mean Sunday. Ironically, Noah Webster does not mention Sunday in either of the latter terms; and goes so far as to specify "the seventh day of the week as the Sabbath instead of the first;" then elaborates on the origin of *Sunday* under "Sabbath." Next, we find:

> "SABBATH-BREAKER: One who profanes the Sabbath by violating the laws of God <u>or man</u> which enjoin the religious observance of <u>that</u> day.
>
> "SABBATH-BREAKING: A profanation of the Sabbath by violating the injunction of the fourth commandment, <u>or the municipal laws of a state</u> which require the observance of <u>that</u> day as holy time."

(*Underlined supplied*)

The fourth commandment, according to Moses, was the keeping of the seventh day Sabbath only (Exo 20:10). The inconsistencies from both the KJV Greek index and Webster's dictionary should make the problem readily apparent. And we will confirm that this *Lord's day* (Rev 1:10) cannot be substantiated as Sunday. However, some day "the municipal laws of the state" may lend stronger reinforcement to the Sunday "sabbath" laws, with greater penalties than they had in early industrial America.

Sadly, the word "Lord," as in "Lord's day," comes from the surname of the Norse god "Thor" as a pagan substitute for the "Tetragrammaton" YHVH; even relegating the Sovereign of the Universe to the status given to an accomplished English gentleman. Nevertheless, we can see the root of this problem takes us back well before even the Protestant Reformation, back before the Dark Ages, back to another time of religious struggle and persecution; when Emperors and their Governors enforced a progressive decree that eventually had very stringent penalties for those who did not comply with their "Christianized" pagan religious laws.

This compromise of faith continues to exist today because of Christian traditionalists, some of the most ardent being pastors, teachers, evangelists and authors, who refer to the "Sabbath" as meaning "Sunday." This is partly because they understand their translation of the Word to mean what it reads, "the first day of the week," even though in their own Bibles there is no scriptural injunction for any change made in the fourth commandment.

Contemporary dictionary writers, many times, just give us the common (majority) everyday understanding of particular words based on their "traditional" usage. Maybe now it may not seem so odd why the original Greek, "sabbat/sabbaton/e," has not been properly classified as a Hebrew transliteration. However, Scripture has told us these kinds of things would happen (Isa 28:7, Mt 15:9, Jn 10:12, 2 Th 2:7, 2 Jn 10, Jude 4, etc.). It is up to each one of us to ultimately determine for ourselves whether a thing is true (2 Tim 2:15; Col 2:8; Heb 12:9; 1 Jhn 4:1). "The readers cardinal sin – trusting the author too much" [Wise, Abegg, & Cook, *The Dead Sea Scrolls, A New Translation*, p.38]. So, to continue our investigation, let us not leave any course unchartered (1 Thes 5:21).

The Tragic Magic

By believing in a Sunday resurrection, we deny the original transliteration for a traditional interpretation. In addition, as the evidence continues to build, there will leave little justification to translate this transliterated word to mean anything more or less than what it was originally transliterated from. So, for the sake of clarity and confirmation, let us look at the two Greek words that have been translated "week," one in literature with one in the NT, and see if there is any relationship between the two. Recall the similarity of the Greek "Sabbat" to the Hebrew "S<u>h</u>abbat," which was before the Greek language.

GREEK ORIGIN	TRANSLITERATED into GREEK
(Gk.) HEBDOMada - week ("given by seven")	*#4520* SABBATismos - Sabbath observance
#1440 HEBDOMekonta - 70	*#4521* SABBAT(on) - Sabbath/(feast), <u>week?</u>
#1441 HEBDOMekontakis - 70 X	*#4315* proSABBAT(on) - day before Sabbath / (feast)
#1442 HEBDOMos - seventh	

Notice the similarity of the words in Greek origin relating to "sevens," and their lack of relevance in spelling and phonetics to the transliterated Greek words from the Hebrew "Shabbat/on/e." The Greek "sabbat," though the seventh day of the week coming from the Hebrew, it does not also refer to seven days comprising a week. In fact, as we continue through the study, you may as well determine along with the author that no evidence exists to convert any "sabbat" or "sabbaton/e" to "week."

"Mia," "Mia" on the Wall

Now consider the next Greek word in question, and all its relations listed in the Strong's index.

#1520 hEIS - one, (a primary numeral)

#1527 hEIS kath heis - one by one

#3367 medEIS - no one, nobody, nothing
medeMIA - (irreg. fem. of *#3367*)
meden - (neuter), none, not (at all)

#3391 MIA - a, an, only, (irreg. fem of *#1520*)

#3762 oudEIS - no one, not any one
oudeMIA - (irreg. fem. of *#3762*)
ouden - (neuter), not even one

[Greek is a gender specific language with some spelling variations dependent upon forms and syntax. Though Strong's does not always delineate these forms, we will examine some of these in our interlinear study.]

As the phrase "the first day of the week" is found but [8X] in the KJV, all in the NT, "mia" is translated "first" only [8X] out of a combined [350X]; (7 of the 8 in "the first day of the week") and "sabbaton/e" is translated "week [9X]" out of [68X], (8 of the 9 in "the first day of the week"). May it become clear to the reader, as we progress, whether the true Greek-to-English conversion, these [8X], should be "a Sabbath," or "the first day of the week."

In less contemporary secular Greek-to-English dictionaries, "mia" is never found to be "first," only in <u>Biblical</u> Greek dictionaries. The only proper word for "first" in Greek is # *4413* "protos" and is found to be unrelated to "mia" / "heis." But if you substitute "'one'(heis) of the 'sabbaths,'" for some it gives the connotation of Sunday as "one" from the sabbath. Yet "from" is not found here, and "heis" in this phrase "first day of the week" is only found in the Greek codices (Codex Sinaiticus, Codex Vaticanus, Codex Macedoniensis, etc.), which came about centuries after the days of the early disciples.

The intentional deceit on the part of the translators to substitute pagan concepts for inspired words, foisted as the true Word of "God" before the conditioned masses, was an abomination in the sight of YHVH. Yet YHVH had allowed this, that the hidden Truth would be ordained to a called-out remnant, according to His ways and timing. Though many "saints" would be persecuted for their testimony, these will be declared righteous before YHVH in His kingdom (Mt 5:6,8,10), at the first resurrection.

The First "First Day of the Week"

The next thing to do, at this point, is to examine the phrase "the first day of the week" within its context. Its first occurrence is found in the Gospel of Matthew.

> "In the end of the sabbath, as it began to dawn toward the first *day* of the week, came Mary Magdalene and the other Mary to see the sepulcher" (Mt 28:1 KJV).

Now if we proceed to dismantle each of the Greek words in this sentence and utilize their more secular English translation in sequence with the proper transliteration, we will find a rather grave discrepancy when compared with the KJV.

Starting with the first three words, "In the end," our Strong's concordance tells us there is a single Greek word for this, *# 3796* "οψε"(opse). Two of the three "opse" [3X] found in the NT, are defined in old English, as "even," referring to "evening or night" (See Mk 11:19; 13:35). The first definition in the earlier Strong's is "late." This definition "late" corroborates with an Oxford Greek Dictionary, which relays the etymology. Only this one time, in Mt 28:1, it is translated, "in the end" as it precedes the Greek word "sabbatone;" which here is translated "sabbath," yet the very next "sabbatone" in the same verse, identical in spelling, they translate it "week." There seems to be a little problem here.

Maybe the theologians forgot to consider this word "opse" in its context preceding the Greek conjunction "δε" or "de." Scholars would typically tell you that "late" or "evening" could be at the end of the day, or at the beginning of the day, if the day starts at even, being dependent of course upon the context. To assure ourselves that "opse" is not really "end," here, after double checking the two verses in Mk 11:19 and 13:35, let us look at the two related words *#3797* "οψιμος" (opsimos) and *#3798* "οψιος" (opsios).

"Opsimos" refers to "belated" or "latter," as in the "early and latter (opsimos) rain" (James 5:7). And "opsios," refers to the coming of evening, as night begins to fall, "when even (opsios) was now come," (Jhn 6:16), which again, according to many scholars, could be the start or end of a day depending upon the context. So, let us look at these three words together from the Strong's:

> G# *3796* OPSE - even, late, night (darkness)
> G# *3797* OPSImos - late, latter, belated (later, tardy)
> G# *3798* OPSIos - late afternoon, nightfall (late of the day)

So "opse" is well into the darkness in comparison to the other action forms of coming into darkness (a better match with Mk 11:19 and 13:35). Next in the Greek is "de." Our Greek lexicon reads "δε σαββατων" or "de sabbatone." "De" is a primary particle, conjunction, or continuative that has multiple variations in English.

> G#*1161* DE - and [1214], but [935], now [168], then [132], when [40], yet [20], for [19], so [15], howbeit [12], nevertheless [12], also [10], yea [10], moreover [9], notwithstanding [8], therefore [4], while [4] . . . " etc.

For some reason, neither "of" nor "of the" is found in the listed definitions in either the earlier Strong's, or the Strongest Strong's as would be expected, for these words "of the" are used here for "de" in the more mainstream English Bible translation at Mt 28:1. The Oxford Greek Dictionary says "and" or "but," not after, or end. Now "de" in French and Spanish can refer to "of," but that is not Greek, which does not use a Latin-based alphabet as these three other languages do. For "opse de sabbatone" at Mt 28:1, in the IB translation does have "after But the sabbaths" (with a capital "B" for some reason). If you look at all the other uses of the Greek "de" throughout the KJV, listed above; and plug any one of these into the location between "opse" and "sabbatone," in Mt 28:1, it would render some aspect of <u>into</u> the Sabbath, not the "end."

The next Greek word "sabbatone," as was shown earlier, literally comes from the Hebrew "<u>s</u>habbatone" meaning a feast day that falls on a seventh-day Sabbath (in this case, Firstfruits (FF) on a "shabbat,"- see "Sabbatone / Sabbaton," p. 13). ["Sabbat" - 7th day; "Sabbaton" – feast day; "Sabbatone" – 7th day Ceremonial feast day].

Continuing further into Mt 28:1 we find, "as it began to dawn." The Greek manuscript reads; "τη επιφωσκω." The word "τη" (tae #5084b) simply denotes that the following word is meant to be in the present tense active form, and "επιφωσκω" (epiphosko #2020) is "dawn," or in this case, "dawning." For grammatical flow this is rendered, "as it began to dawn." The next word is "toward," the Greek being *#1519* "εισ"(eis), another one of those Greek words that has multiple variations:

> G#*1519* EIS - into [543], to [316], unto [206], for [141], in [140], on [59], against [27], upon [24], at [21], among [18], towards [15], toward [14], that [6], . . .

Next, we come to "the first day of the week," analyzed earlier and in the manuscript as "mian sabbatone;" more literally, "a 7th day (Ceremonial) Sabbath" [singular]. So, let us view the first half of Mt 28:1 as we arrange the original words from the Strong's Index (SI), then the words as they were written contextually in the Interlinear Bible (IB).

SI:	οψε	δε	σαββατον	τη	επιφωσκω	εισ	μια	σαββατον
IB:	οψε	δε	σαββατων	τη	επιφωσκουση	εισ	μιαν	σαββατων
	opse	de	sabbatone	tae	epiphoskousee	eis	mian	sabbatone . . .
	late now		7th day feast	at	the dawning	into	a	7th day feast

Now let us make a grammatical reconstruction of this phrase and compare it to the KJV.

> "*It was* late *into the* night, then a seventh-day feast Sabbarh *as it was* dawning into *the* seventh-day feast Sabbath, …"

> "In the end of the sabbath, as it began to dawn toward the first *day* of the week, . . ." KJV.

The scholars will tell you that Sabbath evening is equivalent to our Friday night; so as the sun began to dawn; in other words, as light was coming to the sky, this then would be early Saturday (Shabbat) morning. What this verse is truly trying to convey, as contrary as it may seem, is that our Savior arose from the dead, before sunrise, <u>Saturday</u> morning, just as the original Hebrew writings portrayed it to be fulfilled (on Shabbat). The initial English reaction to all this might be "poppycock!" or "boulder-dash!" Your reaction may be different, but we will continue to answer the more obvious questions as we progress through this study.

Now if we retranslated the English KJV Mt 28:1 back into Greek this is what we would have. (The Greek words CAPITALIZED and <u>underlined</u> are **not** found in this verse):

"The First Day of the Week" Scripture or Tradition?

In the end of the sabbath, as it began to dawn toward the first *day* of the week,...
EIS SYNTELEIA TÔN SABBATO tae epiphoskousee eis PROTOS TÔN HEBDOMADA
εισ συντελεια των σαββατω τη επιφωσκουση εισ πρωτοσ των εβδομαδα

Moreover, as we later examine the other gospel accounts of "the first day of the week," utilizing the same reference tools, we will verify these same results found in Matthew 28:1 (see Mark 16:2, 9; Luke 24:1; John 20:1, 19).

This is one of the reasons why the Word asks us to "Study to show ourselves approved unto YHVH" (2 Ti 2:15) that we might "Beware lest any man spoil (us) through philosophy and vain deceit, after the traditions of men," (Col 2:8) for these "certain men crept in unawares, who were before of old ordained to this condemnation, ungodly men, turning the grace of our God into lasciviousness" (Jude 1:4), "that, if it were possible, they shall deceive the very elect (His chosen people)." (Mt 24:24).

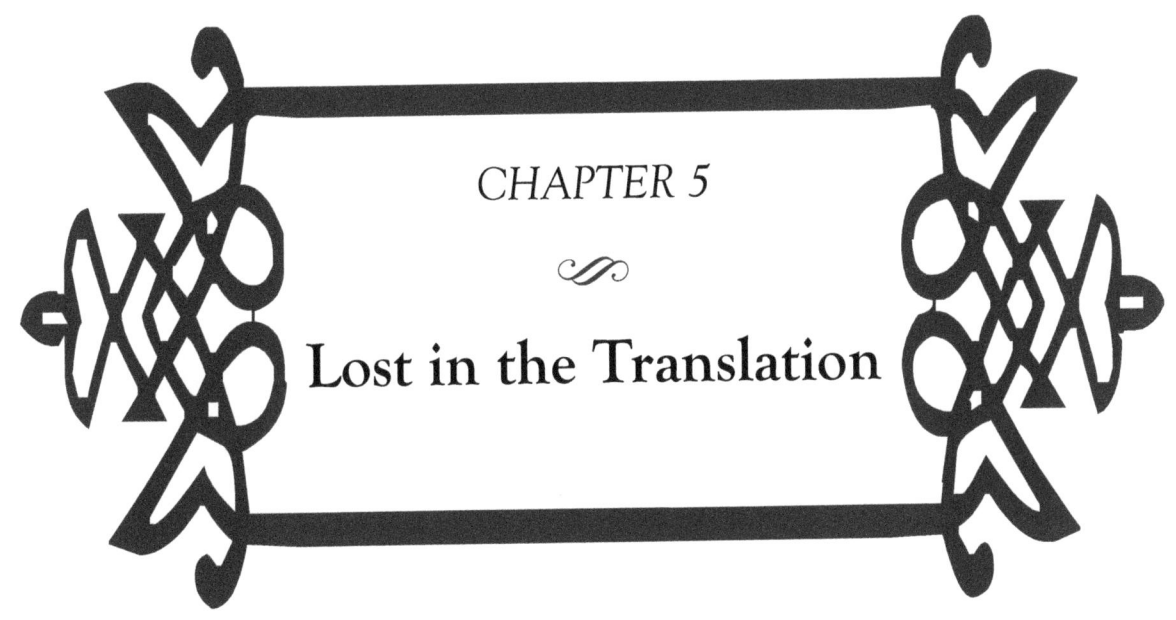

CHAPTER 5

Lost in the Translation

Multinational Transliterations

If we researched "Shabbat" a little more, we would find it to be transliterated (not just translated) into more than 100 known ancient and modern languages. This means that each of these languages had, or have, a similar phonetic equivalent for "Shabbat," (differences in pronunciation are based upon the closest alphabetic sound in a given language with consideration to gender and referent forms.) Between some dialects, identical pronunciations exist. Most of these pronunciations are listed below.

"'Sabbati', 'Sabbatum', 'Sabbedi', 'Sabbado', 'Sabatico', 'Sabotsy', 'Sabtu', 'Sabt', 'Sabulu', 'Sab', 'Saibitai', 'Shabati', 'Shamba', 'Shambe', 'Shapat', 'Shapta', 'Sambada', 'Sanbat', 'Sanbata', 'Saptu', 'Saptoe', 'Sebt', 'Sibiti', 'Sibda', 'Sibbed', 'Sibt', 'Sobota', 'Subbota', 'Subbatum', 'Subota', 'Subuta', . . . 'Szombat'", etc. [Jones, W. M., D.D., *A Chart of the Week,* Etymological col., Washington, D.C., 1886]

With regard to accent variations, these are essentially the articulations of Shabbat that came from different parts of the globe sometime after the miraculous workings of the God of the Shabbat had been done on a Shabbat. Many nations had come to fear this God of the Shabbat for they had heard how Israel's neighboring kingdoms had tried to subdue the Hebrews on the very day the Israelites were forbidden to raise the sword, and many times these nations found themselves supernaturally defeated.

Many cultures, including the ancient Greeks, had named each day of their week after different gods and celestial bodies because of particular events, myths, or legends. The events of the Hebrew's God had apparently, for many people groups, superseded those of their god Saturn; for most of the world referred to this day either by the star of Remphan (Saturn – our Saturday) or of the "rest" (Shabbaton) of the Hebrew God [See Acts 7:42, 43]. (Interestingly, it was the nations furthest away from Israel that used some derivative of Saturn.) Almost all recognized this particular day as the seventh day in a seven-day week. In addition, almost all had some unrelated word for "week," (a few did not have any word, but had only seven days named). The Hebrews did not name the other days of their week, but numbered them consecutively, one thru six. The seventh day was the only day with a name, "Shabbat" "שבת" meaning:

"[שב – *shin* before a *bet*]   'S-ab' –   Learned-Father
[ב – *bet*]   'b' –   House
[ת – *tav*, same as owth (#226)]   'awth' –   Miracle, Sign
(**S-ab · b · ath**) = '**Dwelling Place of the Father's Miraculous Sign**.'"

[Arrabito, J., *History of the Sabbath*, LLT Prod., Angwin, Cal., (1988).]

Not a god, or a star, but a reference to **the** God, YHVH, who is the Author of the Sabbath. And YHVH honored the Sabbath in His only begotten Son, and magnified it in His resurrection (Isa 42:21). And John tells us we should walk as He walked (1 Jn 2:6); as He walked in miraculous renewed life every 7th day Sabbath.

For He had designed this day "Sabbath" for miracles, to be a prophetic sign for the ultimate perfection of His will! The numbered days, such as the "first day of the week," were not typically used as such in the Greek language. As we would call it "Sunday," the Greeks call it "κυριαχη" (kuriache) [*The Classic Greek Dictionary*, Follet Pub. Co., Chicago (1943)] of which "kuria" is the feminine word for "lord," meaning, "lady" (Strong's *#2959*), and "che" is the letter "X." "Kuriache" could be the formal name of an ancient mystical goddess of the Sun. [The Latin Sunday, "Dominica," refers to a goddess (lady) of dominance.]

The Institution of Substitution

To follow another process of substitution let us look at one example of a *literation* from the Hebrew into the Greek. Considered equally as sacred to the early Greek Christians, the proper name of the Father in Hebrew was so inscribed within the Greek Scriptures using the four Hebrew letters "יהוה" (YHVH #3068). ["The first translation into Greek by the Sanhedrin during the 2nd century BCE is called **the Septuagint**, and in its original, the Name was always preserved in its original paleo (ancient) Hebrew, 𐤉𐤄𐤅𐤄." (White, L., *Fossilized Customs*, p. 16. ISBN 0-9584353-6-7). This was the form He used to write His own name in Stone (Later transcribed to Chaldaic-Hebrew, "יהוה") [Paleo-Hebrew was the hand-writing on the wall that only Daniel could read (Dan 5)] This paleo-Hebrew Name of the Father was all throughout the Dead Sea Scrolls (DSS); thus the Greek term "Tetragrammaton" ["tetra" meaning *four*, and "grammaton" meaning *letter* (not in Strong's)].

The later Greek substitution had occurred partly because the mind-set of the previous leadership, the rabbis and scribes who considered the Name too sacred to pronounce, had eventually carried over into the converted Gentile leadership. Prior to our Savior's earthly ministry, and occurring again just a few generations there after, there seemed to be no consensus, like doctrine among so many denominations, on the proper pronunciation. Our Savior gave the true Name plenty of exposure, and this is part of the reason why He and His subsequent followers were despised and persecuted by the Jewish leaders.

This tradition of too-sacred-to-pronounce, perpetuated by a few "silver tongues," prepared the way for the name-substitution when anti-Semitism was in full swing; which caused the repulsion of everything "Jewish;" - the statutes, the commandments, the teaching of the Hebrew language, and the inclusion of the Hebrew Name of the Father and His Son. At the same time, in the name of evangelism, in an effort to bring acceptance and salvation to the pagan masses and deter the persecutions of the believers, the substitution of the names of their Greek gods made their way into the teachings and the Greek copies of the writings, replacing the literations (word interposed from another language without letter conversion or translation), or even Greek transliterations of the names of our Father and His Son. Invariably, this created a distinct line between true believers and those who eventually were called "Christians," which means "followers of anointed one," insinuating the anointed one, but all the Greek gods were "anointed."

Without getting too far off topic, just to make mention of the names of those Greek gods who became the substitutes – "Theos," today meaning "god" or "deity," was foisted as a title, when prior to the "Christians," it was the name of a particular god of the early pagans; (just like "god," a title in English, came from the Teutonic name for the sun, Gott), and Iesous (Jesus), was the Greek god of healing. Today this is pronounced Hay-Zeus [in pictographic-Hebrew (most ancient form) means "hail zeus," which a Hebrew would never say] considered by some to mean the son of Zeus. And we are cautioned about using the names of other deities (Ex 23:13) (see White, L., *Fossilized Customs*, p.15-20. ISBN 0-9584353-6-7 for a more complete explanation). The inscribed substitute # *2316* "θεοσ" (theos) was not the "Tetragrammaton," (Gk: "four letters"), but refers to the *four letters* in ancient Hebrew, as each Hebrew letter in its sequence, **Yod-Hay-Vav-Hay**, expressed the meaning of His true character.

"The First Day of the Week" Scripture or Tradition?

Our phrase "mia sabbatone" was not changed because it was already in Greek letters, only taught differently to substantiate the intended mistranslations. Translated into so many languages the way many believed it to be portrayed by the Hebrews, to count so many days from Sabbath, that it might pose some legitimacy. Yet if the Gospels were originally written in Greek (a separate topic), and they really meant the resurrection to be on the day after Sabbath, they would have used their proper name for it, called "κυριαχ" or "Kuriachi" (pronounced "Kuriakhee") [not in Strong's -- means "Lady X,"]. "Sabbatone" was not the name of another deity, as a possible threat to some celestial being of the Greeks, but the transliterated day the Greeks referred too since the early Greek Septuagint, at least from the 2nd century BCE.

Hypothetically now, let us intentionally substitute the supposed "week" for the same Greek words translated "sabbath" and put it into English. Mark 16:9 is the only "first *day* of the week" that has the legitimate Greek word for "first" "πρωτοσ" "protos" #4413, and the actual phrase translation should be closer to "that first 'sabbath'" in the seven Sabbaths count to Pentecost. Now if this Greek word #4521 (sabbat-on/e) could interchangeably be either "week" or "Sabbath;" then, at the risk of being sacrilegious, let us theoretically transpose the words of our Savior, exchanging the word "sabbath" for "week," and see if we hear His voice.

- The WEEK was made for man, not man for the WEEK
- How that on the WEEK days the priest in the Temple profane the WEEK.
- For the Son of man is Lord even of the WEEK day, (or) also of the WEEK.
- If a sheep fall into a pit on the WEEK day, will he not lay hold on it,
- Wherefore, it is lawful to do well on the WEEK days
- Pray ye your flight be not in the winter, neither on the WEEK day
- Is it lawful to do good on the WEEK days or to do evil?
- Thou hypocrite, doth not each one of you on the WEEK loose his ox or his ass.
- Ought not this woman . . . be loosed from this bond on the WEEK day?
- Is it lawful to heal on the WEEK day?
- And ye on the WEEK day circumcise a man
- Are ye angry at Me, because I have made a man every whit whole on the WEEK day?

We can see the discrepancies and almost absurd statements that would not be characteristic of our Savior. Now to exchange "week" in the NT for "Sabbath."

* In the evening, then Sabbath, as it was dawning into that one SABBATH . . .
* And very early in the morning *that* one SABBATH, they came unto the sepulcher . . .
* Now when *Jesus* was risen early *that* first SABBATH, He appeared first to Mary . . .
* I fast twice on the SABBATH, I give tithes of all that I possess . . .
* Now upon *that* one SABBATH, very early in the morning, they came unto the sepulcher, bringing spices . . .
* But on *that* one SABBATH cometh Mary Magdalene early, when it was yet dark, . . .
* Then the same day at evening, being a SABBATH, when the doors were shut . . .
* And upon a SABBATH, when the disciples came together to break bread . . .
* Upon a SABBATH let every one of you lay by him in store, as God hath prospered . . .

Some may question certain activities conducted by the disciples, if "Sabbath" is truly to be the proper word here. Remember the meaning of "Shabbat" is "the Dwelling Place of the Father's Miraculous Sign." But before we can determine what the true rules and regulations are for the Sabbath, let us review the Greek again. All of these "Sabbaths," but the "I fast twice on the (Sabbath)" (Lk 18:12) are found as "the first day of the (week)," in most Bibles. [7] are "sabbatone," [1] is "sabbatou," and the "sabbath" in "I fast twice . . ." is the "sabbatou," referring to the rich young rulers fasting on both 7th day Sabbaths and the holy feast days.

Objections Overruled

If the 7th day "sabbatone" is truly to be the day of the resurrection, the next question one might ask may relate to women carrying spices to the tomb on the Shabbat; in the early twilight no less. The Pharisees had taught that on the "Shabbat/on," one could walk only so many furlongs, carrying no more than the weight of two figs. This teaching was an adulteration of

Ex 16:29 when Israel was told not to go wondering about looking for manna on the 7th day Sabbath. Their teachings typically added to, or took away from the Torah, and were later written into the Babylonian Talmud. Before a multitude our Savior declared that the scribes and Pharisees "have omitted the weightier matters of the law" (Mt 23:23), taking some things away by adding to it. To the Pharisees, before His disciples, He said, "the 'sabbaton'(feast day) was made for man, and not man for the 'sabbaton'(feast day):" (Mk 2:27).

The feast days were made that man might better understand the plan of salvation and the ways of our Father (Lev 23:6-8,24,39,41); the "Shabbats" were sanctified, and made holy, specifically belonging to our Father, that we might commune with our Father, not to pollute it, or be profaned with the world (Lev 19:30; Isa 56:4; Ez 20:12; 22:8; 23:38; 44:24). As our Savior taught that it was "lawful to do good on the 'Sabbat'" (Mk 3:4; Mt 12:12; Lk 14:3; Jn 5:9), on this "sabbatone," the women came to "anoint" His body on the morning of FF, as the priests were getting ready to do the "anointing" of the new showbread in the Holy Place, and were anticipating in their preparation the waving of all the FF sheaves of Israel before YHVH that morning. Just as our Savior, the Bread of Heaven, was the First Omer to be "waved" before His Father as the Firstfruits of the dead (1 Cor 15:20), then the other graves that the earth had quaked open around Jerusalem, gave up their dead. So, the women (churches) were looking to anoint our Savior's body (Rev 1:6) as the renewed "bread from heaven" without intending to touch His body (albeit incorruptible) before He was to be "waved" before His Father for all those willing to be called "Israel" (as an "overcoming prince of El").

Forty days later, in Acts 1:12, the disciples were returning to Jerusalem from the ascension site on mount Olivet, which the KJV says was "a sabbath day's journey" ["sabbatou echon odon"(IB)], a phrase found only this once in all of Scripture. This translation too is somewhat misleading, designating a prescribed distance allowed for travel on a given day of holy convocation. The phrase reads more literally, "going a Sabbath's way," which essentially tells us this was a way or road, typically used on any sabbath, apparently wide enough to accommodate such a group, and is not specifying that particular day as any Sabbath, or making any limitation for travel. Typically, a Sabbath walk on a well-traveled road was not like traversing a short cut of rocks, hills, and brush, which might not be conducive to meditation or spiritual conversation. Certainly, worshippers could walk and talk on an established "way," in like manner, from their homes to their synagogues.

In respect to carrying things; remember the man by the pool of Bethesda, which had an infirmity 38 years; our Savior healed him on a "sabbat<u>on</u>" day. The Messiah said to him "Rise, take up thy bed and walk." He never specified to him how far, though He knew where he intended to go, and a bed roll is usually quite an armload. The Pharisees and Sadducees placed many unnecessary burdens upon the people that Moses never required on a <u>feast</u> day. In fact, many of the type of healings and kind of miracles our Savior performed were prophetic fulfillments for a particular "sabbaton," or, in some cases, for a "shabbat" in general. Therefore, a "sabbaton" is a day one can do errands, but no "servile" work. No working for employment or pay, but personal chores could be done (Lev 23:7,8,24,25, 33-36,39; Num 28:18,25,26; 29:1,12,35). As opposed to the "Shabbat"s where you are to do no work at all (Ex 20:10; 31:14,15; 35:2; Lev 16:31; 23:3,32; 25:4; Num 15:32-36; Deu 5:14). Yet this day, as likely one woman was carrying spices by a shoulder strap and the other ointments, was a ceremonial 7th day Shabbat, and should not be considered work, especially with their providential attempt to anoint Him on that event-fulfilling Shabbat. (Consider viewing the website listed at the bottom of Literal Translations under Appendix D.)

These "sabbatous" were the only days when most all the common laborers were not working and could help an enfeebled family member or neighbor come to the Savior and to comprise a multitude. These were the "poor in spirit" and "heavy laden," and helping one walk on the Sabbath is not work. The combined tax burden on the average man in Judea back then, both civil and religious, was almost 40% of a man's income, (what many a tax-paying "tither" pays today), without any Welfare or Social Security. Consequently, the "sabbat's / sabbaton/es" were about the only days a laboring man could afford not to work. As one might properly determine the day of the week to the numbered day of the month for certain Biblical events recorded, they would find the 7th day Sabbath to represent deliverance for true Israel, and a day of judgment to its enemies.

Again, regarding the phrase "lay by him in store;" some would argue that a Messianic Israelite would not do a careful checking of accounts on the Sabbath, yet the verse does not say to "reckon your portion," but only to "lay by him in store." It was customary by "prosabbat/on," the day before a Sabbath or feast, to get the last of the work done and complete all preparations before that Sabbath or feast. This would include an accounting of offerings before that Sabbath or feast. A second rendering of this verse is "…let each of you purpose in yourselves to heap together as each has prospered, that there be no collections when I come" (*lit.* 1 Cor 16:2). Paul is simply asking the people to bring together and store their Firstfruits offerings, so that when Paul returned he would take this "liberality (not tithe) unto Jerusalem" (1 Cor. 16:3).

"Fast(ing) twice on the 'sabbatou,'" as opposed to a "week," was considered a very pious thing to not eat at all on a day of holy convocation. The most common Jewish practice on a feast day, or a 7th day Sabbath, was not so much evangelizing Gentiles or visiting widows, but for hearing the Word read, and fellowship gatherings to eat, to "midrash" (Hebrew term for doctrinal discussions), and spiritual fellowship. Traditionally though, most ate two meals on a "sabbatou," so as not to be burdened with too much meal concocting on preparation day (Ex 16:23-25), nor too much cleanup after a "sabbatou." The statement to "fast twice in the week" is not very concise. This could mean fasting two meals or two days. In an era of manual labor, two days would tend to make one gluttonous on the other days of the week, infers no regularity of worship, and two meals in the week infers no specific precept, as this ruler describes his piety.

Regarding the doors that were shut on the Sabbath, or "locked" as the Interlinear Bible delineates, the verse states that our Savior came and stood in the midst, literally walking through a locked door. This occurred the same day that He arose (Jn 20:19), right after He had miraculously left the two from their walk on a way or road to Emmaus, after blessing and breaking bread (Lk 24:30). And our Savior returned to the upper room in a similar manner "after eight days" (Jn 20:26), on the following Sabbath (counting Sabbath-to-Sabbath is "eight" days, by their customary inclusive reckoning), to appear before a doubting Thomas.

As our Savior came to be the "bread from heaven," broken for mankind that each of us might be partakers of His body unto everlasting life, we recognize He was the showbread foreshadowed in the earthly Sanctuary; patterned after the heavenly, which was typically exchanged for "new" showbread every Sabbath morning (Lev 24:8). Then it was anointed, and the week-old bread was eaten by the priests in the holy place on that same morning, in type, partaking of His body.

So, in order for our Savior to truly be the anti-typical showbread, He had to be *renewed* Sabbath morning to become the glorified Bread of Heaven. This lends added significance to our Savior's Words when He said, "For the Son of man is Lord (master) even of the 'sabbatou'" (Mt12:8; Mk 2:28; Lk 6:5), for He had fulfilled all the ceremonial days with healings and miracles specific for the day, and ultimately conquered death on the 7th day First Fruits Sabbath. These were all the concepts that John understood, when he wrote, "I was in the spirit on the Lord's day," (Re 1:10). Maybe he was in the spirit on the FF 7th day feast Sabbath.

Black Sabbath

The next consideration may generate more of a concern among "sabbatarians," who revere the Friday crucifixion/Sunday resurrection concept on the premise that our Savior had fulfilled the "rest" required on the Sabbath. However, this concept has our Messiah, not preaching, praising, or healing on the "miracles" day, but asleep in death from Friday sunset, all through the 7th day, as if to "rest," and to rise unto everlasting life <u>after</u> the Sabbath, early on "the first day of the week," which gives precedence to "Christians" that the Sabbath is a completed prophecy no longer binding. As if the Law had died on Sabbath, and the resurrection on the next day (Sunday) signified a new covenant. To them, the empty tomb on "the first day of the week" is a sign of acceptance for people of all Sunday (catholic) religions, now exonerated since the tower of Babel. This made it legitimate to venerate only the Christ on "the day of the sun," that YHVH might be the one true God to all, as if "'God' may be all in all" religions, which is a catholic belief.

For Sunday-keepers, and many a Sabbath-keeper alike, by believing in a Sunday resurrection, they unwittingly bless and sanction the high day of Pharaoh and Caesar. Sunday-keepers ignorantly follow the worship practices of the pagans, congregating every Sunday morning, at the "rising" of the sun, often with their large stain-glass windows facing East (Ez 8:16,17). They might argue the point that this Sunday resurrection initiated the "new" covenant for all mankind, but would have to consent that this would abrogate the 4th Commandment, which in turn would eliminate the other nine (Jms 2:10).

The Sabbath-keeper, on the other hand, to consent to death as the culmination for the Sabbath, as the only full day our Savior was dead, (based on a Friday/Sunday scenario) would lend their minds to idleness and "lay" activities on the Sabbath, rather than consummate "praise and honor and glory"(1Pt 1:7) for renewed life, and an invigorated faith. For even a Sabbath-keeper, who might believe in the "third angels message" (Rev 14:9, 10), to believe in a Sunday resurrection is counter-consciousness, discounting the day of sanctification for renewed life on the day of the Adversary.

Remember "Shabbat" is "the Dwelling Place of the Father's Miraculous Sign", and this "sign"(#226) "אות – awt," means "a symbol, a signal or event that communicates; a supernatural event or miracle as a sign from God" (like a Shabb'awt' resurrection, and the letter "tav" "ת" itself means "sign" as the vowel point that accompanies it in the word "Shabbat" mimics the phonetics of "awt" that represents the same in paleo Hebrew).

The Shabbat was made a perpetual covenant since the dawn of Creation for all mankind, not since Sinai for a select group of people. It was "blessed" and "sanctified" before the universe, at the very time "the breath of life" was breathed into man's nostrils (Gen 2:3,7); early <u>on</u> the Sabbath, as YHVH finished His work of Creation "<u>on</u> the seventh day"(Gen 2:2) (See Appendix C). When our Father "blessed"(#1288) and "sanctified"(#6942) the seventh day (Gen 2:3), it was "set apart" for "a holy purpose," made clean, and pure, free from guilt and corruption. Understanding the sanctity of Shabbat, and to say our Savior was dead on Shabbat is to make Him cursed and desecrated every Shabbat. This would abdicate victory to the adversary, who made a pagan Greek god of healing (Iesous) to resurrect on "the first *day* of the week" in translation; to take the ignorant captive back to the adversarial religion, that Satan might become the god to this world, if he could substitute himself that "he" arose on "the first *day* of the week."

The Sabbath is called to be a "delight," "holy" and "honorable" (Isa 58:13), and death is none of these things, especially for our Savior. In fact, no correlation exists between "rest" and "death" in either Greek or Hebrew. On the seventh day, in the end, the Father says, "all flesh shall come to worship before Me" (Isa 66:23); just as our Savior came before His Father on resurrection morning, before Mary touched Him, before He appeared to His disciples later that day (Jn 20:17).

Scripture states, "the dead know not anything" (Ecc 9:5), they "praise not YHVH" (Ps115:17), nor is there any "remembrance" or giving "thanks" (Ps 6:5). As we cease from our labors on the Shabbat it should be a day of joyous gratitude and worshipful celebration; a day of willing re-creation, regeneration, and healing as the proper definition of "rest" (#7673), of which death is the complete opposite.

Interlinear Comparison

Now we are ready to look at all "the first day of the week" phrases as they are found in two commonly used Interlinear NT, the same Greek words with different interpretations.

INTERLINEAR New Testament	Trinitarian Bible Society (1976)	Baker Book House (1981)
	Interpretation:	Interpretation:
"μιαν σαββατων" Mt 28:1 mian sabbatone	"the first of (the) week"	(the) first (day) of (the) week"
"μιασ σαββατων" Mk 16:2 mias sabbatone	"the first of the week"	the first (day) of the week"
"πρωτη σαββατου" Mk 16:9 protae sabbatou	"the first of the week"	(the) first (day) of the week
"μια των σαββατων" Lk 24:1 mia tone Sabbatone	"one of the week"	the first (day) of the week"
"μια των σαββατων" Jn20:1 mia tone sabbatone	first of the **sabbaths**	the first (day) of the **week**
"μια των σαββατων" Jn20:19 mia tone sabbatone	first of the **sabbaths**	the first (day) of the **week**
"μια των σαββατων" Ac20:7 mia tone sabbatone	one of the **sabbaths**	the first (day) of the **week**
μιαν σαββατων 1Cor16:2 mian sabbatone	one of a week	first (day) of the week

"The First Day of the Week" Scripture or Tradition?

Ironically, even the same group of scholarly translators can determine the same Greek phrase differently. Consider "mia tone sabbatone," as "one of the week," as "first of the Sabbaths," and "one of the Sabbaths." Was the intent of the original author to mean all three? Now, let us evaluate all the forms of *#4521* "sabbaton" in the NT, and see if we can ascertain some consistency in an attempt to clear up this confusion.

Interlinear Bible(IB)	INTERLINEAR BIBLE TRANSLATION			as found in
Forms of *#4521*	Singular	Plural	"week"	KJV
1. Sabbasi	S	P		S/P
2. Sabbasin		P		S/P
3. Sabbata		P		P
4. Sabbato	S			S
5. Sabbaton	S	P	W	S/W
6. Sabbatone		P	W	W
7. Sabbatou	S		W	S/W

There are seven NT forms of *#4521* "sabbaton" [see Appendix B and F]. Each of these Greek words reflects the Hebrew in transliteration. And even though Greek words can be masculine, feminine, or neuter; and regular or irregular; they can only be singular or plural, not both. Strangely enough, in this case, neither the Interlinear Bibles, nor King James and his scholars can fully agree upon the proper classification of several of these forms. Each are in agreement that "sabbata" is plural and that "sabbato" is singular, but notice that the IB has "sabbaton" as "S"["sabbath" (Singular)], "P"["sabbaths"(Plural)], and "W"("week"), and disagrees with the KJV on this and two other forms.

Of greater interest is how another form can be both singular and "week," without ever being used as a "P" (plural) (sabbatou -10X), as it had been presumed that "week" can only be derived from a plural form, "a *se'nnight*, i.e. the interval between two Sabbaths." (earlier Strong's). [Just to be persnickety, an "interval" is "A space between two objects," (Collegiate Dictionary) that would mean their use "sabbaton" for "week" would be a six-day week.] Remember that confusion was not authored by YHVH (1 Cor 14:33).

Part of the problem stems from the fact that fallen man has a greater affinity for tradition than for truth (Jer 17:9). Whenever "sabbaton/e" relates to fulfilled prophecy in the NT, the KJV scholars have translated them to "week" for the purpose of converting "Sabbath" observance to "the first day of the week" (Jer 17:5; Pro3:5, 6).

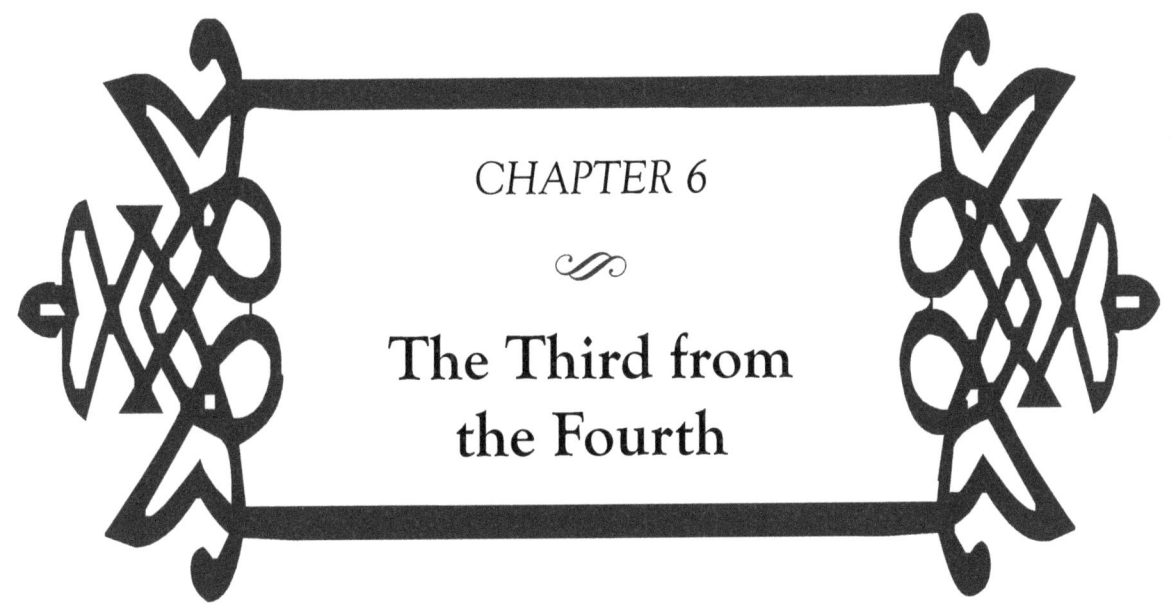

CHAPTER 6

The Third from the Fourth

"Let God be True, but Every Man a Liar"

Man is naturally rebellious and is uncomfortable with change. Remember in the secular Greek dictionaries, the Greek word "hebdomada" was defined solely as "week," and "sabbaton" was never found to have this interpretation. Now you will find that some new Greek dictionaries do have "sabbaton" as "week," but most of these are your Greek <u>Bible</u> Dictionaries that are simply reflecting the translation according to the KJV scholars, as do the KJV concordances, and their progeny.

Therefore, in reviewing "mia sabbatone," could we not have "a (feast day) 7th day Sabbath?" Could "mia tone sabbatone" possibly be "the one (feast day) 7th day Sabbath"? Could "prote sabbatou" possibly relate to the first feast time of the year (i.e. UB)? At least all these are consistent and make some sense. But even with certain errors being brought to light, the intention is not to discourage KJV readers, but to attend the self-learned mind to particular traditions, which have made their way into this foundational translation, or "version," as the King James translators call it.

Again, Scripture informs us that these things would happen (2 Th 2:10,11; Rom 1:25; Jude 4; Rev 22:18,19). For just as the Greeks eventually replaced the Hebrew "Tetragrammaton" from the earlier Greek manuscripts, and the Romans eventually kept the sacred writings from the people (replacing truth for tradition); controlled Protestantism reluctantly gave the Word back to the people, in their own language. Only after leaders had edited a few things, out of concern for reputations, to maintain harmless tradition; based upon their own understanding, to keep peace among the majority. Oddly enough, these translations were not censured or burned by any authority.

The Bible tells us that "the heart (of man) is deceitful above all things, and desperately wicked" (Jer 17:9), and that even, if possible, "the very elect" (devout believers) can be deceived (Mt 24:24). However, if we ask our gracious Father to exchange our "stony heart" for the heart He would give us (Eze 11:19; 36:26), then He would provide a way of understanding if we search for Him with all our heart (Jer 29:13; Jn 15:15).

The Word tells us that "the express image" of our Father, is "the Way, the Truth, and the Life" (Heb 1:3; Jn 14:6); so, "with patience," let us run after the "express" definition of His Words, as He is the Word, by the prayerful use of commentaries and concordances with our dictionaries, Bibles and Interlinear, being as wise "as" a serpent, but in the Spirit of the Father to "lay aside every weight" (Heb 12:1) that would keep us from the Truth (2 Jn 1:4).

Our heavenly Father implores His little children to love one another not "in word, neither in tongue: but indeed and in Truth" (1 Jn 3:18) for He wants to lead every one of us and "guide (us) into all Truth" (Jn 16:13). But without Him, each one of us is prone to lean unto our own understanding (Pr 3:5). May our Father attend us as we continue to rely upon Him, asking Him to take us through the next section of our study.

"The Third Day"

The most frequently asked question at this point concerns the length of time our Savior was dead. Several times, toward the end of His earthly ministry, our Savior tried to impart to His disciples that He would "suffer many things" of the religious establishment "be killed," and rise again "the third day" (Mt 16:21; 17:23; 20:19; Lk 9:22; 13:32; 18:33); so if the morning of the 7th day Sabbath was the time of the resurrection, then Friday certainly could not be the day of the crucifixion and be congruent with Mt 12:40.

All the popular modern English "translations" refer to the three days as, the "preparation day," "the sabbath," and "the first day of the week," or three separate days, implying a three day week-end. Our Savior did decree three days for himself. The Book of Acts also informs that three days did happen (Ac 10:40), and Paul mentions "the third day" in this context "according to scripture"(1 Cor 15:3,4). It is true that back in the OT, the "third day" did lend some significance to the resurrection, as on this "third day" our Father:

- * Released us from darkness (Gen 42:17,18: Exo 10:22,23)
- * Prepared us with fasting (Est 4:16; 5:1)
- * Had us come before Kings (1Kng 12;5,12; 2Chr 10:5,12)
- * Purified us for cleansing (Num 19:12,19)
- * Gave us healing (2Kng 20:5,8)
- * Allowed us to enter the Promised Land (Jos 1:11)
- * Finished the Temple (Ezr 6:15)
- * Prepared us to come before Him (Gen 22:4; Ezr 10;8,9)
- * Revealed the Former and Latter Rain (Hos 6:3)
- * Will raise us up to live before Him (Hos 6:2)

* Prepares a feast   (Gen 40:20)
* Brings deliverance   (Exo 15:22-26; 1Sam 20:5,12; 2Sam 1:2)
* Allows Himself to be revealed   (Exo 19:11,16)

In light of our study, the question should be asked: Would these "third day" accounts be more significant to culminate on the first day of the week or the Sabbath? Granted, we have no empirical evidence whether any of these events ended on a seventh-day Sabbath, but several of them relate to feast elements that with a consistent calendar may have terminated on a 7th day Sabbath. None of them can be proven to end on the first day of the week. The following are the Gospel texts stating the "three days" period:

	"in three days"	"after three days"	"the third day"
Matthew	26:61; 27:40	27:63; 12:40 (and 3 nights)	16:21; 17:23; 27:64
Mark	14:58 [by]	8:31	
Luke			9:22; 24:21, 46
John	2:19-21		

Because our Savior is consistent in His Word, we can regard each of these phrases to refer to the same timeframe. Even the priests of the day quoted our Savior as saying, "after three days," and asked Pilate to have the tomb guarded "until the third day" (Mt 27:63,64). Part of this apparent discrepancy is related to the fact demonstrated in Mt 27:62, which literally states: (details - p.96)

"Then on the day following that which **belongs with** the preparation, …"

Passover (the preparation) was considered part of the 1st of UB as it was "with" the 1st day of Unleavened Bread. This is confirmed in the previous chapter just before this time, in Mt 26:17:

"And on the **first** *day* of the *feast of* **unleavened bread** the disciples came to (our Savior), saying unto Him, 'Where would you want us to prepare for you to eat the **Passover**?'" (*Emphasis supplied*)

As Passover was indeed a day of unleavened bread that afternoon, after the sacrifice of the Passover lamb, the children of Israel would certainly eat unleavened bread. Hopefully, this may help clear up the "after-unto" problem regarding the "third day;" but the Pharisees understood that our Savior was trying to be the Firstfruits offering, on a day of deliverance, when the priest was to wave the sheaf of the Firstfruits in the Temple on the *morning* of the 7th day Sabbath. Some of them were expecting the disciples to steal the body and declare the disappearance as a resurrection; others anticipated the Roman guards to thwart a resurrection – only they wound up paying-off the Roman guards not to share what they had seen.

This "third day" is just another illustration of "inclusive reckoning," a common means of counting time in the ancient world. A classic example of this is found in 2 Kng 18:9,10, a time period beginning with the 4th year of Hezekiah and the 7th year of Hoshea, ending in the 6th year of Hezekiah and the 9th year of Hoshea. Some might call this period 2 years, subtracting 4 from 6, or 7 from 9, but the OT describes this as "the end of three years;" evidently counted as 4,5,6, and 7,8,9, three years inclusive. Therefore, intending to be clear and not leave any uncertainty, our Savior had specifically stated to the scribes and Pharisees that there would only be <u>one</u> sign given to this "evil and adulterous generation … the sign of the prophet Jonas" (Mt 12:39).

The Sign of Jonah

This "sign of the prophet Jonas" is probably the most disputed and falsely analyzed words of our Savior regarding the timeframe of His death and resurrection; specifically connected with His being "three days and three nights in the heart of the earth" (Mt 12:40b). This verse should firmly set the red flag over the Friday crucifixion /Sunday resurrection. The conventional reckoning of His going into the tomb Friday afternoon before sundown and resurrecting before dawn Sunday morning would be rendered in the Hebrew mind as only two days and two nights.

Some denominations theologize "the heart of the earth" as starting with our Savior in the Garden of Gethsemane, sweating "as it were great drops of blood falling to the ground" (Lk 22:44), but you should recognize the problem with that as we continue. In regards to the events of the passion week, as we read through each one of the gospel accounts, we find each day is described as follows: "the preparation (day)," "the sabbath," "a high day," and "the first *day* of the week." Without Mt 12:40, it could easily be understood why most Christians would render a Friday/Sunday scenario, but what is not typically brought out is that these passion days in the Gospels were comprised of two different preparation days before two separate holy convocations; one a feast day sabbath, the other a 7th day Sabbath. This would mean a "preparation" day before a feast day "sabbath," followed by another "preparation" day before a 7th day "sabbath." Here is an IB analysis.

"the preparation"	"the sabbat**on(ou)**"	"the preparation (sabbatou past)"	"mia sabbat**one**"
Mt 27:57		Mt 27:62	Mt 28:1
Mk 15:42		(Mk 16:1)	Mk 16:2
Lk 23:54	Lk 23:56		Lk 24:1
Jn 19:14, 42	Jn 19:31(ou)		Jn 20:1,19

Cognizant that "sabbatou" is a general term that makes reference to both holy convocations, typically during a feast week, it is not a "sabbatone," which is specifically a feast on a 7th day Sabbath. Each convocation has a preparation day before it. The 1st preparation is **before** a "sabbaton" (or "sabbatou"), and the 2nd preparation, **after** that "sabbato(n/u)," is **before** the "sabbatone." As Lk 23:56 specifically denotes the 1st "sabbath" a "sabbaton," a feast convocation.

This is why the Pharisees requested Roman guards to secure the tomb to the "third day," as they could not have their own guards working outside the Temple through late Friday evening, for this was the beginning of their sacred hours of their 7th day Sabbath (see Appendix D). Now let us take a more comprehensive look at our Savior's Words in Mt 12:40, so as not to take anything out of context.

> "For as Jonas was **three days** and **three nights** in the whale's belly; so shall the Son of man be **three days** and **three nights** in the heart of the earth." KJV

If we go back to the book of Jonah and review Jonah's pleading with his Heavenly Father from the belly of the whale, we find:

> "I cried by reason of mine affliction unto the Lord, and He heard me; out of the belly of **hell** cried I, *and* thou heardest my voice." Jnh 2:2 (KJV).

The word translated "hell" is the Hebrew word "sheol" H#7585, which means "common grave" (see KJV margin). Moreover, in verse 6: "… yet hast thou brought up my life from corruption …" KJV. The word "corruption" in the same margin is "pit." In Hebrew, it is "shachath" H#7845, which is another term for "grave."

So when our Savior made the correlation of His pending experience "in the heart of the earth" to Jonah's "three days and three nights in the whale's belly;" He meant that He too would be three days and three nights in the common "grave." "Heart of the earth" in the Greek here is "kardia" "ges" (G#2588, G#1093), which alternately means "soul of the world" (as in the "globe," or sphere), and refers to the land of Israel (with Jerusalem as the S-A node of the heart). And to the Jew, if one was not "dead" for 3 days and 3 nights, by inclusive reckoning standards, he could not be legitimately declared dead (1 Sam 30:12). As all awaiting souls will emanate from the earth when our Savior returns (1 Thes 4:16), so too our Savior awaited the specific call of His Father spoken to "the heart of the world" - Israel (as many saints there arose from the dead, Mt 27:52); yet unto three days and three nights. Therefore, if our Savior did indeed resurrect Sabbath morning, just before the rising of the sun (not to be construed with "sun rise" worship even on the 7th day Sabbath), then to determine the day of the crucifixion, all we need to do is count back three nights and three days and see if that day of the week fits the prophecy of such in the OT. This means of verification would technically be a third witness.

Inclusive Reckoning

The hour before the sun came up on that empty-tomb-Sabbath morning was still considered late into the third night from our Savior's entrance to it; so three nights back from this point would take us to our Wednesday night. The three "days" would have to be Fri-day, Thurs-day, and Wednes-day, as our Savior would then have been taken off the cross and placed into the heart of the earth, specifically the tomb of Joseph of Arimathaea, before the sun went down late Wednesday afternoon.

Now there are those who have tackled Mt 12:40 by partial analysis to declare the three days and three nights to mean three full days and three full nights, or 72 perfect hours; saying that our Savior was placed in the tomb Wednesday afternoon, then left the tomb at the same hour Sabbath afternoon. Of course, this would be in disregards to the true English renderings of the Greek, and have the empty tomb discovered by the three Hebrew women nearly 12 hours after the earthquake, early on "the first day of the week."

If this scenario was true, any amount of time after 72 hours would be classified as the fourth day. Recall, after the resurrection, that Cleopas and a fellow disciple, as they traveled the road to Emmaus "that same day," they informed the wayfaring "stranger" that came by their way, all the things that came to pass in Jerusalem; including how "certain women of our company made us astonished, which were early at the sepulcher;" stating that:

> "… even besides these **all** being completed (our Savior in the grave and the Passover complete) <u>now</u> is the third day <u>since</u> these things were <u>done</u>." Lk 24:21 (*lit.*) (*Emphasis Supplied*)

With "<u>all</u> being <u>completed</u>" includes " …the day following that which <u>belongs with</u> the preparation…"(*lit.*) Mt 27:62 (see Appendix D). Yet, before the dawning, when the women had found the empty tomb, this was before the fourth "day" since the crucifixion - (Lk 24:13-29; Ac 10:40, 41). Regarding the "day" here in Lk 24:21, the earlier Strong's has the following note:

> G#2250 ημερα (HEMERA) - " … *day*, i.e. (lit.) the time space **between dawn and dark**, … (but several days were usually reckoned by the Jews as inclusive of the parts of both extremes)."

Referring to the day light hours, hence our Savior's reference of 3 days and 3 nights. It is understood by ancient historians that any part of a day was referred to as a "day" by many cultures, including the Hebrews; just as it was with "years," as seen in the Hebrew reckoning of the reign of any king of Israel or Judah; as the number of months were generally not mentioned, unless their reign was considerably less than a year.

One particular reign, that of the boy king Jehoiachin, who reigned "three months and ten days" (2 Chr 36:9) is the longest reign of those who reigned less than one year, and is the only one that includes the number of days, (which likely, was not "ten days" to the hour.) An interesting point in the passage is that in the next verse, v. 10, it reads:

> "And **when the year was expired**, king Nebuchadnezzar sent, and brought him to Babylon, … and made Zedekiah his brother king over Judah and Jerusalem" (KJV). (*Emphasis supplied*)

Is this account implying that there was a period between the end of his reign and the end of the year? Certainly many societies have had a fixed date in a given year for the inauguration of their leaders. Did Israel do the same with their kings? Worthy of thought is the concept that Israel's first king, Saul the Benjamite, was anointed in coronation before the congregation of all Israel at Mizpah (1 Sa 10:17-25) on Pentecost Sabbath.

A little off topic, but in defense for this we should see a pattern. All Israel would congregate three times in the year at the place of YHVH's choosing (De 16:16), and Mizpah was that place before David; and of the three feasts, Pentecost was the one that was a single day; the other two lasted a week plus (Unleavened Bread and Tabernacles). And on each of these feasts, Moses told the Israelites when they came together, they were not to come empty handed (De 16:16, 17). At the presentation ceremony of their new king, Saul was lost in the crowd before the formal event, and was found inspecting all the "gifts" that were brought by the people ("stuff" in KJV, H#3627 - "keliy" - 1 Sam 10:22). This is verified by vs. 27 as the ill-repute of Israel, we are told, "brought him no presents," but they did come to this apparently required special convocation.

In the entire chapter of 1 Sa 10, from the anointing oil upon Saul to the departure of the people after services, including offerings that are in accord with Pentecost, such as the two leavened loaves (vs. 3, and 4), the Spirit descending upon Saul (v.6), the burnt offerings (v.8), Saul's prophesying (v.10), it all happened in one day (v.25), (compare 1 Sa 10 with Lev 23:17-21). So with this apparent point of the year, would it not make sense for the king to be anointed in coronation on the day of the out pouring of the Spirit?

Hence, all subsequent kings may have been anointed and received official coronation on the same day of the year, and, before the nation of Israel split in the days of Rehoboam, the three previous kings had each reigned "40 years" (Ac 13:21; 2 Sa 5:4; 2 Chr 9:30). In respect to inclusive reckoning, 1 Chr 3:4 tells us that David reigned "seven years and six months" in Hebron and "thirty and three years" in Jerusalem, yet in 1 Kng 2:11 it says he reigned "seven years" in Hebron and "thirty and three" in Jerusalem, and in 2 Sam 5:4, 5:

> "David *was* thirty years old when he began to reign, *and* he reigned **forty years**. In Hebron he reigned over Judah **seven years and six months**: and in Jerusalem he reigned **thirty and three years** over all Israel and Judah." (*Emphasis supplied*)

Since no months are mentioned in respect to Jerusalem, could there have been some inclusive reckoning unaccounted for? Did David reign in Jerusalem thirty-two years and so many months? Let us look at 2 Chr 36:10 again where it says, "when the year was expired," that word "expired" in Strong's is as follows:

> H#8666 תשובה "teshubah" – a *reoccurrence* (of time or place); … (as *returned*)"

Could the boy king Jehoiachin, because "he did evil in the sight of YHVH," or not being thirty years of age (Num 4:3, 23, 30 etc.), that he resumed the throne some "three months and ten days" before the turn of the year, before Pentecost, and was consequently not anointed? For the literal words are "And at the turn of the year …" (2 Chr 36:10). Nebuchadnezzar had him brought to Babylon, "at the turn of the year," (Rosh HaShannah) as if there was a period from the "three months and ten days" and his being taken to Babylon, before his brother Zedekiah was made king. Therefore, the reign in years for all the kings could have been in respect from Pentecost to Pentecost. Hence, no months are typically mentioned in the reigns longer than one year. All of this is brought to light to show that so many months being inclusive in a year, so too the number of hours can be inclusive to a day. Consider that even a portion of the "day," here (#2250 "hemera"), is still part of that "time space between dawn and dark."

So when the Gospel account records that our Savior died upon the cross at about "the ninth hour" (6am - **3pm** = 9th hour of the day - Mt 27:46; Mk 15:34; Lk 23:44), if it was at the top of the hour, there was 3½ hours of "day" light left on that Wedneds-"day." This time is referred to as "between the evenings" (Ex 12:6 YLT).

> "Within the Temple, the day was divided into quarters. The quarter between 12:00 noon and 3:00 pm was called the minor evening oblation, while that between 3:00 and 6:00 pm was called the major evening oblation. Therefore, 'between the evenings' means between those two periods or 3:00 pm." (*Rosh HaShanah and the Messianic Kingdom to Come*, p. 20)

This would allow enough time to get permission from Pilate, whose palace guard sent a flag signal from atop Fort Antonio, a towering edifice in the corner of the city by the Temple, to notify the guards at the crosses on the hill at Golgotha, that permission was granted. Then sympathizers helped remove, lower, and partially cleanse the body, in order to properly carry It to the tomb, as Joseph of Aramathæa and Nicodemus likely arrived from Pilate's presence.

At this point, Joseph and Nicodemus were able to oversee the critical procedure of preparing the body and the wrapping of It while in the tomb, all of this well before sunset to constitute "a day." With even enough time left for both Joseph and Nicodemus to get to their homes, likely cleanse themselves if they prepared the Savior's dead body, all before sundown, so that they might officiate the Passover with their families (Lev 22:4-8). Even this 4th day of the week, "Wednes"day, named after a pagan god (formally called "Woden's Day"), was celebrated by the burning of a cross at sundown. Could this be the origins of "Ash Wednesday"? [see - White, L., *Fossilized Customs*, p. 8, 9].

Pope Dope

In a letter from Pope Nicholas I to King Boris of Bulgaria, dated in 866 BCE., the Pope is attempting to encourage this King's conversion to "Christianity," and consequently that of his people, by answering some of the King's questions. In regard to his question about the customary fasting on Wednesday that occurred in his region, the Pope replies:

"Chapter V. One should engage in lamentation more on the fourth day of the week (Wednesday) than on the other days except the sixth (Friday), because the Lord had already been buried in a certain way on this day in the heart of the earth, i.e. in the heart of the traitor Judas, when he was planning to betray Him to death (re: Mt 26:14-16). If one of you wishes to eat meat on this day however, he absolutely can do so, unless perchance it is known that a priest has forbidden him this …"

It seems to be more fitting that the Christian world, at least as late as 866 CE (Christain Era), would fast every Wednesday, "because the Lord had already been buried in a certain way on this day in the heart of the earth," rather than for what Judas may have contrived in his heart. This would also be the day of the week of our Savior's Ascension if we count "forty days" from the "sabbatone"(Ac 1:3). These events may very well have been the impetus for the Wednesday night prayer meeting; but by the time of the more organized reformation period, in the days of Martin Luther, the concept of a Friday crucifixion / Sunday resurrection, known as the Easter celebration, had already become a tradition throughout most of Christendom.

CHAPTER 7

Right on Time

Extra-Biblical Extras

Before we confirm this Wednesday crucifixion from secular and astronomical sources, let us garner confidence from these sources by first looking at the time of our Savior's birth and work forward. From *The Antiquities of the Jews*, written by 1st century historian Flavius Josephus in 93 AD, we read in Book 17, Chapter 6, Section 4:

> "Herod deprived this Matthias of the high priesthood, and burnt the other Matthias, who had raised the sedition, with his companions, alive. And that very night there was an eclipse of the moon."

This lunar eclipse is the only eclipse mentioned by Josephus in any of his writings, confirmed by the US Naval Observatory in the region of Palestine, and occurred on March 13th in the Julian year 4710, which was 4 years Before the Christian Era, or 4BCE. It was shortly after this event that Herod had died; the same Herod that called for the death of all the children in Bethlehem "from two years old and under, according to the time which he had diligently enquired of the wise men" (Mt. 2:16). It seems reasonable to conclude that our Savior's birth had to have been before this period, even though the Christian majority points to various astrological signs that may create a bright "star" closer to the traditional transition time from 1 BCE to 1 CE (AD).

If planetary conjunctions can be considered to be "his star in the east" (Mt 2:2), there was a rare conjunction of Jupiter, Saturn, and Mars in 6 BCE. In consideration of the Magi, an ancient Babylonian clay almanac from 8 BCE had described coming celestial events for the next 13 months. The tablet calculates Jupiter and Saturn remaining together in the constellation of Pisces for 11 months, coming into close conjunction 3 times. The tablet refers to the coming period March/April 7 BC – March/April 6 BC. The brightness in the night sky that year may not have correlated to our Savior's birth at the feast of Tabernacles as we once thought, but likely on the true Rosh HaShannah, Abib 1 (Nisan 1) (see Youtube: Jonathan Cahn, *When was Messiah Jesus Born?* [See also Jonathan Cahn, *The Mishkan Clue*, DVD, and Appendix E]).

Many believe our Savior came to "dwell"(tabernacle) with mankind, being born at the start of the feast of Tabernacles (Jn 1:14), which would place the birth of John the Baptist at the previous Passover, six months prior (Lk 1:36). Tabernacles was called "Sukkoth," or feast of Booths, as Israel would gather together to share the bounty of their harvest and stay in shelters they made of palms, willows, and leafy branches; open to the elements, to remind them of their ancestors dwellings when YHVH brought them out of Egypt (Lev 23:40-43). This may be why tradition had our Savior born in a stable. If indeed He was born on the first of Tabernacles, He would have been circumcised on the eighth day of Tabernacles, both of these days, the first and last of Tabernacles, are holy convocations.

Relevant to the likelihood of His birth on Abib 1 (Nisan 1) ("Rosh HaShannah" meaning "New Year,"- late March – which coincides very close to the vernal equinox) the Gospels mention that "there were in the same country shepherds abiding in the field, keeping watch over their flock by night" (Lk 2:8). The only time shepherds would be with their sheep at night is when the ewes were ready to lamb. This happens no sooner than early spring, never in winter, and not in the fall. The angel told the shepherds that the Savior was born that day (vs.12, in a "manger" as the "Lamb of God"). This would be fulfilling the type-to-anti-type as the literal, earthly Tabernacle in the wilderness was completed on this day, Abib 1 (Ex 40:2, 17), for He will be called "Emmanuel," or "El *Tabernacling* with us" (Mt 1:23), as Jn 1:14 says:

" …the Word was made flesh, and dwelt (tabernacled) among us, …"

The Greek word for "dwelt" is "εσκηνωσεν" in the IB, from G#*4637* "**skenoo**" - "to *tent* or *encamp*; to *occupy* (as a mansion), to *reside* (as God did in the **Tabernacle** of old, …"

This Abib 1 was also the birth date of Levi (Jub 28:14), whose tribe ministers the tabernacle. The rare conjunction of Jupiter, Saturn, and Mars in 6 BCE started in the spring of that year (to His conception) and Jupiter and Saturn continued through to 5 BCE. All these things may be why the shepherds, and Mary, marveled at the "words spoken to them" for the timing on which these things occurred (Lk 2:17-19).

The references to "tabernacling" is understandable why many "non-Christmas" believers would consider the feast of Tabernacles. Only the ewes would not foal in the fall, even in Palestine, as the young lambs would not likely survive any winter without cover. To place the Savior's birth at the feast of Tabernacles would also place Mary's travel to visit Elizabeth, from Galilee to Judea, in the winter; whereas with Messiah's birth at Rosh HaShannah (1st of the 1st) would place her travel in early or mid-June (maybe when Joseph went to Jerusalem for Pentecost), which is much more conducive to traveling and sleeping in the elements along the way.

To confirm these thoughts, the father of John the Baptist, Zachariah, was of the Levitical family "Abijah" (Lk 1:5), which is the "eighth" of the twenty-four Levitical families that serve the Temple (1 Chr 24:10); but the only reference we have to determine the time in the year of the "eighth" service is found in extra-biblical sources. These are the Dead Sea Scrolls and the Talmud.

Both of these sources corroborate "the course of Abijah" that lend to the conception of John at Hannukah (early-to-mid December) and the conception of our Savior about six months later (Lk 1:36), possibly at Pentecost, with their subsequent births six months apart. The interesting point here is that in type, Moses went up the mount on Pentecost and was there "forty days and forty nights," in which he receives the statutes and the commandments; and possibly 3 weeks into his time there, he may have received the directives and dimensional layout for the Tabernacle, which would place the dedication of the Tabernacle precisely 9 months later on Abib 1.

John being born very near, or on the Feast of Trumpets (1st of the 7th - to be "one 'shouting' [G#994 - boao] in the wilderness" Jn 1:23), and our Savior on the day of Rosh HaShannah (Abib 1, also meaning "New the Age")[Mary could have conceived on Pentecost with the birth at Abib 1, placing her 3 weeks overdue (more of a possibilty with a first-time pregnancy)], as the Father brings His "Bread of Life" (Jn 6:35) to Bethlehem (House of Bread)[Bethlehem on the turn of the year (Abib1) would be more likely the time and location for the couple to be taxed, than on Tabernacles – requiring attendance in Jerusalem (Lk 2:1,3,5)].

Our Savior was always the true reflection of the pattern in Heaven in all that He did, and with His being brought here to be the "Lamb of God" (Lk 2:12) it would make sense that He would have been born on the 5th day of the week ("5" - Tabernacles and Divine favor) answering the same day of the week when sin entered the world (Jub 3:17; 2 Cor 5:21). With either Abib 1 or the 1st of Tabernacles as His birth, this would be on the 5th day of the week with His circumcision on the following 5th day of the week. But with an Abib 1 birth, His name given at circumcision (Lk 2:21), would then have been unto the "third day" of our Father choosing His Lamb on the 7th day Sabbath (10th of the 1st - Ex 12:3); which, if His mother was overdue, would still allow His dedication to be on Pentecost Sabbath (Lk 2:27, 32, 38), as both Mary and Joseph went to Jerusalem when the time of Mary's purification was past (Lk 2:22, 24; Lev 12:2-4, 6), for Joseph was to be in Jerusalem for Pentecost (Ex 23:14-17), and they were there together (Lk2:22).

Moreover, even at this point, this disruption of the Truth should be well recognized, from the day of His birth switched to the three days after the winter solstice, and to the day of the resurrection abdicated for the pagan feast of Easter, (the first Sunday after the vernal equinox), when the sun's light overtakes the night's darkness on the day of the sun - commemorated each week on the pagan day of worship "the first day of the week" (Sunday), and the pagan feast of the rebirth of the sun on December 25th (the first day of observable lengthening of daylight after 3 days [and 3 nights] of no measurable movement from December 21st). So we will return to the astronomical points for a Wednesday Crucifixion after some more foundation is laid here.

Re-Pentecost

Now that we have secured some reasonable documentation for this case, let us see if we can determine what year our Savior began His earthly ministry and what significance that might have to a Wednesday crucifixion. Our Savior began His ministry when He received baptism of John in the wilderness of the Jordan river and this was likely on the Day of Pentecost (a sabbatone), the 7th day feast of the holy Spirit, (not a Sunday – see "Fact, Fiction, or Fraud," p. 36) in preparation for the years turn in the sabbatical cycle on the Day of Atonement (Lev 25:8). What better time to receive the baptism of the Spirit, but on Pentecost Sabbath.

The fiery revelation of YHVH on Mount Sinai before Moses on this "sabbatone" (Ex 19:1, 11, 15, 16), was a similar type of fire that came upon the disciples in the upper room on the same day of the year. The same Spirit descended upon our Savior, but not in the form of thunderous lightening, a consuming fire, or tongues of fire accompanied by a "mighty rushing wind," but as an exceeding bright light that completely surrounded and pervaded Him on that same day.

The Gospel translators say that the Spirit descended upon Him "like a dove" (Mt 3:16; Mk 1:10; Lk 3:22; Jn 1:32). The word "dove" in the Interlinear Bible (IB) is "περιστεραν"(peristeran) in all four accounts, which comes from (#4058) "**peristera.**" Let us take a look at the definition and then break this Greek word up into its two component parts and reconsider the definition:

G#4058 PERISTERA – "**of uncert. der.**; a *pigeon*: - dove, pigeon."

G#*4012* PERI – "prop. ***through*** (all *over*), i.e. **around**; fig. *with respect* to;"
G#*4731* STEREOS – "*stiff*, i.e., *solid, stable* (lit. or fig.): - steadfast, **strong**, sure." (*Emphasis supplied*)

Notice in the description for "peristera" the prescribed meaning has an "uncertain derivation," which alludes to an unknown etymology in this very common translation as a "dove." To take the proposed definitions of "peri" and "stereos" and recombine them we have something that is "strong, pervasive and all encompassing." A dove is not strong, and does not envelope anything - unless you consider the traditional representation of the dove as a winged god of the heavens as the pagans did. At least His cousin John witnessed this bright, shadowless light as he was foretold that the coming Son of God would be the One who receives a physical manifestation of the Spirit that would remain on Him (like the disciples in the upper room), the physical manifestation of His Father's Light upon Him on Pentecost (Lk 3:15,16). Our Savior, now in turn, would best "baptizo" G#*907* (immerse) others with the holy Spirit (Jn 1:32, 33), as He so prepared His many disciples (Jn 20:22), and then through Peter, He "baptizo" 3000 Israelites the same day four years later, in the middle of a week of years (Acts 2:41), on Pentecost Sabbath.

Would it not be like the Father to do "all things decently (promptly) and in order (fixed sequence)" (examine the Gk in 1 Cor14:40), to place His Spirit on His Son on the very day He had in type, poured out His Spirit upon the patriarchs and kings in the days of old as a Divine appointment? In order for our Savior to impart the "immersion" of His Father's Spirit onto others, it would make sense that He Himself should receive the impartation of His Father's Spirit with "immersion" on the day prophesied for the outpouring, that he in turn would do the same for His disciples with the same timing, as they were "to walk, even as He walked," even "in the light" (1 Jn 2:6; 1:7).

Pentecost is always represented with a bright transcending light upon the Spirit-filled believer, and this is why the Israelites were to "kindle no fire" (Ex 35:3) specifically on the Pentecost Sabbath (found 1X - see context from Ex 34:29), so as not to construe their own initiated sacred light, or "strange fire," as Nadab and Abihu attempted to do (Lev 9:24-10:2). This is just what the prophets of Baal tried to do before Elijah's Pentecost sacrifice was accepted (1 Kng 18:24,29, 36-41) on that 7th day feast sabbath. And Jezebel (Heb."Iyze·ba̱l" ["pure for Baal"] "bal" - fem.of Baal, not "el" [title for the Almighty]) made a covenant with the gods that she would kill Elijah "by tomorrow," or herself be killed. If indeed this was a Sabbath, or Pentecost Sabbath, the next day would be Baal's day, "the first day of the week" (1 Kng 19:2); and Jezebel's death could have likely happened on that very day, some years later (1 Kng 21:23).

Remember, the 7th day Sabbath means "the Dwelling Place of the Father's Miraculous Sign," and a Pentecost baptism (Mt 3:15 - certainly not for the remission of His sins) was an outpouring of the Father's Spirit upon His Son that can also be surmised by calculating the approximate time from this point leading to our Savior's reading of the Isaiah scroll before the people of His home town on the Day of Atonement (Lk 4:16), which was the 10th day of the 7th month (Lev 23:27; 16:29,30).

So, in reading of His baptism, Mt 3:5-17, we envision a sizeable crowd venturing into the wilderness by the Jordan, looking for an outpouring of the Father's Spirit in baptism, likely on the day of Pentecost, for even "many of the Pharisees and Sadducees" (v.7) had made the excursion - maybe to police those carrying more than a fig weight, or looking for a sign, or some reason to condemn John and stem the tide of his influence.

Recall now that after our Savior's baptism He was led "immediately" (Mk 1:12 "Spirit driven") across the Jordan into the same wilderness of the children of Israel and "fasted 40 days and 40 nights" (Mt 4:2), just as Moses did in the mount, at the same point in the year, for the same amount of time; and maybe our Savior had been taken up Mount Sinai (Mt 4:8). [John was likely baptizing at the same location the children of Israel crossed into the promised land (Jn 1:28).] After being tempted of the devil, our Savior returned -

"[I]nto Galilee and there went out <u>a fame of Him through **all** the region</u> round about. And <u>He taught in their</u> <u>synagogues</u> being <u>glorified of **all**</u>. And He came to Nazareth, where He had been brought up. . . [and] went into the synagogue on the '**sabbatone**,' and stood up for to read." (Lk 4:14-16).

Some twelve Shabbats since His coming into Galilee from the wilderness, is likely the amount of time needed to visit all the synagogues throughout that region and develop a reputation by word of mouth before coming into His hometown on the next "sabbatone," which would be the Day of Atonement, a 7th day feast; for a total of 4 months from the previous "sabbatone" of Pentecost.

At One-ment

On this particular Day of Atonement, the first in our Savior's ministry, the trumpet of the Jubilee may have been blown throughout the land (Lev 25:9); which would have marked the beginning of the hallowed fiftieth year, in the middle of the forty-nine year, or the seventh Sabbatical. The Sabbatical cycle always starts in the middle of the year, specifically on the Day of Atonement, the 10th day of the 7th month.

If it was the day of Jubilee (the Day of Atonement in the 49th year), our Savior fulfilled the requirement of returning to His hometown of Nazareth (Lk 4:16) as Scriptures says, "you shall return every man to His family" (Lev 25:10); and He read aloud Is 61:1,2a before the synagogue, the requirements for the year of Jubilee. Slaves are set free, debts cancelled, and liberty is proclaimed, which would be the <u>acceptable</u> ("desirable, delight" #H 7522 –"ratson") year of YHVH, (Lk 4:19; Lev 25:12); and He added, "This <u>day</u> is this scripture fulfilled in your ears"(Lk 4:21). And "this" day that our Savior addressed His hometown congregants was on a "Shabbat," a 7th day Sabbath (Lev 16:31; 23:32). As the Interlinear reads in English at Lk 4:16 (IB):

"… And He went in as the custom **to Him**, on the day of the 'sabbatone'…"

This day was certainly a 7th day feast Sabbath, as the Day of Atonement always was in the days of the prophets and kings. From the rabbis own literature they make inference to this, calling the Day of Atonement the "Sabbath of Sabbaths" ("Shabbos Shabbason"), or the "double Sabbath" (*Biblical Holidays,* p. 319; www.torahmusings.com), acknowledged to be the day of the new year in the count of years in the sabbatical cycle (Lev 25:9, 10), but as it is traditionally called a "double" Sabbath, it may give some insight to it being a consistent 7th day Sabbath in the past (as the 7th month has never been mentioned as a Shabbat month -), with our Savior in Nazareth this day, early in His ministry, this could have been at the end of a Sabbatical year, kicking off the last seven year count-down to a specific Jubilee, a special week of years, as a Teshuvah (turning - repentance) of years, a type of seven year dispensation – (see Appendix E).

Now Scripture says that at His baptism He "began to be about thirty years of age" (Lk 3:23). In Hebrew culture, a man's age included his gestational time spent in his mother's womb (see also Appendix H); so any commemoration of his years would be closer to his day of conception, rather than at his birth. Recalling from our brief study that if our

Savior was conceived on Pentecost in 7 BCE, then at His baptism he certainly "began to be" 30 years of age (1 Cor 14:40), if He was baptized on Pentecost in 24 CE as He would be just entering His 30th year, again as the Hebrews would allocate the time from conception [Remember, no Ø BCE (BC), or Ø CE (AD)].

This would place the Magi's visit and the time of Herod's killing of all the children in Bethlehem to 5 BCE, a Sabbatical year (one year before Herod died - 4 BCE), when our Savior was still under 2 years of age. The "star" the Magi saw may have been brighter at the Savior's birth than at the time of their visit, yet no doubt they observed the conjunction in their land. Because of the ancient influence of Daniel in that region of Shinar, the Magi came to concur the meaning; and possibly, after some political maneuvering and coordinating two or more kings to travel together, they arrived in Jerusalem inquiring of the Messiah's whereabouts nearly a year after the main conjunction.

In order for a priest to do "service," "work," or "ministry," in "the tabernacle of the congregation" he had to be "from thirty years old and upward" (this phrase mentioned 7x's in Num Ch.4). From His baptism on Pentecost, maybe in the last seven year count down to the declaration of the 50th year to commence on the Day of Atonement of 31 CE. But in the year 24 CE our Savior had officially announced His ministry from His home town on the Day of Atonement that year. The Mosaic time-keeping of His crucifixion, 3½ years later as the Passover Lamb, did coincided with the Pharisees lunar Passover that year (28 CE), which they and the Sadducees have kept since the days of the Babylonian captivity, always falling on a full moon. This Passover so coincided with YHVH's timing, that the Pharisees and Sadducees would have no excuse of missing the prophecy.

Blue Moon

As the Babylonians would worship their Moon god on the full moon, their captive Pharisees and Sadducees were taught to lead their fellow captive Israelites to determine their feasts accordingly. There was no such thing as a Pharisee, or a Sadducee prior to the Babylonian captivity. These were the groups of families amongst the Levitical priests most willing to compromise their previous beliefs and teachings, who were consequently given the most authority over their own people. Over the next succeeding generations, the inevitable confusion fostered denominationalism amongst Judaism, beneath which emerged a remnant group, the Essenes, who refused to compromise and eventually resorted to the wilderness to escape the oppressive Pharisees. These were those who comprised the Qumran community by the Dead Sea. "For the movement behind the scrolls, the Pharisees were public enemy number one." "The Pharisees were the forbearers of the rabbis and rabbinic literature." [Wise, Abegg, & Cook, *The Dead Sea Scrolls*, p. 272, and 17].

Remember that the Judeans were now oppressed servants of Babylon, who had to outwardly comply with the wishes of their captors. Hence, the lunar calendar would invariably gain prominence with the majority, within a couple of generations if enough sanctions are imposed. Even to this day the Judaic lunar calendar retains the Babylonian names for all 12 months in their Aramaic dialect, not unlike our present day Gregorian calendar in Latin. The 4th Jewish month is obviously not the name Moses would have used, called "Tammuz." Yet the Jewish majority had continued to follow this time-keeping even after the Babylonian empire fell, for the Medes and Persians kept a lunar calendar and the compromising priesthood became well established through these governing bodies, secured by the development of secret societies that today have no boundaries. In fact, all the nations represented in Nebuchadnezzar dream (Dan 2) had used the lunar calendar, which includes fallen Judaism, with the exclusion of some tribes of Ephraim in the "diaspora" (dispersed Israel). This was all in accordance to YHVH's providence (Rom 11:25).

Now, to the astronomical signs for the Wednesday crucifixion: According to the US Naval Observatory (USNO), the full moon in the month of Passover in the spring of 28 CE fell on a Wednesday. The majority of churches teach that our Savior died in 30 CE, because the month of Pascha (Abib) that year had a Friday full moon; which denies the previous historical/astrological accounts of Him being born well before 4BCE, and being baptized as He began to be 30 years of age.

Some churches teach 31 AD, with a Friday crucifixion; which denies both astronomical accounts and ancient history, as the USNO has the Jews Passover full moon that year on a Wednesday as well. Again, our Father had preordained His calendar (the intercalated 360 = 364 days) to coincide with the lunar month in that year of His crucifixion (28 AD / CE). Hence, that the Pharisees and Sadducees would have no excuse of missing the Messiah (this synchronization would happen at least once every three (3) years, since the lunar calendar is typically corrected every three years).

The Twilight Zone

Our Savior triumphantly entered Jerusalem, on the back of a young colt, on a 7th day Sabbath; not a Sunday like most of Christianity believes. There are several points to verify this. In Jn 12:1-3,12,13, we read:

"Then Jes-s six days before the Passover came to Bethany (Friday) (inclusive reckoning), ...There they made Him a supper (Friday even)... ...Then took Mary a pound ...of spikenard, very costly, and anointed the (head and) feet of Jes-s, ... (the evening before the people would choose a Passover lamb) ... On the next day (IB: "on the morrow" or "in the morning") much people that were come to the feast, when they heard that Jes-s was coming to Jerusalem ("waved" their "firstfruit" offerings), ... and cried, 'Hosanna: Blessed is the King of Israel that cometh in the name of the Lord.'" KJV.

The "next day" was the 10th of the 1st month, the Chosen Lamb Sabbath, the same day the people would ceremoniously carry their first sheaf offering into Jerusalem to wave before the priest in the Temple (Exo 12:3; Lev 23:10-12); it was not "Palm Sunday," it was "Wave Sheaf Sabbath." [In fact, Palm Sunday has a problem with a Friday crucifixion, which would be six days inclusively, when the days from Lamb choosing to Passover are five days (10th - 14th)].

On the following 7th day Sabbath morning, the third day after our Savior "Passed-over" His people as the "Lamb of God," even after the "great earthquake" (Mt28:2) and the empty tomb, before all this was acknowledged by the priests on the 17th of the 1st month, the high priest garnered the FF Omer and waved it before YHVH in the Temple; then the priests started to wave these first fruits of the people before YHVH (Lev 23:11). So, if by the Mosaic calendar, the 14th day (Passover) [Exo 12:18; Lev 23:5] was consistently a Wednesday, then the 10th day was consistently a 7th day Sabbath. This is the day all of Israel would choose the lamb and take it to the family home.

In fact, the rabbi's admit that the choosing of the lamb in Egypt was on a 7th day Sabbath, and they call it the *Shabbos HaGadol* (The Great Sabbath) in commemoration of the miracle that the Egyptians did not interfere with Israelites intention to sacrifice, what represented to the Egyptians, another one of their gods (*The Chumash*, The Stone Edition, p. 351).

Once more, in our Father's providence, the Pharisaic Lunar calendar of Babylonian origin coincided with the true Mosaic calendar in the month of our Savior's passion; that the priests of the day would have no excuse for not seeing these prophecies fulfilled to the appointed time. (The length of a Lunar month alternates from month to month, being either 29 or 30 days long [the lunar cycle is approximately 29 ½ days]).

On the 10th of Abib (Nisan), that 7th day Sabbath, when our Savior rode into the city before the praises, and the waving of their "wave sheaves," Scripture says there were "much people" in Jerusalem that day. This was the fulfillment of Scriptures Zec 9:9 and Ex 12:3. At the website for the US Naval Observatory (USNO), the corresponding Pharisaic month of Nissan (Hebrew - Abib), you can find the night of the full moon. Most denominations determine the crucifixion between 27 and 34AD; but within those years only 28 and 31AD had a Wednesday full moon on this month. According to Pharisee and Sadducee standards, the first full moon of the Hebrew year would be the night of Passover, which by USNO findings, the Biblical account, and secular recordings, had to be 28 AD, on a Wednesday (see also Appendix's D and E).

All good Israelites would choose a spotless Passover lamb on the 10th of the 1st month. Before our Savior's passion, before this 10th day, in the "evening" (afternoon)(the 9th); Mary had anointed our Savior for His sacrifice and burial (Mk 14:8; Jn 12:7). "On the next (morning)," (the 10th) there were many people in Jerusalem for these official preparations of the Feast of Unleavened Bread.

Many came to have their chosen Passover lamb inspected, and to wave their first barley sheaf of the season before the priests (Lev 23:10). Very likely many came to understand this "Son of David" was fulfilling prophecy as He came through the streets of Jerusalem on the back of a foal; for they had heard of Him and hoped Him to be the coming Redeemer to fulfill the appropriate feast, at the appropriate time. The people not knowing then, that He would literally be their Passover Lamb, as their last sacrifice typified.

On this same 10th day, our Savior drove out the moneychangers from the Temple, for the second time (Mt 21, Lk19); as they had made the Temple courtyard a marketplace, "a den of thieves," buying and selling their "superior" lambs on the 7th day Sabbath (see Ne 13:15-22). The Temple had to be clean (free of leaven) before the Father could present

His only begotten Lamb for sacrifice, to sanctify all of Israel. Therefore, YHVH cleansed His house in order to declare His Son as the worthy, spotless Lamb, just as the people were preparing to cleanse their own dwellings and bring their lambs for inspection. (This event may have tainted the minds of many people against the Savior in the ensuing days before Passover.)

It is very likely that Daniel had remembered and understood the Mosaic calendar, from before he was captured as an adolescent Israelite, before the Babylonians required the Hebrew nation to accept their pagan culture and lunar timekeeping. Daniel had likely kept the Passover with his family on a Wednesday each year, on the 14th day of the 1st month; being taught on that very day of that week that Moses had compelled the Israelites in Egypt, that Abraham was spared from sacrificing his son, that Noah had so prepared his family before the flood, and Adam and Eve had commemorated the mercy extended to them, being spared the immediate death of sin on this very day. All of these "Passovers" were according to our Fathers perfect timing. Even Cain and Abel brought their wave-sheaf and spotless lamb, respectively, before YHVH for their house at this same time (Gen 4:2-4), only Cain's offering was not his firstfruits, and maybe Abel rebuked him.

Daniel and his three friends (Hananiah, Mishael, and Azariah) were part of the remnant of Israel, brought to prominence in Babylon to witness for and maintain the Truth. And to Daniel it was revealed that there would come an "exceeding dreadful" beast with ten horns (horn = king, Dan 7:24), having another horn that shall rise after them; diverse from the first, and "he shall speak great words against the most High," "and think to <u>change times</u> and <u>laws</u>"(vs.25). Was this other horn Emperor Constantine, King James, or some other high office that represents all successive kings in the line of Babylon, whose very origin was from the Tower of Babel?

So it was on a Wednesday, our Savior was nailed to the cross, at the time of the morning sacrifice, and died on the cross at the time of the evening sacrifice literally hanging between heaven and earth in the midst of the day, in the midst of the literal week, in the midst of a week of years, dying at the moment of the Passover sacrifice, possibly in the midst of the millennial week of controversy between good and evil. For our Father's ways are perfect (De 32:4; 2Sa 22:31; Ps 18:30, 19:7; Mt 5:48; 1Co 13:9, 10; Jas 1:17).

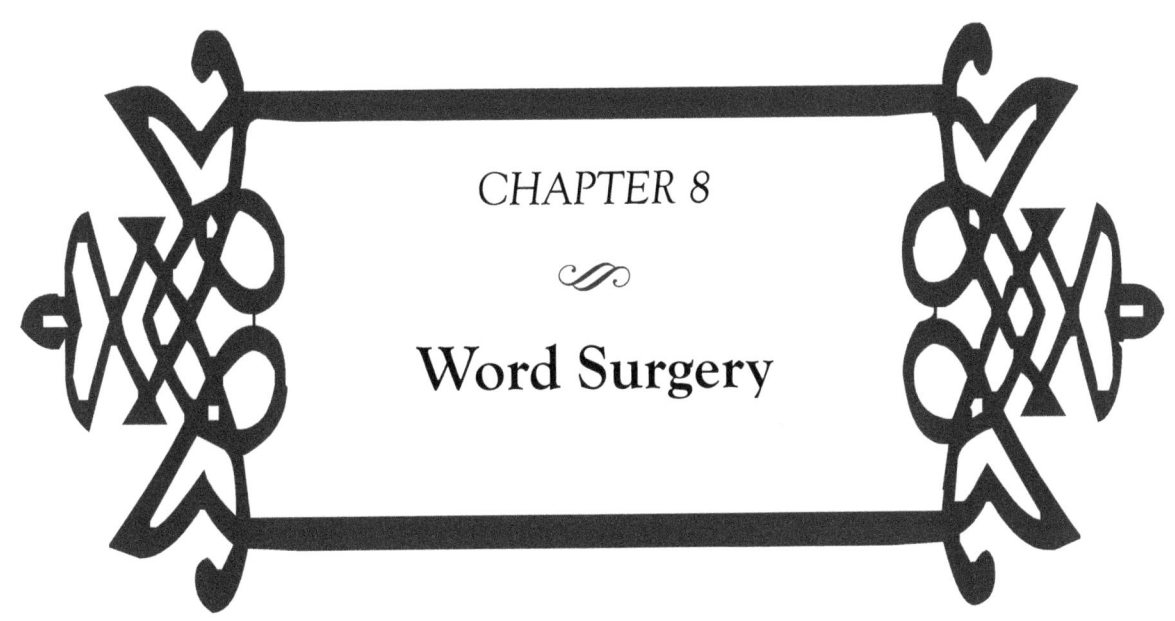

CHAPTER 8

Word Surgery

The Shell Game

What better way to change times and laws for a more unified Christian world, than to change God's Word through translation, and teach well-intentioned ministerial students of virtually every tongue, a skewed understanding of the Hebrew and Greek. The problem is not just found in the English conversion, but in every state-recognized school of theology in every Christian country. For if you have people who are yearning, insistent upon understanding that they might prove for themselves the Word of God in their own tongue; only those who are literate (clergy - *literate*) in any Christian land can teach those who are less *literate* what a word might mean in another language; so long as the less literate don't create any significant interference with any mainstream belief system.

Heaven forbid that a true "Protest-ant" might arise from those who have become literate, "rightly dividing the Word of Truth," to affect some well-established doctrinal teaching; for this might threaten a whole company of believers to separate from the brethren, and that could cause confusion, distrust, weaken the faith, and disrupt grace in love. Nevertheless, the common denominator of all true denominationalism is exposure of a properly translated word in its context, to ultimately reduce denominationalism toward a unity of belief (Jude 3).

The unity amongst the Christian majority today is composed of Scriptural versions that do not differ substantially from the KJV in terms of major doctrine. All these popular *versions* coupled with the near-similar teachings of the major "Christian" denominations, give the impression that the "Passion Week," after our Savior's betrayal and arrest, fell on a Friday, Saturday, and Sunday; the "preparation" day, the "Sabbath," as "a high day," and the "first day of the week." Recall and consider that there are two "preparation" days, and two "sabbath" days that literal week (the first half of the seven days of UB), one of which is a feast sabbath, and the other a 7th day Sabbath.

"Precept upon Precept; Line upon Line"

We have already evaluated OT prophecy, the original Hebrew and Greek writings, and the words of the Savior, to determine whether indeed our Messiah resurrected before dawn on a 7th day Sabbath, or "the first day of the week." Now let us put it all together in its proper context following the Greek, beginning with Matthew. The KJV reads:

"The First Day of the Week" Scripture or Tradition?

"Now the next day, that followed the day of the preparation, the chief priests and Pharisees came together unto Pilate," Mt 27:62

We need to concern ourselves with the first half of this verse. So, as we had done with Mt 28:1, let us again utilize our Strong's Index (SI) and Interlinear Bible (IB) and determine the English equivalents for these words in the Greek.

KJV:	the	Now	(next day	that	followed	the day of)	the	preparation,
IB:	τη	δε	επαυριον	ητισ	εστι	μετα	την	παρασκευην
SI:	#(3588)	1161	1887	3748	2076	3326	(3588)	3904

The two words τη (tae), and την (taen) are found alphabetically in the Strong's, under #5084, with a referral to #3588 for definitions. Observing the accent marks in the IB, and looking to the earlier edition of Strong's, we find both of these words are in their neutral form, and the IB, for Mt 27:62, has τη translated as, "on the." The various Strong's definitions of δε are laid out in "The First 'First Day of the Week,'" p. 50 of this study, and are straightforward. However, the next four Greek words (G# *1887*, G*3748*, G*2076*, G*3326*) will require some critical retranslation. Looking up the next number in our Strong's Index:

G#*1887* EPAURION - next day [7], on morrow [7], day following [2], morrow [1].

The index informs us that this word is composed of G#*1909* (epi) and G#*839* (aurion). The prefix "epi" is somewhat diverse depending upon the context in which it is found. Let us just take a look at the more frequent usage in the KJV.

G#*1909* EPI – on [182], upon [148], in [122], over [49], unto [45], at [43], against [38], to [36], for [30], before [17], into [16] of [16], with [9], by [8] together (+*846*+*3588*) [7], above [5], toward [5], about [4], after [4], among [4] . . .

Now all the KJV definitions of the suffix:

G# *839* AURION – to morrow [9], morrow [4], next day [1], on morrow [1]

Though, in comparing "epaurion" with "aurion," we do find three (3) identical translations in common; the majority usage between the two is "next day" vs. the "next morning."

The earlier Strong's gives the working definition of "epaurion" to be "occurring on the succeeding day," or "on - the next day," now on to the next three (3) words:

G#*3748* HOSTIS (IB form: HAETIS) – which [82], who [30], whosoever [10], that [7], they [3], whosoever (+*302*) [3], till (+*2193*) [2], . . . in that [1], such as [1], what [1], . . . **earlier Strong's**: which same, in that they, (they) that, (they) which . . .

G#*2076* ESTI – he, she, it, is (no itemization); . . . **earlier Strong's**: is, are, **be** (**-long**), call, come, consisteth, (**that**) **is** (**to say**), make, meaneth, + follow, x have, x must needs, . . .

G#*3326* META – **with** [345], after [76], after (+*3588*) [12], among [5], afterward (+*3778*) [4], against [4], hereafter (+*3778*) [4], in [2], and [1], to [1], unto [1], upon [1] . . .

The word "**hostis**" is a combining of #*3739* (hos) and #*5101*(tis):

G#*3739* HOS – which [452], whom [267], **that** [144], who [85], whose [53], what [45], . . .

G#*5101* TIS – what [258], who [101], why [66], whom [25], **which** [16], how [10], whose [9], . . .

As the IB has this word as "haetis," the earlier Strong's informs us that "hae" is the neutral form of the feminine "hos." Therefore, since "haetis" cannot be translated to anything relative to gender, such as "who," "whose," or "whom," and it is not found in the form of a question in Mt 27:62, this compound Greek word could be translated "that which." These are more intricate dissection procedures of what it takes sometimes to get to the truth in "rightly dividing."

Now the next two words, "esti meta," precede τὴν παρασκευὴν, or "the preparation," and should also be translated contextually. The primary interpretations of these two words are listed in the Strong's individually as "is" and "with," combined as "is with," which could suffice, but more accurately, "esti," is "belonging to, or being part of something," and "meta" is "with," or "among" in the sense of being a part of something. Your standard English dictionary definition of "meta-" (as from the Greek) has six (6) definitions; commonly "after, beyond, over, higher;" when used as a prefix. We had touched on this word earlier, and it is only "with" when it is used by itself in the Greek, but when it is conjugated with another word it has the connotation of "after, beyond" etc.

The reason "with" is not a definition here in the English dictionary is because we never use an unconjugated meta in our language, but is always used as a prefix (see "On the Time Appointed" p. 109), having given the example of <u>meta</u>carpals, <u>meta</u>morphosis, and <u>meta</u>physics – advancing just a little further in ability, structure, and mechanical law, but all are "with" the other.

Another consideration in making the proper translation is the need for harmony with the Old Testament. With all this taken into account, now we can properly transform this Greek phrase into the English:

> "Then on the day following that which belongs with the preparation, the chief priests and the Pharisees came together unto Pilate"(*lit*. Mt 27:62).

It was common knowledge among believers that the "preparation" for the Passover commenced in the latter hours of the 14th day of the 1st month (Ex 12:6) "at the going down of the sun" (Dt 16:6), which is any time after noon. Passover ended just before sunrise on the 15th [Ex 12:10, "let nothing of it (the lamb) remain until the morning" –"morning" H#1242 (boqer) – dawn, or break of day].

Passover observance then, technically, includes the hours after "midnight," and it has been celebrated this way, at least since the time of Moses (Ex 12:6,10; Dt 16:6,7). As such, the Passover "preparation" would begin with the killing of a spotless lamb, preparing the animal, and placing its blood on the doorposts, and lintel, before eating the Passover, with the "passing over" actually occurring at "midnight" (Ex 11:4; 12:29) encroaching upon the 1st "day" of Unleavened Bread (UB), a holy convocation. Most KJV margins at Ex 12 have the Passover lamb slain between the 9th and 11th hour, or between 3pm and 5pm; as much as a few hours before sundown.

Returning then to Mt 27:62, "the day following that (day) which belongs with the preparation," would have been the 16th, which is the day following "that (day) which belongs with the preparation" (which is the 15th); the day then following, the 16th, was a Friday, now entering the third day after the crucifixion and burial. Wednesday afternoon on the 14th our Savior had died, at the time of the Passover sacrifice, as a great earthquake rent the *veil* of separation between His people and the Almighty, literally and spiritually.

Thursday morning, after the "passing over," was a time of holy convocation on the 1st day of UB; a coming together of the people to hear the words of Moses. It was a day of eating unleavened bread with no servile work, which is why the chief priests and Pharisees did not approach Pilate until Friday. That Friday was not any kind of sabbath, or holy convocation, but a preparation day before the 7th day Sabbath. Though a day of unleavened bread, it was a servile day, and within the law for an Israelite to conduct his business in Jerusalem, which, in this instance, was on the preparation day before the end of the prophesied "three days and three nights" to the 7th day Sabbath.

Another reason why the priests inquired of Pilate, to secure Roman guards at the tomb of the "deceiver"(vs 63), on a Friday, was because these Jewish priests could not have any of their own Temple guards posted outside the Temple courtyard during their 7th day Sabbath.

Otherwise, Temple guards would make for a better witness that could be easily trained to corroborate with the interpretation of a priest, instead of paying less-cooperative Roman guards to be quiet or maintain a consistent story. Consequently, just before the end of the third day, the priests assured the presence of the body, made the tomb sure by "sealing the stone," (Mt 27:66), on a Friday preparation day, before the early evening hours of their 7th day Sabbath, and the Roman guards were stationed to assure that no one would attempt to steal the body after the "third day," and no one would get out.

"Not by Bread Alone, but by Every Word"

As a second witness, let us look at the next preparation verse, Mk 15:42. This verse gives us the timeframe in which our Savior was placed in the tomb of Joseph of Aramathaea (vs 43-46). The KJV states:

> "And now when the even was come, because it was the preparation, that is, the day before the sabbath,"

This verse is essentially translated correctly, except for the last Greek word. According to the IB, it is "προσαββατον" or G#4315 (prosabbaton), which is more accurately translated "day before the feast day sabbath." Notice the Greek word is pro–sabbat<u>on</u>, referring to the preparation of the Passover before the 1st day of UB. The word "even" here, G#3798 (**opsios**) according to Strong's, is more precisely "late afternoon, or early evening," which would relate to somewhere between 3 pm and 5pm.

A third witness, referring to the same event of placing our Savior in the tomb, is Lk 23:54, which states in the IB that this preparation was before "the 'sabbat<u>on</u>' drew on." The two verses of Jn 19:14 and 42 are straight forward referring to the preparation of the Passover day, without the word *sabbath*, but we will need to dissect vs. 31 and retranslate it in accordance to the form of "sabbath" given to us in the IB. To simplify the process, only the words that are in contention, or need further clarification, will be considered. The KJV reads as follows:

> "The Jews therefore, because it was the preparation, that the bodies should not remain upon the cross on the sabbath day, (for that sabbath day was a high day,) besought Pilate that their legs might be broken, and that they might be taken away." Jn 19:31

The word "preparation" here, G#3904, is in the plural form, referring to the idea that either there is more than one preparation day during the week of UB, or that there are many "preparations" before the several days of UB, which is not a crucial point. The following word "that" is:

> G#2443 HINA – that [537], to [71], for to [5], after [1], albeit [1], because [1], must [1], so as [1], so that [1], **to the intent that** [1], to the intent [1], would [1] . . . **earlier Strong's**: "in order *that* (denoting the *purpose* or *result*)" [Italics so quoted].

The word "remain" is:

> G#3306 MENO (IB form: MEINHAE) – abide [27], abideth [20], abode [12], **dwelleth** [10], remain [8], continue [7], tarry [7] . . . endureth [2], . . . be yet present [1] . . . **earlier Strong's**: to stay in a given place.

These definitions should help us gain a clearer concept before the retranslation process. The next point to clarify would be "on the Sabbath," which in the IB is "εν τω σαββατω." Notice we are not dealing with a feast day sabbath at this point, but a 7th day Sabbath, "sabbato." The Greek words "εν τω" (**en toe**) are more appropriately translated "into the," or "unto the." The word "εν" G#*1722* is ordinarily translated "in [1877 X]," and the Strong's does not index "τω"(toe), listing it only in the appendix. Yet, if one were to scan the IB, they would find its most common translation to be: "to the" (i.e. Mt 21; 30; Mk 5:16; Lk 14:21; Jn 9:17, etc.). In addition, even though "en" has been translated "unto [9]," it would be best to give an example of its use with "toe."

In Jn 17:11, "en toe" is found twice. In this verse our Savior is in the garden of Gethsemane praying to His heavenly Father on behalf of all those who would follow Him. In the KJV, He states in His prayer: "I am no more 'in the' (en toe) world, but these are 'in the' (en toe) world, ..." At the end of our Savior's ministry while on this earth, He is saying "I am no more 'into' or 'unto' the world." Obviously, He is still "in the" world in the sense He is not yet crucified, and His disciples were not "in the" world, or to be "of" the world, but "are 'unto' the world," to minister through the Holy Spirit (Jn 7:39). Therefore, "en toe" should be translated either "into the" or "unto the." Now to the phrase in parenthesis, "(for that sabbath day was a high day)," in the Greek IB it is:

IB: ("ην   γαρ   μεγαλη   η   ημερα   εκεινου   του   σαββατου")
SI: # *2258* *1063*   *3173*   (*3588*) *2250*   *1565*   *5120*   *4521*

There are three key words here that are poorly translated, G#*3173*, G#*2250* and G#*4521*. In the IB G#*3173* is "**megalae**," which the KJV has here as "high." Let us examine this word more closely, utilizing the other translations for this word as it is listed in the Strong's, and consider the Strong's comments.

> G#*3173* MEGAS (IB form: MEGALAE [fem.]) – great [148], loud [33], greatest [2], high [2], large [2], ... **earlier Strong's**: "*big* (lit. or fig., in a very wide application);..." **Strongest Strong's**: (commentary) "spatially: **large**; **of quantity** or degree: loud, intense, violent; *of time*: **long (time)**; of position: great, important" (*Emphasis supplied*)

Since we are dealing with time here, "megalae" should refer to a "long" period, or "quantity of time" in the sense of more than one day. Can it indeed mean more than one day? The next word in question may clue us in:

G#*2250* HEMERA (IB form: [same]) – day, time of day, time, **period of time**, longer than 24 hours: - day [199], **days** [154], … time [3], years [2], a good while ago (+575+744)[1], age (+1722+4260) …

Because the preceding word is "megalae" we can see that "hemera" in this context should be more than a day. The third word is "sabbath;" in the IB it is "sabbat*ou*," inferring a feast time that can include a 7th day Sabbath, which appropriate to the context is more than one day. During the week of UB, this would include the FF Omer on the 7th day Sabbath. The word # *5120* "**tou**" is "(often not translated)" by both the KJV and the IB, but can be translated to "his, her, its, here [-by], +such manner of, that, thence [-forth], thereabout, **this**, thus." Therefore, the Greek-to-English, more accurately should look like the following:

("ην	γαρ	μεγαλη	η	ημερα	εκεινου	του	σαββατου")
# 2258	1063	3173	(3588)	2250	1565	5120	4521
are	for	many	the	days	of that	(this)	feast time

Not just a feast "sabbath" (as in "sabbat*on*") but referring to the many days of the week of UB leading to the special "sabbato," the FF 7th day Sabbath. Because the lunar calendar has feasts fall on different days of the week every year (354-days), as opposed to YHVH's consistent calendar of the same day of the week for the same date (364-days, divisible by 7), the Pharisees and Sadducees always had the FF fall on a different day within the week of UB each year; yet many rabbis say that FF should be the "third day" from Passover (according to the rabbis – see "The Third Day," p. 70).

Since the FF is not listed in Lev 23:11 as a specific dated feast, but a Shabbat; the Greek refers correctly to the coming 7th day Sabbath within UB as a 7th day Sabbath, "sabbato." Our Savior brought His students back into YHVH's timepiece. This is reflected in the NT writings congruent with the OT, written before Judah fell into Babylonian captivity. To put the entire verse back together again, it should more closely resemble: (*Emphasis supplied*)

"Therefore the Jews, because it was preparation time, to the intent that none of the bodies should dwell on the cross unto the **7th day Sabbath**, (for **many are** the **days** of that **feast time** *of UB*), asked Pilate that their legs might be broken, and they be taken away" (*lit.* Jn 19:31).

Therefore, we are not talking about a single particular day, but several days that led up to the 7th day Sabbath in this case. It was well known throughout the Roman world that crucifixion was a slow and painful death that typically could last for several days, [this is why Pilate "marveled" that the Savior was "already dead" within a matter of hours (Mk 15:44)]. The legs of the two thieves were broken, so they could no longer place their body weight on their feet to take the pressure off their arms, so they could catch a breath. In this way crucifixion, technically, is death by slow and painful, exhausting suffocation. The next verse to consider is Mk 16:1. In the KJV we read:

> "And when the sabbath was past, Mary Magdalene, and Mary the *mother* of James, and Salome, had bought sweet spices, that they might come and anoint him."

The primary point of concern here is the first phrase of this verse; "And when the sabbath was past." Let us look at the Greek IB and then see what our Strong's has to say.

```
KJV: And when    was past        the     sabbath,
IB:    και     διαγενομενου     του     σαββατου
SI:   # 2532      1230           5120     4521
```

G#*2532* KAI - **and** [<u>8167</u>], also [517], even [100], both [47], but [41], then [25], so [18], neither (+*3756*) [16], likewise [12], . . . **and when** [<u>1</u>], . . .

Notice "and" is used many more times than "and when." Next:

G#*1230* DIAGINOMAI (IB form: DIAGENOMENOU) – after [1], **past** [1], spent [1] . . . composed from words #*1223* and #*1096*;

Since we only have a few occurrences of G#*1230*, maybe we ought to check out the translations of the two words that comprise G#*1230* to get a better concept of this word.

G#*1223* DIA – **by** [<u>247</u>], through [86], for [58], therefore (+*3778*) [43], for sake [35], because of [24], because (+*3588*) [21], with [17], for this cause (+*3778*) [14], for sakes [12], because [9], in [8], wherefore (+*3778*) [7], after [3], always (+*3956*) [3], by reason of [3], of [3], throughout [3], . . . **earlier Strong's**: "*through* (in very wide applications, local, causal, or occasional) . . . In composition it retains the same general import."

Strongest Strong's: "through, by means of; (acc.) because of, for the sake of, therefore"

G#*1096* GINOMAI – **was** [103], be [84], made [67], came to pass [65], done [63], come [27], were [26], become [21], came [21], is [20], became [17], God forbid (*+3361*) [15], **come to pass** [15], . . .
earlier Strong's: "to *cause to be* ("gen"-erate), to *become* (come into being), used with great latitude" . . .
Strongest Strong's: "to be, become, happen; to come into existence, be born."

With contextual restructuring for a proper translation:	και	διαγενομενου	του σαββατου
	And (when)	by was (come to pass)	this feast time

The term "this feast time," refers to the two days, the Passover preparation with the 1st of unleavened bread (UB), (a holy convocation) together [as in the day "which belongs with the preparation (day)" (Mt 27:62)]. The other Gospel accounts refer to only the 1st of UB (explicitly Lk 23:54), which is a holy convocation (Lev 23:7). This then could be simply referred to as a "sabbaton."

In grammatical English: "And **when this feast time came to pass by**, (*lit.*)
IB: Mary Magdalene, and Mary the *mother* of James, and Salome, bought spices, so that coming they might anoint him."

Now in context, relevant to the previous verse, Mk 15:47:

"And Mary Magdalene and Mary *the mother* of Joses beheld where he was laid." KJV

The two Marys' acknowledged where He was laid just before the Passover, and returned home to prepare some spices and ointments they already had (Lk23:56). After Passover, and after the day that goes with it (1st of UB), now Friday, these two women went out and "bought (more) spices" to add to what they already prepared (Mk 16:1), in order to finish their anointing compound for their Savior's body. There was more than enough time to accomplish all this. If the 7th day Sabbath "was past," it would have all been on Saturday night, with no late night convenience stores available to buy spices.

Now to support the foregoing interpretation that the women had started to prepare some spices before the Passover, before the feast day sabbath, as opposed to just prior to the 7th day Sabbath, let us turn again to Lk 23:54. Remember, "that day was the preparation, and the ('sabbat<u>on</u>') <u>drew on</u>" KJV. The next two verses in Lk 23 are before the Passover.

> "And the women also, which came with him from Galilee, followed after, and beheld the sepulcher, and how his body was laid. And they returned, and prepared spices and ointments; 'και το μεν σαββατον ησυχασαν κατα την εντολην.'" Lk 23:55,56

The last phrase of Lk 23:56 is "kai to men sabbat<u>on</u> haesuchadzan kata taen entolaen." The first half of this phrase, "kai to men sabbaton," should read, "and on the feast sabbath." The next word:

> *G#2270* HAESUCHAZO (IB form: HAESUCHADZAN) – held peace [2], **ceased** [1], quiet [1], rested [1] . . . **earlier Strong's**: *to keep still*, i.e. *refrain* from labor.

This form of G#2270 is plural, referring back to the object in this sentence which is "they." And the last word in the sentence,

> *G#1785* ENTOLE (IB form: ENTOLAEN) – commandment [42], commandments [27], **precept** [2] . . . **earlier Strong's**: *injunction*, i.e. an authoritative *prescription*.

If one were to contextually analyze all 71 occurrences of this Greek word "entole," they would find that many of the "commandment(s)" are referring to Mosaic Law as a NT admonition rather than the Decalogue, or the Ten Commandments. This is because the translators do not want to emphasize the statutes of Moses that they have contrived in their versions to have been done away with at the cross, and certainly do not want to make any distinction between sabbaths, so as to expose the problem with the "first *day* of the week." This verse, Lk 23:56, is more accurately rendered as: (*Emphasis supplied*)

> "And they returned, and prepared spices <u>and</u> ointment; and on the **feast day** they **ceased** their labor according to the **precept**." (*lit.*)

To cease from labor on a holy feast convocation is in accord with a statute, not any of the "commandments." Every Gospel account that regards the timeframe from the cross to the moment before the resurrection has been reevaluated from the Greek writings, and with each instance, the language portrays a consistent chronology that is different from the KJV translation; which shouldn't be very surprising at this point.

"The First Shall be Last; and the Last Shall be First"

Now we return to the time when the tomb was found empty, or what is considered the moment of the resurrection, which the KJV refers to as "the first day of the week." Every time we find this phrase in the Gospels (6 times), it deals with the renewed life of our Savior, insinuating a Sunday resurrection. We had previously stepped through the first Gospel account of this phrase in Matthew 28:1, determining a more viable translation, and listed all the Greek forms of the questionable KJV translation; but since we ought to have at least a second witness, we need to walk through the next recording of this event in Mk 16:2.

"And very early in the morning the first *day* of the week, they came unto the sepulcher at the rising of the sun." KJV

The IB reads, "And very early on the first of the week, . . ." the actual Greek being:

"και	λιαν	πρωι	της	μιασ	σαββατων
kai	lian	proi	taes	mias	sabbatone
G#2532	3029	4404	(3588)	3391	4521

The word "taes" is actually listed as G#*5084*, with reference to G#*3588* in Strong's, which only gives general translations for the several Greek articles listed, thus leaving the reader at a loss for which Greek form means what. According to the Strongest Strong's, half the time these articles are "*usually not translated* [9495]," and by a simple read in the earlier Strong's, when this word is translated, it can be " – the, this, that, one, he, she, it, etc."

Therefore, to do the best we can with "taes," we need to see if we can determine the proper tense and form of the next word. The **earlier Strong's** has "mia" as the irreg. fem. of "heis," and that "heis" is considered the Greek cardinal number "one." The **Strongest Strong's** delineates "heis" as:

G#*1520* HEIS – one [289], a [13], first [8], some [6], the other [6], **certain** [5], any [2], an [2], man [2], . . . another [1], . . . only [1], . . .

With "mias" still irregular feminine, this form could easily be translated to any one of the less frequent definitions listed (other than "man"), so long as it is within the context. Because "mia/heis" is always singular (one), we could have the following translation:

"And very early *on* that **one** (certain) **7th day feast Sabbath** (FF), they came unto the sepulcher at the rising of the sun" (*lit.* Mk 16:2).

To be consistent, consider the remaining phrases of "the first *day* of the week." The next is found in Mk 16:9:

"Now when (our Savior) was risen early the first *day* of the week, he appeared first to Mary Magdalene, out of whom he cast seven devils" KJV.

The "first *day* of the week" here is found in the IB as "προτη σαββατου," or "protae sabbatou." The word "protae" comes from:

G#*4413* PROTOS (IB form: PROTAE) – **first** [86], chief [10], before [2], former [2], beginning [1], best [1], chiefest [1], first (+*1722*) [1].

Here we have the true Greek word for "first" translated correctly, and is so used with "sabbatou" here as it is the 1st of the 7 Sabbaths leading to Pentecost, relating to the "first" 7th day Sabbath in the count of the Feast of Weeks, starting in the midst of the feast of UB, so our translation could more easily be:

"And rising early on the **first 7th day feast Sabbath** (of seven), He appeared first to Mary Magdalene, out of whom He cast seven devils" (*lit.* Mk 16:9).

Again, this is referred to as the "first 7th day feast Sabbath" as Firstfruits (FF), as the first Omer in the count of the seven 7th day Sabbaths in the Feast of Weeks leading to the Pentecost, which happened between Mk 16:19 and Mk 16:20, with the events detailed in Acts 2. Now, the last three Gospel accounts of "the first *day* of the week" are all "mia tone sabbatone" (Lk 24:1; Jn 20:1, 19). The word "tone"(των) cannot be found alphabetically in the index, but in coming across this frequently used word throughout the IB NT, it is found typically to be translated "the," or "of the," if translated at all. Consequently, utilizing the IB, we can restructure these three verses as follows:

> "Then on the 7th day feast Sabbath (FF), while still very early, they came to the tomb, carrying spices which they prepared, . . . " Lk 24:1a.

> "And on the 7th day feast Sabbath (FF), Mary Magdalene came early to the tomb, darkness yet being *on it*. . . . " Jn 20:1a.

> "Then it being late afternoon on that day of the 7th day feast Sabbath (FF), and the doors having been locked where the disciples were assembled, . . . " Jn 20:19a.

Remember, "mia tone sabbatone," at least at Jn 20:1 and 19 in the IB, showed each "sabbatone" translated "sabbaths," as opposed to "week," yet, even so, there is no delineation found, even in the IB NT interpretation, between a "feast sabbath" and a "7th day Sabbath." In Jn 20:19a, the proper derivation of G#*3798* (opsios) is "late afternoon." (see also *Concordant Commentary on the NT*, p.136) Therefore, maybe the publishers had not allowed for the true Greek transliterations from the Hebrew, as for them, certain words could only mean certain things when they are found in certain verses (i.e. traditional understandings).

"On the Time Appointed"

Moving beyond the Gospels now to the next "first *day* of the week" in Acts 20:7, we find another "mia tone sabbatone." Nevertheless, to deal with this verse properly, we first need to reconsider the translation of the previous verse (vs. 6) to maintain the proper context.

> "And we sailed away from Philippi after the days of unleavened bread, and came unto them to Troas in five days; where we abode seven days" Acts 20:6 KJV.

We are told that Paul had sailed away from Philippi to meet with awaiting disciples in Troas "after the days of unleavened bread." Sadly, we find another misuse of the word "after," which in the Greek here is "meta" G#*3326*. To complete our understanding of this word the **earlier Strong's** has in commentary:

G#*3326* META - "denoting *accompaniment*; *'amid'* ("**with** [345]")*; modified ... according to the case (gen. a*ssociation*, or acc. *succession*) with which it is joined; . . . among, x and, + follow, hence, hereafter, in, of, (**up-**) **on**, . . . since, (**un-**) **to**, . . . used in composition, in substantially the same relation of *participation* or *proximity*, and *transfer* or *sequence*."

*(Itemization from the **Strongest Strong's**) The Strong's listing of "meta" as " . . . **after** [**76**], after (+*3588*) [12], . . .," gives the illusion that "meta" by itself, unconjugated, can be both "with" and "after," because there is no indication here in the highlighted of any conjuncting with no "+" to any other Strong's number. In this context of Acts 20:6 a dichotomy would arise as these two variations in translation here are not interchangeable to still retain a consistent thought. In analyzing all the "meta's," a more accurate list would be as follows:

" . . . **after** (+*1161*) [20], **after** (+*3778*) [16], **after** (+*2532*) [14], after (+*3588*) [12], **after (alt. forms 'met,' 'meth')** [10] . . ."

The remaining [**16**] of the [**76**], are indeed singular "meta's," yet investigating each, it is determined they would best be translated in their context as either "unto," or "with;" so the more accurate meaning of an unconjugated "meta," would be "with," "unto," "alongside of," or "just ahead of," not "after." Accordingly, in vs. 6, it was not meant to be "after" the days of UB, but "just ahead of" the days of UB, as UB started just "after" that day. Moreover, a couple of other key words in verse 6 are mistranslated. Looking at the short phrase, "in five days," we find the Greek IB has "αχρισ ημερων πεντε," or "achris haemerone pente;" these are interpreted as:

G#*891* ACHRIS – until [12], **unto** [12], till (+*3739*) [4], till [4], until (+*3739*) [4], as far as [2], for [2], while (+*3739*) [2], even to [1], even unto [1], hitherto (+*1204*+*3588*) [1], into [1], in [1], . . .

G#*2250* HAEMERA (IB form: HAEMERONE) – day [199], days [154], daily (+*2596*) [15], . . . time [3], years [2], . . . **day's** [1] . . .

G#*4002* PENTE – **five** [36], fifty thousand (+*3461*) [1], threescore and fifteen (+*1440*) [1],   - "<u>**unto day's five**</u>" -

Notice the highlighted words would actually give us "unto day's five." This is not arbitrarily chosen, for the Greek word "haemerone" is the genitive case of "haemera," which can be either a separative or a possessive form depending upon the context. This particular context in Acts 20:6 allows "haemerone" to be possessive, which would render this phrase as, "unto day of the five," or "unto day's five," as in the numbered day in respect to a week. Otherwise, what is the significance of Paul mentioning that it took five days to get to Troas "after" the feast days? If he truly mentions that it took him five days to get there from Phillipi, would there not be a reason given? Unless he intended to relate a particular land-sea travel record back then. (Some other examples of the possessive "haemerone," in the IB, are: Mt 11:12; Mk 2:1; Lk 17:22, 20:1; Ac 1:3, 7:45).

Remember this fifth day of the week, Thursday, or "day five" as a Hebrew would refer to it in respect to the week of UB, was consistently the 1st day of UB according to the Mosaic calendar; and of course UB lasts for seven days from that point (Lev 23:6, etc.), which would be why Paul mentions that he and his company stayed there "seven days." They stayed there in worship and fellowship with these other disciples in Troas for the entire week of UB. Moreover, if they did start that feast on "day five" of the week, it would support the idea that Paul, and the disciples he communed with, recognized the Mosaic time keeping as prophetic.

The Mosaic "day five" of that week was unlikely to be the same day observed by the Pharisees on any given year because their lunar calendar could place that day on any day of the week, depending upon which day of the week the first visible crescent appeared at the beginning of that month.

With the predictable 364-day calendar, based upon what we have uncovered thus far, if we set the 1st day of UB (15th of the 1st) on the 5th day of the week (Thursday), and we count our days ahead from there, we find that the Day of Atonement (10th of the 7th) is indeed a 7th day Sabbath. This is the beauty of YHVH's-ordained 364-day calendar, as every element of it is consistent and matches true gematria (see "Perfect Timing," p. 25). From the feast commemoration on the very weekday of the original event giving expression to the number, to the consistent meaning of intercalation on the last day of each season due to the flood of Noah; all the days of meeting are all part of the perfect "cycles" of righteousness whose significance becomes concentric the more you study it. Even with the entrance of sin occurring on the weekday that has come to be referred to in gematria as the day of "Tabernacles" and "Divine favor" (5th day - Thursday) [Bullinger, E.W., *The Companion Bible*, Appendix #10, p. 14] (see Jub 3:17-21), for the sinner would approach the "Tabernacle" on this meeting day in the feast season, desirous of "Divine favor."

This sin event, initiated in the garden, had long been redeemed annually with Passover on day 4 (Wednesday) as the preparation for the "passing-over" of the death angel at midnight before daylight of day 5 (Thursday), the day of sin, until the Babylonian captivity, exercised for nearly 3300 years (except maybe the years of Egyptian servitude). [It should be noted here that the adversary's symbol is the inverted pentagram (5), because he gained dominion on day 5]. This is the reason why YHVH had all the dimensions of the Tabernacle, used for the disposal of sin and to restore relationship, be divisible by five (5) - to leave the clue in gematria; knowing in the future His people would forget, and His remnant would come back to it; for this was, and is, the same "pattern" in the wilderness, in pre-Babylonian Israel, and in the Tabernacle in Heaven.

Of course this counters rabbinic teaching coming from the very instructors who know full well that their own language states the Day of Atonement is a 7th day Shabbat (Lev 23:32; 16:31). Instead of entering into a discussion of relevant etymology, the reform, conservative and orthodox rabbis will extol and expound upon Talmudic compositions and bicker amongst themselves regarding what day of the week this "fringe" calendar of the outcasts starts; knowing it is consistent.

To promote confusion and discourage any investigation amongst any non-conformists, a conservative rabbi would promote their confident rationale as to why this calendar starts on a Wednesday (4th day), while a reformist would chime in to dismiss their argument and say it starts on a Friday (6th day), and the orthodox would say that its all a waist of sacred time, but none of the rabbis are willing to declare the truth from the writings of Moses to bring out from their own language that this calendar would have to start on the very day between their two arguments (i.e. Thursday); because their covenant ordination forbids them. As rabbinic scholars comment on certain DSS today, we must remember there were Jews among the first forensic linguistic team deciphering the DSS, in some places arranging scroll fragments to fit their model, as they understood it.

In fact, if the conservative rabbis say this calendar starts on the 4th day of the week (Wednesday)(on the 1st of the 1st month), then they would have to admit that this would place the day that Solomon began the work of building the Temple on a 7th day Sabbath, the 2nd day of the 2nd month (1 Chr 3:2) (instead of Sunday, as it would be if this calendar started on a Thursday), and maybe that is why they reject it. In turn, if the reform rabbis say this calendar starts on the 6th day of the week (Friday), then they too would have to explain why the Essenes would observe the Day of Atonement on a Sunday, which would be an abomination, which is what they would have likely taught their followers about the Essenes, in order to create the contrived reason to cause the people to despise and reject the Essenes, even attempt to destroy them. Yet other less prominent DSS specifically mention that the Day of Atonement was to be on a 7th day Shabbat.

Any correlation to world events involving governments, commerce, or false religion as it is portrayed in the <u>media</u> (comes from "medium"), will have signs and judgments that follow the lunar calendar that has its foundation in Babylon; but YHVH's prophecies and His Divine protection over His remnant will be according to His true timepiece. Even the sabbatical year is off with the lunar calendar according to the DSS and the concept of the disciples utilizing a different calendar is confirmed with a proper translation of Col 2:16 (see "Question Authority," p. 18). Therefore, Acts 20:6 should read:

> "And we sailed away from Philippi **unto** (just ahead of) the days of unleavened *bread*, and came to them at Troas unto **day's five**; where we remained seven days."

Moving on now to verse 7, you will notice the word "sabba<u>tone</u>" in your interlinear, which now relates specifically to the FF Omer Sabbath. We should note that the breaking of bread on a 7th day Sabbath morning was common practice among Hebrew priests in the sanctuary; meant to prefigure the partaking of a renewed Messiah, as the Bread of Heaven. This "sabbatone" now fits the pattern, and certainly had greater significance for the believers in Messiah on this commemoration of the FF Resurrection Sabbath.

The phrase "ready to depart on the morrow" has a slight twist in the translation as an apparent attempt to make it look like Paul was planning on leaving town after the long "first day of the week" service. As if Sunday was a sanctified day and he could not travel until the day was over. But as he was there for "seven days," then that would mean he would have arrived on a 7th day Sabbath, the day a believer was not to travel with their belongings, according to the commandment (Ex 20:10).

If indeed Paul stayed in Troas for the entire feast of UB, arriving on "day's five," or Thursday, which is consistently the 1st day of UB on YHVH's Calendar; this meeting on "sabbatone" being on a 7th day Sabbath, is only in the middle of the feast which continues to the following Wednesday, always the last day of UB; so to leave after the 7th day Sabbath would not be "seven days."

The majority of translations have a phrase that is similar to what the KJV has in this verse where it reads, "ready to depart on the morrow." Understanding that the word "morrow" is from the old English before the days of King James, which means "morning," taken from a familiar Greek word we have analyzed before "epaurion"(IB form) (see "Precept upon Precept:" p. 96). Therefore, "morning" is correct. The problem word is "depart," and the Greek word here is:

> G# *1826* EXEIMI (IB form "EXIENAI") – to leave, go out, go away: - departed [1], depart [1], get [1], gone out [1]. **earlier Strong's**: "**from *1537* and *1510*.**"

However, notice here the actual IB root word is somewhat different. For proper clarification of "exienai," we will need to rebuild this word from the following three related words to restructure the definition correctly. The two relations listed here in the earlier Strong's, and one other related word:

> G#*1537* EK or EX – logically: the means or source of an activity, disassociation or separation: - of [441], from [185], out of [112], by [55], on [34], … **earlier Strong's**: "used in composition … often of *completion*."

> G#*1510* EIMI – is [829], be [366], was [349], are [345], were [155], am [139], art [85], being [37], been [24], have [23], had [16], … **earlier Strong's**: "*I exist*. ... See also G#*1511*"

> G#*1511* EINAI – to be, exist, **be present** (no itemization) … **earlier Strong's**: "*to exist*: am, are, come, is, x lust after, x please well, there, is, to be, was."

This word "exienai" is found only one other time in the NT, at Acts 27:43, and is translated "get" in the KJV, yet revaluating the prefix and root, we could have any of the following:

EXIENAI = EX + EINAI = of to be, complete to be, complete being present, (as in) "ready to 'complete being' on the morrow" or "ready to continue until the morning."

Therefore, since the previous activity was "preaching," Paul would have "completed his being" in the act relevant to this verb. If Paul was "ready to depart on the morrow," why did he not get some rest if his intentions were to "depart" early the next day, on foot (v. 13)? Mind you, he is an older man here with failing vision. So, having covered the words "tae" and "epaurion" earlier, we can now connect these phrases using the IB conjunctions, and place the two verses together.

> "And we sailed away from Philippi **unto** the days of unleavened bread, and came to them at Troas unto **day's five** (in the week); where we remained seven days. And on that **one 7th day feast Sabbath** (FF), when the disciples assembled together to break bread, Paul preached to them, ready **to be present until** the morning; and he continued his speech until midnight." (lit. Ac 20:6,7).

Moving on in this chapter, "and he continued his speech until midnight," this point in the night is mentioned because "a certain young man named Eutychus" had fallen asleep in a window and fell some 20 plus feet to the ground (hitting at least one thatching of three on the way down – ["loft" refers to thatched decks], v.9). For the sake of context, let us continue from v. 9, and go into the next few verses, in the IB. Paul was preaching "for a long time" and Eutychus, . .

> "being overborne with sleep, he fell from the third floor down and was taken up dead. (10) But Paul, going down, fell on him and embracing *him, he* said, 'Do not be terrified; for his soul is in him.' (11) And going up (back to the third floor) and breaking bread and (partaking) and conversing over a long *time*, until daybreak, **thus he went** (came) **out**. (12) And they brought the boy alive, and were comforted not a little." Ac 20:9b-12 (IB)

In vs. 11, the IB has "thus he went out," as opposed to "so he departed" in the KJV. This "departed," leaves you with the impression that Paul left the city at that time, but this word in the Strong's is:

> G#*1831* EXERCHOMAI (IB form: EXHAELTHEN) – to *issue* (lit. or ig.):- come (forth, out), depart (out of), escape, get out, from *1537* and *2064*;"

Word Surgery

G# 1537 EK or EX - (previous two pages)

G#*2064* ELTHO – to come or go (in a great variety of applications, lit. and fig.): - accompany, appear, bring, come, enter, fall out, go, grow …"

The Greek word "exhaelthen" is found with this same spelling 10 other times in the KJV; each time being translated in the KJV as "came out" or "came forth," only this one time with this same spelling is it "departed." Therefore, Paul was not planning to "depart" the region after Sunday services, as the KJV tries to portray, but intended to finish speaking and leave the building after the (FF) Sabbath, by "daybreak," with fellow believers, assisting or carrying the young Eutychus alive (Acts 20:11,12).

This retranslation of Acts 20:6-12 can be somewhat of a paradigm shift, but is much more true to the Greek. The King James translators, under government scrutiny, had to downplay the more literal translation of these verses so as not to emphasize any feast keeping here, Sabbath convocation, or any correlation to the week, so as not to leave any blatant evidence to the truth, while at the same time attempting to "doctrinize" the false concept of Sunday worship.

The next verse that accentuates the false impression of Sunday sacredness is the KJV interpretation of 1 Cor 16:2. This last occurrence of "the first *day* of the week" is "mian sabbatone" and should be restructured in its context as:

> "According to the 7th day feast Sabbath, let each one of you lay by him in store, however YHVH has prospered you, that when I come, there should be no gatherings at that time." (*lit.* 1 Cor 16:2)

Just prior to each 7th day feast Sabbath was a point of harvest; barley for the Firstfruits, wheat for Pentecost, and most other fruits prior the Day of Atonement in preparation for Tabernacles. Every man was expected to go to Jerusalem and bring a type of "firstfruits" offering from each of their harvests to be "waved" before the God of Heaven at each of the three 7th day feast Sabbaths (Ex 34:20-22). This was an offering, distinct from any compulsory tithe. In this case, the Corinthians were asked to "lay by him in store." The IB says "let each of you put by himself," as in, store it in your own place, or set it in store yourself "upon" the 7th day feast Sabbath, so that no one would be out in their fields at the last minute "gathering" food, or trying to make "collections" (vs 1) by selling some, on whatever day Paul was to come.

Hence, Paul's instruction of "no <u>gatherings</u> when I come," refers to the same order he gave to the "churches of Galatia" (vs 1), to do these things ahead of time, preferably before the 7th day feast Sabbath, to be set aside on that day in a particular place; so that "<u>when</u> I come," says Paul, "I will send your <u>liberality</u> unto Jerusalem" (1 Cor 16:3).

To this point, we have untwisted several passages of Scripture back to their proper understanding in these two languages; revealing a pattern congruent with the use of a consistent calendar. Each evaluation has demonstrated their day-of-the-week date to match a common start-day to this calendar (1st of the 1st month); all traced to the gematrial day of "tabernacles" and "Divine favor" - the 5th day of the week.

This same conspiracy extends its collaboration to the modern day Pharisees (Rabbis) as they had taken the authority to interpret faded parchment and arrange all the Essene fragments (DSS) with their belief of a Wednesday commencement, which causes the construction of Solomon's Temple to start on a 7th day Sabbath (2nd of the 2nd month - 2 Chr 3:2), throws off the crucifixion week, all the feasts, and disrupts gematria (Jub 6:33-37). But they did miss at least one, as the Mishmerot E fragment 4Q394 has the 12th month ending with an "[addi]tional [day on Wednesday.] The year is complete: three hundred si[xty-four] days." (intercalary day) as the 4th day of the week (Dead Sea Scrolls, Wise, Abegg, & Cook, p.320), placing the commencement of the year where it should be, on the 5th day of the week.

CHAPTER 9

Two-edged Sword

"Faithful is He that Calleth You"

In the tradition of the King James translators, most of the formally trained Greek and Hebrew scholars today are denominationally employed and are careful not to stray too far from the meanings and definitions that have been previously established. In a sense, they are holding to the "command," in 2 Th 3:6, of keeping to the "traditions," as it is translated in the KJV; comprising some truth linked together by teachings that do not reflect the OT prophets.

> "Now we command you, brethren, in the name of our Lord Jes-s Christ, that ye withdraw yourselves from every brother that walketh disorderly, and not after the tradition (# *3862*) which he received of us." 2 Th 3:6 KJV.

> "Therefore, brethren, stand fast, and hold the traditions (# *3862*) which ye have been taught, whether by word, or our epistle."
> 2 Th 2:15 KJV.

Therefore, the word "tradition" found in the Greek is:

G#3862 PARADOSIS (IB form: PARADOSEIS) - tradition [10], traditions [2], ordinances [1] (# *3844* + # *1394*) **earlier Strong's**: " a *precept*; spec. the Jewish ***traditionary law***: ordinances, tradition."

The two syllables examined individually:

G#3844 PARA – ***near***, i.e. (with gen.) *from beside* (lit. or fig.), (with dat.) *at* (or *in*) the *vicinity* of (obj. or subj.), …"

G#1394 DOSIS – a *giving*; by impl. (concr.) a ***gift***: - gift, giving."

Paul is not being emphatic about the cultural norm, neither is he referring to the "tradition" of the Jews, as in the Pharisaical law that is hinted here in the comments; but alluding to the "ordinances" that he had confirmed with them before, many times stating "as it is written."

Interestingly, the word "tradition(s)" is not found in the OT at all; and oddly enough, redefining the Greek word "paradosis" by evaluating the prefix and root separately, we have a "near giving," "beside a gift," which, essentially, is not really receiving the gift. You might be able to see it, get a chance to shake the box and guess what it is, or just admire the wrapping that it's in from a distance, or maybe you're expecting something that you heard was coming to you, but you never do get the benefit of it.

In the secular Oxford Greek Dictionary the definition for "paradosis" is "surrender, tradition, teaching," and one would certainly "give" up, or "surrender" his or her time, and mental energies to study, and they in turn would be taught or conditioned. Depending upon their desire to know truth, or the customs of man, determines the "gift" they choose to attain in life.

Maybe now we can appreciate how important it is to use what YHVH has given us, and use those reference tools He has made available today; to dig for Truth, no matter how deep and dirty the ways of man might get (Mt 13:44). It is not until you hit something hard, and begin to sweep away all the vain traditions and philosophies of men (Col 2:8), can you then see the beautiful gift and come to understand and appreciate the perfection of the precious gems of Truth (Mt 15:3,6; Mk 7:8,9,13; Gal 1:13-16; 1 Ptr1:18).

The verse says, "Faithful *is* He that calls you, who also will do *it*" (1 Th 5:24). Contextually, reading this with the previous few verses, He calls us accordingly as we "Prove all things; holding fast to that which is good" (v.21). Those things that are "good" *# 2570* "καλόσ" (kalos) are "beautiful, valuable, virtuous, worthy, and honest." As the promises in the NT are for those who are referred to as "saints," which means those who are called "out," out of the world, out of the mainstream, who are "blameless," as Paul states in v. 23; - the Greek word "saint" is consistently the same throughout the NT:

> G# *40* "ἅγιος" HAGIOS – *sacred* (phys. *pure*, moral. *blameless* or *religious*, cer. *consecrated*)[comp. **53, 2282**]: - (most) holy (one, thing) saint(s)."

Though this concept was introduced earlier, it would be best to layout the index quotes here. Note again the comparison made to a number that is not italicized, indicating this to be the Hebrew index number, # 2282. Looking at this number's definition on the next page, make recognition to the similarity in the Hebrew pronunciation, as best as can be accomplished between the two languages, which gives indication of this Greek word having its origin from this Hebrew word – otherwise known as a transliteration:

H#2282 "חג" "HAG" – religious **feast, festival**; festal procession: - feast, feasts, keep a feast (+2287), sacrifice, **solemn feasts**, solemnity." **earlier Strong's**: *CHAG* (the first Hebrew letter here, "ח" [as the Hebrew reads from right to left] is called a "chet" or "heth" as some pronounce it, and has a hard "h" sound as in Ba*c*h, the closest sound in Greek is the "ha" sound.)

Thus, throughout the Greek NT, a "hagios" is someone who keeps "hag," which by the transliterated definition is one who keeps the Hebrew "religious feast" as a "festival" in "solemnity," such as Unleavened Bread (UB), and the Firstfruit (FF) feasts, which our Messiah had kept and exemplified in His death and renewed life. Consequently there is no room for a "saint" to observe any of the "holidays" as a substitute for the OT "holy days."

Our Father anticipated giving us these feasts as he did His Son, from the foundation of this world, as His Son had become the chosen Lamb since the fall of man (Gen 3:15; 4:2-4). From the Flood in the second month Passover (Gen 7:4,7,11; Ex 16:1; Nu 9:11, by 360-day calendar) to the coming out of Egypt due to the Passing-over, and the counting of the "Shabbat's" through the course of the Feast of Weeks in the wilderness, to the outpouring upon Moses on Mount Sinai for the people in the Shabbat Pentecost (Ex Ch.16-19); He gave us these spring feasts, and the fall feasts, to rehearse all these salvific celebrations that we might learn and understand and be able to teach His story (true History), to others and our children (Deut 6:7).

Paul had written to the new believers in Colossia (2:16,17) that they might believe these holy days "are a shadow of things to come" for those in Messiah in the coming last days; in the same way our Savior had perfected them. Paul had specifically stated:

> "Let no one condemn you in eating (offerings), or in drinking (offerings), or in your obligations of a feast day, or of the new month, or of holy feast (convocations); Which are a shadow of things to come for the body of Christ (the assembly of believers)." (*lit.* Col 2:16, 17).

Paul, in these two verses, is conveying a message regarding the feasts and feast sabbaths, without mention of the 7th day Sabbath. Paul had called himself a Pharisee of the Pharisees (Ac 23:6), having been a student of Gamaliel (Ac 22:3), who came to reject many of their teachings as our Savior had struck Paul down on his way to Damascus and told him "about all things appointed for you to do. …for YHVH … has appointed for you to know His true word … to hear His voice from His mouth" (Ac 22:10,14). (*Emphasis supplied*)

Paul was about to receive a major paradigm shift. He was carrying with him warrants to the synagogue in Damascus to take any of those belonging to "the Way" (Ac 9:2), and bring them bound to Jerusalem [those at Qumran also referred to themselves as members of "the Way" (1QS, 4Q255-264a, 5Q11)]. This is implying that Paul, having the equivalent credentials as a Suma Cum Laud Harvard graduate, did not have full knowledge of the Truth, as he later recounted the traditions of men as dung (Php 3:8). He had come to learn many Truths from the very people he persecuted, this included the true Calendar of Moses from these early disciples, some of whom had direct contact with the Savior. To the Thessalonians Paul writes in 1 The 5:1:

> "But of the **times** and **seasons**, brothers, you have no need that I write unto you."

The Thessalonians already understood and kept the Mosaic Calendar, but of the Colossians, both Jew and Gentile, there in the day, were steeped in pagan and traditional influences, for that was a merchants crossroad town. They had been determining their feasts and holidays by the moon. Paul was trying to encourage the new believers in Colossia to hold to the true calendar he had taught them; not to be swayed by disciples of others who might follow that Babylonian lunar calendar that he himself used to follow.

In fact, in one of the Dead Sea Scrolls called the Damascus Document it argues that YHVH revealed to his chosen, "things hidden, in which **all Israel had gone wrong**: His holy Sabbaths, His glorious festivals, His righteous laws, His reliable ways" (DD1, 3:14,15) (*Emphasis supplied*); as He so revealed to Paul, as he made his way to Damascus, the very town it came from. Recall what YHVH said to one of the prophets **after** the Babylonian captivity:

> "I hate, your feast days; and I will not delight in your solemn assemblies" (Amos 5:21).

"For the Time is at Hand"

In the DSS, Noah prophesies:

> "And all the children of *the* prince of the Almighty will forget and will not find the path of the years, and will forget the new months, and seasons, and sabbaths and they will go wrong as to all the order of the years" (Jub 6:34)

Just as Moses, in the same writing, relays YHVH's warning for the children of Israel, a prophecy that will come upon them some time after they have entered the promise land and transgressed the covenant and rebelled, saying:

> "And many will perish and they will be taken captive, and will fall into the hands of the enemy, because they have forsaken My ordinances, and My commandments, and the festivals of My covenant, and My Sabbaths, and My holy place which I have hallowed for Myself in the midst of the land, that I should set my Name upon it, and that it should dwell (there)" (Jub 1:9).

The Book of Jubilees was the most frequently found complete scroll amongst the DSS (15 discovered) and is classified as Pseudepigrapha (which essentially means commentary with an unknown author, like 1&2 Chronicles, which also is classed as Pseudepigrapha). It is considered by many scholars to be the lost writings of Moses edited out of the Torah during the Babylonian captivity; compiled and brought back during a revival era of the Maccabees, which gave us the feast of Hanukkah. In respect to these prophecies and that quote of Amos from YHVH (5:21), Israel did lose its way; - losing sight of their Father's timing and directives for the calendar and traditions of their captors. The Book of Jubilees, as if from the pen of Moses, has written that:

> "Noah and his sons observed it (Pentecost), ... till the day of Noah's death, and from the day of Noah's death his sons did away with (it) until the days of Abraham, ... Abraham observed it, and Isaac, and Jacob and his children observed it, up to the days ... (that) the children of Israel forgot it until you celebrated it anew on this mountain." Jub 6:18, 19

Mosheh (Moses in Hebrew), here in the Jubilees, continues to explain the origin of the 4 intercalation days that Enoch had prophesied about that was to be added to YHVH's calendar at the great deluge (En 75:1):

"...with the 4 intercalary days, which cannot be separated from their places, ..."

And these, we are told, were put in their place by the following events (Jub 6:25-28):

1st of the 4th month – the Fountains of the deep were CLOSED.
1st of the 7th month – the Fountains of the deep were OPENED.
1st of the 10th month – the Tops of the mountains were seen.
1st of the 1st month – the Earth became visible.

These intercalary days, as we can see, were one day for each of the four seasons (referred to as "new month") to begin the next season, accounted as the "intercalary" day between the seasons (noted as the day after the 30th being the 31st- En 72:19, 20; 82:19), for it says in the previous verses (Jub 6:23, 24):

> "And on the new (month) of the first month, and on the new (month) of the fourth month, and on the new (month) of the seventh month, and on the new (month) of the tenth month are the days of remembrance, and the days of the seasons in the four divisions of the year. These are written and ordained as a testimony for ever. And Noah ordained them for himself as feasts for the generations for ever, so that they have become thereby a memorial unto him." (R.H. Charles translation)

Based on this writing, scholars have mentioned that the new month celebration, construed as new moon, was actually at the beginning of a month beginning each new "season," as the alternate meaning of the Hebrew word #4150 "moed" refers to "season." With these four seasons, Noah completed a 364-day year cycle (Jub 6:28-30) as:

> "…on the seventeenth day of the second month the earth was dry. And on the twenty-seventh thereof he opened the ark, and sent forth from it beasts, and cattle, and birds, and every moving thing." Jub 5:31, 32 (R.H. Charles translation)

For the 17th day of the 2nd month in the previous year was the commencement of the Flood (Gen 7:11). The Jubilee account of the flood is completely compatible with that of Genesis, with some complimenting details. Some Rabbis will say that the lunar calendar went from 360 days to 354 days after the Flood. Whether the moon had a perfect 30-day cycle prior to the flood, we are not told, but it certainly is not in the pattern of Gen 1:14. Some have argued that the dates from the 17th of the 2nd month thru the year to the following 27th of the 2nd month of the next year would have been 354 + 10 = 364. Notably, it is the 360 days + the 4 intercalary days = 364 days, taking you to vs. 31 to "the 17th of the 2nd month" again, to make for the full year. However you slice it, the lunar model is not YHVH's time piece as Jubilees 6:36, 37 testifies:

The Warning

> "For there will be those who will assuredly make observations of **the moon** – how *it* disturbs the seasons and comes in from year to year **ten days too soon**. For this reason **the years** will come upon them when they **will disturb** *the order*, **and make** an abominable *day* the day of testimony, and **an unclean day a feast day**, and they will confound all the days, **the holy with the unclean**, and the **unclean day with the holy**; for **they will go wrong** as to the **months** and **sabbaths** and **feasts** and **Jubilees**." (*Emphasis supplied*)

Months, feasts, jubilees, and even the Sabbath as to when it commences, all in accord to the Adversary's attempt to change "times and laws" (Dan 7:25) to every aspect of time. The passage before vs. 36, 37 is a lengthy prologue to this prophecy:

> "But **if they** do neglect and **do not observe** them according to His commandment, then **they will disturb** all their **seasons** and the **years** will be **dislodged** from this (order), and they will **neglect** their **ordinances**. And all the children of Israel will **forget** and will not find **the path of the years**, and will forget the **new months**, and **seasons**, and **Sabbaths**, and they will go wrong as to all the order of the years. For I know and from henceforth will I declare it unto thee, and it is not of my own devising; for the book lies written before me, and **on heavenly tablets the division of days is ordained**, lest they forget the feasts of the covenant and walk according to the feasts of the Gentiles after their error and after their ignorance." vs.33-35 (*Emphasis supplied*)

Maybe now we can see why the Pharisees decided, as more and more people were hearing more truth from the "way," why they decided to get rid of Enoch and Jubilees.

> "For this reason I command and testify to thee that you may testify to them; for **after thy death thy children will disturb** (them), so that they will not make **the** year **three hundred and sixty-four** (364) **days** only, and for this reason they will go wrong as to the new months and seasons and Sabbaths and festivals, …" Jub 6:38 (*Emphasis supplied*).

Without quotes such as these (and there are others) it would be easy to assume that following the feasts of either template should be close enough, so long as we observe them. Yet, this is what many Sunday-keepers say about weekly worship. Nevertheless, one might otherwise ask, "If our Savior's passion was right on time to the lunar calendar, didn't He keep the other feasts alongside the Pharisees?" This is a reasonable question. In the book of John, consider the Words of our Savior as He spoke to his disciples:

> "Go ye up unto this feast: **I go not up yet unto this feast; for my time is not yet full come**.... Then the Jews sought him at the feast, and said, 'Where is he? ... Now about the midst of the feast (our Savior) went up into the temple (complex), and taught. " Jn 7:8,11,14 KJV

> "...I am not going up to this festival, for the season for Me has not yet been ..." Jn 7:8 CLNT

Some have argued the point that He did not go up then because He knew the Pharisees would take Him, yet He showed up 3 days later while they were still there. Now the reason our Savior had His disciples "go up" before Him may have been to influence the people gathering and being proper witnesses before the Pharisees. Another point of interest for our Savior keeping a different time-piece was on another occasion where John records the feeding of the 5000 being just before Passover (Jn 6:4), as our Savior had blessed the 5 barley loaves and 2 fish. The word "loaves" in the Greek here, mentioned [3X] in this story (Jhn 6:9,11,13), each time it is:

> G#740 "αρτοσ" ARTOS – **from 142**; *bread* (as raised) or a *loaf*:"

> G#142 "αιρω" AIRO - ... to lift; ... fig. **to** *raise* ... bear (up), carry, lift up, loose, ..."

The Greek word "artos" refers to <u>leavened</u> bread, which they had 12 baskets full of "artos" bread later that day (Jn 6:13) just as this "feast of the Jews was nigh" (Jn 6:4). The emphasis here should be on the "Jews" feast, as opposed to that of our Savior. If this was the proper timing for the coming Passover, would not our Savior, knowing that many of the people were going to take these blessed bread fragments home to their family members; would He not have given them miraculous <u>un</u>leavened bread?

A third witness to the fact that our Savior had kept a different time piece is found in the last event of Luke, Chapter 2. When our Savior was 12 years old, He accompanied his parents to the feast of Passover in Jerusalem. We are told that when His parents "had fulfilled the days," they left Jerusalem not knowing that their son was not "among their kinfolk" (Lk 2:41-49). After searching for Him desperately for three days His parents found Him in the Temple listening to the learned teachers and asking them questions.

It would seem likely from our standards that His parents would be pretty upset with Him, but what did the young Son of YHVH say to them? "Why were you searching for Me?" Now why would this perfect soul say such a thing to His bereft parents? Unless, of course, He knew they should have known better. Then He adds, "Didn't you know that I had to be in My Father's House?" Making it evident that He had taught His parents a different timepiece; likely having informed them that He was obligated to keep His Father's timing to continue in His House at least 3 days later than the usual "custom" that year. Even at this young age, our Savior was attempting to correct wrongs that He came to understand, as His Father directed Him through His own Word.

The Pharisees missed the timing of our Savior's birth, but crucified Him right on time. If you read all the events of our Savior's ministry carefully, you will find a few apparent discrepancies between the Pharisees activities and the timing of our Savior's miracles; insinuating two different timetables. He rebuked them saying, "Ye hypocrites! Ye can discern the face of the sky and the earth; but how is it that ye do not discern this time?" (Lk 12:56), and again saying, "(thy enemies) shall not leave one stone upon another, because thou knewest not the time of thy visitation" (Lk 19:44). Will we miss His coming, and partake of His retribution when we least expect it? We are encouraged "to walk, even as He walked" (1 Jn 2:6).

Each of the spring feasts were an image of our Savior's first coming, as our spotless Passover Lamb, delivering us from our Egypt, (H# 4714. "Mitsrayim" means "tribulation" [miserable]), chosen on YHVH's time, sacrificed in the very midst of the week, being our Unleavened Bread of Heaven during that week (removing our sin); and risen precisely in accord to the meaning of the only day our Father sanctified, as a covenant for us (Gen 2:3; Ex 31:13), as the Firstfruits of the dead (1 Cor 15:20; James 1:18; Rev 14:4), rehearsed since ages past at this very time by all the patriarchs, prophets, and kings. On that same Firstfruits 7th day Sabbath, our Savior breathed on His disciples that they might be prepared to receive the baptism of the Holy Spirit on the 7th day Pentecost Sabbath (Jn 20:22; Ac 2:1-4). (See also Appendix C)

"The First Day of the Week" Scripture or Tradition?

To emphasize YHVH's character in His utilization of the 7th day Sabbath, and the importance that these elements might play in the last-day prophecies, let us take a look at the occurrences of the other dates given to us in the OT that we haven't touched on yet, as they correspond to a Thursday start to the 364-day calendar, beginning with the 7th day Sabbath.

Other 7th day Sabbath Events in the OT

As a Day of *Deliverance*, *Judgment*, or *Convocation*

	Day Month
Israel declares pedigrees after their families (Num 1:18)	1st of 2nd
Aaron dies on Mount Hor (Num 33:38)	1st of 5th
Moses repeats all YHVH has given him (Deu 1:3)	1st of 11th
Israel crosses the Jordan (Jos 4:19)	10th of 1st
Jeroboam ordained a feast of desecration (1 Kng 12:32)	15th of 8th
Nebuchadnezzar came against Jerusalem (2 Kng 25:1)	10th of 10th
Jehoiachin released from prison (2 Kng 25:27; *Jer 52:31)	27th of 12th
Hezechiah dedicates the cleansed Temple (2 Chr 29:17, 20)	17th of 1st
Ezra (brought to) Jerusalem (statutes and ordinances) (Ez 7:9,10)	1st of 5th
Early Former Rain poured out on Jerusalem (Ez 10:9)	20th of 9th
Nehemiah calls for reform on solemn assembly (Ne 9:1)	24th of 7th
Haman to kill Israelites, receives his own death (Es 3:13)	13th of 12th
Word of YHVH came unto Ezekiel (Eze 24:1, and 40:1)	10th of 10th
Word of YHVH came unto Daniel (Dan 10:4)	24th of 1st

It seems reasonable that these events would occur on a 7th day Sabbath based upon the following points. In order for Jeroboam to desecrate something it would have to be on a 7th day Sabbath, as there are no feasts in the 8th month, and the verse says, "like unto the feast (#2282 – solemn assembly) that is in Judah." As judgment came upon Israel, with their cup of iniquity full, it seems appropriate that Nebuchadnezzar would be able to march on Jerusalem on a 7th day Sabbath. In Jer 52:31 the date given here is the 25th, two days before that of 2 Kng 25:27, as it says in Jeremiah that the king merely "lifted up the head of Jehoiachin," as he was likely given two days to clean himself, adorn new clothes, and prepare his statement before being taken to the king. Ezra coming into, or more accurately "brought forth" (ceremoniously) to Jerusalem on this 7th day Sabbath date, was to so "teach statutes and ordinances in (renewed) Israel" (Ez 7:10), which included proper feast observance. Now let us consider other dates mentioned in the OT that fall on feast sabbaths and other 5th days of the week (Thursdays).

5th day (Thursday) Events in the OT

	Day Month
Sin enters the Garden of Eden (Jub 3:17) [360-day calendar]	(17th of 2nd)
Children of Israel go out from Egypt (Ex 13:4; Num 33:3)	15th of 1st
Children of Israel come to Sinai desert (Ex 19:1)	4th of 3rd
Setting up the Tent of Tabernacle (Ex 40:2, 17)	1st of 1st
First day of Unleavened Bread (Lev 23:6; Num 28:17)	15th of 1st
Feast of Trumpets (Lev 23:24; Ez 3:6)	1st of 7th
First day of Tabernacles (Lev 23:34, 39; Num 29:12; Eze 45:25)	15th of 7th
Eighth day of Tabernacles (Lev 23:36, 39; Num 29:35-38)	22nd of 7th
Cloud taken up from the Tabernacle (Num 10:11)	20th of 2nd
Began to Sanctify and came to the Temple (2 Chr 29:17)	1st & 8th of 1st

Ezra goes up from Babylon, heading for Jerusalem (Ez 7:9)	1st of 1st
Ezra counsels certain chiefs of the fathers (Ez 10:16)	1st of 10th
Covenant of Transgression ends on this day (Ez 10:17)	1st of 1st
Wall of Jerusalem finished on this day (Ne 6:15)	25th of 6th
Word of YHVH came unto Ezekiel (Eze 29:17)	1st of 1st
Word of YHVH came to Zechariah (Zec 7:1)	4th of 9th

It makes sense that most of the things recorded on this day of the week are relevant to the Tabernacle or Temple ("5" means "tabernacle" or "Divine favor," as mentioned earlier); or the need for a "three day" preparation completed by the "third" day from the 5th day. Now look at all the dates represented by the 1st day of the week (Sunday).

1st day (Sunday) Events in the OT

	Day Month
Solomon began to build the Temple (2 Chr 3:2)	2nd of 2nd
A day of feasting and gladness after the death of Haman (Es 9:17, 19, 21)	14th of 12th

There are only two (2) known dated events that are listed for the 1st day of the week (Sunday); the beginning of a work week and the 2nd day of Purim to celebrate the victory over the pagan god of Haman on the pagan god's day, as Haman intended to kill all the Jews on the day previous, a 7th day Sabbath, as there was celebration on the 13th before the 14th. Now for a summation of all the days of the week as they occur by their dates as we understand the beginning of the 364-day year:

Sunday	Monday	Tuesday	Wednesday	Thursday	Friday	Sabbath
<u>4</u> times	13 times	3 times	20 times	<u>27</u> times	10 times	<u>31</u> times

The more we study these elements, the more beauty of perfection we come to see in our Father's plan of salvation. As the Psalmist says, "His way is perfect" (Ps 18:30) and

His "way" is found "in the sanctuary," (Ps 77:13), so then everything about the sanctuary should be perfect, including the timing of the feats as Divine appointments. The Hebrew feasts are like blueprints for the Father to build a dwelling place in our hearts according to His specifications. When you follow a set of blueprints all your measurements have to be correct, your angles exact to have a sturdy house on a firm foundation that cannot be moved. Is it any different with YHVH building His dwelling within us? (See Appendix H for feasts by genetic blueprint).

CHAPTER 10

His Way is Perfect

"Thy Word is Truth"

The only instruction on the lunar calendar is found in the Babylonian Talmud, and our only basis to consider such an inconsistent timepiece is rooted in Jewish tradition and an improper interpretation of "rosh chodesh," (a phrase not even found outside the Torah), construed to be "new moon." At certain points of OT time instruction there is only "moedim chodesh," "yom chodesh," and "hag chodesh," conferred in translation as "new moon" because of this tradition. Yet every one of the seven times "rosh chodesh" is found, it is found in the Torah, and is correctly translated as the beginning point of a month, and "new moon" is not found in any commonly recognized translation of the Torah (five books of Moses) by this writer:

"Rosh Chodesh - 7x's in Torah"

Gen 8:13 – "first *day* of the month"
Exo 12:2 (2x) – "chief of *the* months" and "first of the months"
Exo 40:2 – "first of the month"
Exo 40:17 – "first of the month"
Num 10:10 – "beginning of your months"
Num 28:11 – "beginning of your months"
(Num 28:14) – "every month for all *the* months of the year"

Just as "rosh ha shannah" means "new the year," "rosh chodesh" literally means "new month." Outside the Torah, when "chodesh" is coupled with "moed(im)" [appointed time(s)], or "yom" (day), or "hag" (feast), insinuating a Divine appointment, it is purposely mistranslated 20 separate times as "new moon" to retain this contemporary standard of ancient "tradition." Amazingly, with all the Rabbinic talk of "rosh chodesh" referring to "new moon," these two Hebrew words are never even translated as such anywhere in Scripture! Now Num 28:14, listed above within the Torah, does not have a "rosh," but it also does **not** have "every **moon** for all *the* months of the year." Neither do you ever see, "first of the moon," "beginning of the moon," or "chief of the moon." Chodesh was never meant to be "moon," as it is conveniently translated so, to retain what has seemingly always been (See Appendix A).

Remember Daniel 7:25 says the adversary will "think to change time**s** and law**s**," plural. Understanding that YHVH's desire for us is to worship Him on Sabbath, not

Sunday; with the difference of a day, maybe the right timing of the feasts might be equally important to Him (Am 5:21). And since there is no Scriptural moon to follow, the question might be asked, "What was the criteria that the remnant used to determine YHVH's true 'Rosh HaShannah' (New Year)?" Though there is no explicit instruction in the Scriptures for determining the year's beginning, there is enough in the Word to know it is not related in any regard to moon. Take note of the following Hebrew word, found four times [4X] in Scripture:

> "H#8622 "תקופה 'tequphah': - a *revolution*, i.e. (of the sun)"

> "H#8622 - a finished circuit of the sun, - at the turn of the year -"

The last quote is from The Brown-Driver-Briggs, Hebrew and English Lexicon, utilizing Strong's referencing, as this word is found in:

> Ex 34:22, 1 Sam 1:20, 2 Chr 24:23, and Ps 19:6.

Now Enoch had prophesied of the need to intercalate the 360-day calendar ("4 intercalary days" En 75:1 - 364 days) with the coming flood of Noah's day (En 10:4), and Enoch is the oldest known of the Scriptural writings - The book of Enoch was considered part of Scripture prior to the oral law being encrypted into the Babylonian Talmud, when Enoch was "excluded" from the formal "canon," by the leading body of non-believing Jews in 90 AD at the Council of Jamnima; along with other writings that have been found among the Dead Sea Scrolls (DSS), which mention that both Noah and Abraham referred to the Book of Enoch.

Enoch, whose <u>writings</u> are mentioned in Jude 14,15, and his Mazzaroth (stars and planets) in Job 38:31,32; and 2 Kng 23:5, is the one who tells us when the 364-day year starts. With chapter numbering differences between publishers, the translations of Enoch tell us [not to be confused with Enoch II, whose earliest known manuscript is Slavic – circa 1400's CE (AD), a counterfeit created in the early days of the reformation to discourage truth-seeking scholars] the time of year when both day and night have equal parts (as the day encroaches upon the night), and this would be the turn of the year in 364 days:

> "On that day the night decreases and amounts to nine parts, and the day to nine parts, and the night is equal to the day and the year is exactly as to its days three hundred and sixty-four. ..." En 72:32, 33 (www.earth-history.com)

" ... the exactness of the year is accomplished through its separate three hundred and sixty-four stations." En 75:2, 3 (R.H. Charles translation)

This is declaring that the next day is the first of the year (Rosh HaShannah)(Abib 1) and would be the day after what is called the vernal, or spring equinox. [Enoch Chs.72-82, give detailed instruction on the 364-day calendar.] This is compatible with what even the Rabbis say about the beginning of this 364-day calendar. Invariably, when the sabbatical year comes around, one week is added, [as an intercalation "week" (1 day for each of the seven years)] to give an overall annual average of 365 days per year, without disrupting the days of the week paired to the numbered day of the month. Obviously, with 364 vs. 365, the beginning Thursday in respect to the vernal equinox will creep back just a little more than a day per year until the next Sabbatical, yet it is most of the time within the week of the vernal equinox, starting consistently on the right day of the week.

There is a reasonable <u>theory</u> posed by scholars that accounts for the remaining ¼ day / year of the solar cycle (as this is not addressed in any known Scriptural or DSS writings) with an intriguing intercalation that matches the gematrial pattern. As was mentioned briefly before, this is to add a second week of intercalation on the 4th Sabbatical year [4 x 7 = 28 years; ("redemption, earth" x "spiritual perfection, life" = "earth" comes into "perfection" with time, as an act of "spiritual redemption")], instead of the usual one week. (Yet based on the present solar time, with these intercalations only, this would cause an extra week and a day in 1000 years, which may have some prophetic correlation to Rev 8:1).

As the intercalation week, reserved for the sabbatical year, is symbolic of the year of the creation week initiating the sabbatical cycle; the cancellation of debts in the sabbatical year would set president to cancel the debt of time as well. So, the two weeks of intercalation could have been added at the Jubilee [a sabbatical (1 week) of sabbaticals (another week), as a cancellation of debts with property returns], for a "double spiritual perfection" (7 x 7). These extra weeks of celebration would be more conducive in the sabbatical years when there is no sowing or reaping. Again the scholarly answer would be to add one week to the Feast of Unleavened Bread, as we have record of such in Hezekiah's day (2 Chr 30:23), and one to the Feast of Tabernacles in some multiple of a sabbatical year, maybe adding the second week to the Week of Awe just prior to the Day of Atonement, for a complete balance of all debts on the very day of Jubilee. So as these intercalations balance the debt of time, the first day of the 364-day calendar year will most often have the 5th day of the week (Thursday) on the vernal equinox or the day after.

This idea of a sabbatical timing pattern can also be inferred in the analysis of the 24 priestly divisions that serve in the Temple, mentioned in 1 Chr 24:7-18. With 24 divisions covering exactly 52 weeks a year, each division would serve twice a year, and 4 divisions would serve a 3rd week. Six full years would complete the priestly cycle for all 24 divisions precisely (6 x 52 = 312; 312 ÷ 24 = 13 service periods), and this procedure is confirmed in the DSS (text 60, *Synchronistic Calendars*). The Sabbatical year had different requirements of the priests, and the people, as likely the High Priest took a larger role. Although these accounts allude to the possibility of them adding a week on a Sabbatical, outside of Enoch, they are not conclusive and circumstantial at best.

For those who may be comfortable with the idea of adding the week of intercalation on a Sabbatical year, the next step would be to find the precise timing of the Sabbatical pattern. Determining the Sabbatical year has always been a challenge and controversy for centuries, as it was likely lost in the years of the "diaspora" (the dispersion of the Hebrews out of Palestine, to the four corners of the world). Our Savior seems to point out the Sabbatical, but we do not know precisely what year He declared it (Lk 4:19), other than our calculation.

One thing to keep in mind when searching for any secret is to understand that YHVH is always the same (Heb 13:8), and does not change (Mal 3:6), hence, just like His consistent calendar, the days of the week, and the 7th day Sabbath; the Sabbatical cycle of years should have had its beginning with Adams creation. If we knew for certain the year of Adams beginning, the Sabbatical years must have commenced from then.

The well-accepted Bible chronology work of James Ussher (commissioned during the reign of King James and completed in the days of his son Charles I in the 1630's), is still used extensively by theologians today. It is generally considered a reliable and valuable resource, with the exception of at least one point – the year of Abrams birth, as it correlates to the age of his father Terah (Gen 11:32). Making the correction and counting backwards would place Adam's creation to the year 3989 BCE, placing 6000 years since his creation to the year 2012 CE (no Ø BCE or CE), instead of 1997 by Ussher's reckoning (just as the Aztec's and Chinese determined 2012 a world changing year). (See www.timelyministries.com for the correction).

Doing the Sabbatical math, places the most recent Sabbatical year to the fall of 2011 to the fall of 2012 (1990/91 being the last Jubilee). Not that the Sabbath Millennium, the 1000 year reign, had commenced at that time, for that would not start until after 6000 years of sin, since the time Adam had actually fallen. Contemporary Scripture gives no clue as to when Adam sinned, but one of the DSS does. The Book of Jubilees says that Adam sinned after being in the garden "seven years exactly" (Jub 3:17). That means 6000 years of sin would be up seven years beyond the 2011/2012 year, making it 2018/2019, which happens to correlate with other end-time studies, and specific patterns in Daniel and Revelation (See also Appendix E).

In light of this Sabbatical pattern, there is an interesting correlation with the vernal equinox falling on the 5th day of the week in these sabbatical years. Consider the following table with March 22nd as the first full-day after the vernal equinox:

										03/21
2009	2010	2011	**2012**	2013	2014	2015	2016	2017	2018	**2019**
Sun	Mon	Tues	**Thrs**	Fri	Sab	Sun	Tues	Weds	Thrs	**Thrs**

As March 21st is the day when the "moment" of equinox occurs within the Gregorian calendar, we see the beginning of the year is precise according to Enoch, when compared with the rest of Scripture. Yet there is still a need for adding a week to the 364-day calendar in 2019, recalling that this does not disrupt the pattern (2 Chr 30:23) [this "Thrs" comes out as the right start of the year because this is the 28th year from the last proposed Jubilee (1991)]. All this minutia gives some plausible evidence of the timing of the sabbatical cycle, and that the sequence of the weekdays has never changed since the creation, or at least since the flood; though many scholars might declare foul.

It is true that there have been isolated regions within various empires that have tried an eight-day week, at different points in history. Even France, as recent as the French Revolution, had tried a ten-day week until all the beasts of burden refused to move, even when goaded; so the country went back to a seven-day week with the rest of the world. Our Heavenly Father has retained His cycles upon His creation, for He had designed all His creatures with His biological template, and made a covenant with His people that His remnant will continue to retain (Ex 31:13). This includes these "cycles of righteousness," misconstrued as "'paths' of righteousness" (Ps23:3). The word "path" is:

H#4570 מעגל MA'GÂL – from the same as **5696**; a track (lit. or fig.) … (as *circular*):"

H#5696 עגל ÂGÔL – from an unused root mean. To **revolve**, **circular**: - round."

"He restoreth my soul: He leadeth me in the **cycles** of righteousness for His Names sake." (Ps 23:3).

"Concerning the works of men, by the Word of Thy Lips have kept *me from* the **cycles** of the destroyer. Hold up my goings in thy **cycles**, *that* my footsteps slip not" (Ps 17:4, 5).

YHVH wants us to be punctual in keeping His Divine Appointments, otherwise, why would He refer to them as appointments? As the "shadow of things to come," we should make the reasonable effort to gain some semblance of meaning from the feasts, and rehearse them according to His perfect calendar that is purely a matter of counting your days (Ps 90:12). This is the Scriptural choice, rather than conjuring some ethereal meaning from the occasional mistranslations and misinterpretations. To substantiate the beginning of a month by a pagan method of moon-watch that one priest might see and another might not, only stands a 40% chance that it would be in sync with a given month in the 364-day model with each passing year (100% that one month would be in sync every 3 years), for a high probability of making "an unclean day a feast day … the holy with the unclean" (Jub 6:37). The rabbis say:

" …only the court can proclaim *Rosh Chodesh* based upon the testimony of witnesses who observed the re-appearance of the moon, and upon this proclamation, the Jewish calendar is based. Unless the month can be proclaimed there is no calendar, and without a calendar there can be no festivals." *The Chumash*, Stone Edition, p. 348

A system completely controlled by the "court," when we ourselves are responsible to count our days (Ps 90:12). If you want to follow Torah, - you cannot utilize a lunar calendar to determine the feasts, for Moses never used it. The books of Enoch and Jubilees were taken out of accepted Scriptures by the leading Jewish authority at the Counsel of Jamnima in 90 CE because both books denigrated the use of the lunar calendar. The evangelizing disciples of the "Way" were using the 364-day calendar, without a priest, to count and determine their feast-time. Consider this quote that is recorded in the book of Peter, as he quotes from the book of Jubilees:

> "But, beloved, be not ignorant of this one thing, that **one day *is* with (YHVH) as a thousand years, and a thousand years as one day.**"
> 2 Ptr 3:8 KJV (*Emphasis supplied*)

As a direct quote, this statement is only found in the book of Jubilees (Jub 4:30). Some commentaries might point you to Ps 90:4, but this is not a quote, and half the thought at best, as Peter makes reference to a direct phrase.

"In the Fullness of Time"

The mystery of iniquity (lawlessness) was already working in Paul's day (2 Th 2:7), as he had also written to the Thessalonians, "…you received not the word of men, but as it is in truth, the word of God" (1 Th 2:13). Because Paul knew several languages (1 Cor 14:18) YHVH had commissioned him to go to the Gentiles as he came to understand, between language barriers and cultural paradigms, how things could get lost in the translation. As part of that mystery, he knew these same arguments would continue, as they do today. So, taking up Paul's defense, let us look at a couple more points that Paul had dealt with.

A rabbi today would defend the concept of reaping the first wave sheaf offering when it is ripe, having dependence upon trends in the weather, as they would factor a 13th month at the end of every third year or so. The majority of modern Israelites and Messianic believers today utilize some form of the lunar calendar that was revised and standardized by Meton of Athens in 432 BCE, which was later adopted by the leading authorities in Israel, and other nations previously influenced by Babylon.

Lunar calendars are 354 days per year, about 11 days off per year, 10 days off per the 364-day calendar, so the Meton approach was to add 1 lunar month at the end of every third year (30 = 3 x 10), what they call a second Adar (Adar II)(Adar = 12th month), being sure to do this 7 times in 19 years, to balance out the 354-day year to the actual average (365-¼). This is why they looked to a ripening to bring the harvests back in line with the feasts by adding this month. There have been as many as 26 different lunar calendars in use amongst various Semite groups in different ages. Many of them worked, and some corrected more easily to the solar than others, yet the question we should ask is: "Were any of these YHVH's calendar?" The book of Leviticus, the instruction manual for the priests, does not give any teaching on the use of any lunar calendar.

The Book of Leviticus

No "new moons" described No "moon(s)" mentioned at all No mention of a 354-day year No mention of an intercalary month	No mention of a 13th month No mention of 3 or 19 year cycles, but of sevens No mention of sighting a crescent No mention of any disruption of a seven day cycle

There is no such instruction on the use of the moon anywhere in the Torah, or the OT. The Pharisees and their posterity, with the observable need to move the harvest three or more weeks ahead, they would add another lunar month in the middle of the growing season, at the end of the year, to attain their ripe barley by the second week of the first month; forgetting, as Noah had prophesied, that they would loose their way in "the new months, and seasons," going "wrong as to all the order of the years"(Jub 6:34). They did this by creating a tradition, disassociated from the other writings of Moses, as a misconception before the people, which presupposes the need for other misinterpretations.

This misconception promotes the assumption that every first-sheaf harvest is done when the grain berries are ripe; as one is encouraged to rely upon the priest for the lack of written instruction. Today, the believer tends to lean toward the idea that our Savior will come and thrust in His sickle on the day when all His grain is ripe; but His return occurs when all the fruits of His labors are ripe, as each church generation ripens and is stored (reserved) before the next; this includes the corn, olives, grapes, etc. Many of these are brought in at the Feast of Ingathering, or Tabernacles, and will be commemorated spiritually by the nations, year by year in the Sabbath Millennium (Zec 14:16-19).

Consequently, Lev 23:14-17 and Num 28:26 clue us into the idea that ancient Israel, in this early part of the latter rain, ate "green," or "new" grain (Hos 6:3; Deut 16:9; Isa 55:10,11). The word "green ear" here is #3759 "karmel" which is where we get the word "caramel" from, when the green fruit is in the sweet milk stage. If one would put their thumb nail into a green berry and get a milky substance, this was considered edible, and worthy of a wave-sheaf offering (Lev 23:14).

By vernal equinox standards, the barley was usually ripe in the region of Jerusalem in the 1st month, and typically ripe in the lowlands in the 12th month, yet not always ripe in the highlands until the 2nd month; but there were "green ears," as scripture implies, in each locale by the second week of the 1st month, some a little greener than others, but still "karmel" when all of Israel brought their First Wave Sheaves into Jerusalem.

Our Savior's triumphal entry into Jerusalem, in accordance with Zec 9:9, was on the 10th of the 1st month, a "shabbatone," (Hb). At that time many of the Israelite pilgrims were coming into Jerusalem with their lambs and early sheaves (which look like small green "trees" – the grain heads like so many branches, the stalks bundled together as the trunk) and they waved these "branches" before the righteous "Branch" of Jesse (Isa 11:1; Jer 23:5, 33:15), while the disciples declared Him on the rightful day as the fulfillment of prophecy, with the KJV saying, the people "strawed *them* in the way" (Mt 21:8; Mk11:8).

"And a very great multitude spread their garments in the way; others **cut down branches** from the **trees**, and **strawed** *them* in the way." Mt 21:8

SI   (IB)

"**cut down**" - G#*2875* KOPTO (EKOPTON) – "to *beat*, to '*chop*', ..."
(repeated action)

"**trees**" – G#*1186* DENDRON (DENDRONE) – a branching out from center
(Eng. Def.)

"**branches**" – G#*2798* KLADOS (KLADOUS) – "or *bough*" – frond-like branch
(Eng. Def.)

"**strawed**" – G#*4766* STRONNUO (ESTRONNUON) – "to '*strew*', i.e. *spread*"

So to restructure this half of the verse:

"...others beat the boughs of (απο) the branchings, even (και) spread in the way"

The words that were "from" and "and," can contextually be "of" and "even."

G#*575* APO "απο – from [386], **of** [149], ... by [9], ... with [4], ..."

G#*2532* KAI "και – and [8167], also [517], **even** [100], … then [25], so [18], likewise [12], or [12], that [12], …"

Some of the Israelites repeatedly *beat* (as in beating the air) "waved" their (tree-like) "sheaves" (spreading) "undulating" the branches thereof in the (way) "course-way," as the word *them* is supplied in the KJV. Sounds a little out there? Let us look at John's account in the KJV:

"much people that were come to the feast … **Took palm branches** of **palm trees**, and went forth to meet him, … " Jhn 12:12,13

It turns out these words "**palm branches** of **palm trees**" in the Textus Receptus are actually Phoenician words and are not original to the Greek language.

"**branches**" G#*902* BAION – "<u>bah</u> –*ee'-on*, - a **palm** *twig: - branch*" from G#*896* BAAL – "<u>bah</u>*'-al,* - a <u>Phoenician</u> deity"

"**palm**" G#*5404* PHOINIX – "*foy'-nix,* of <u>uncertain derivation</u>: - **palm** (tree)"

Notice the "uncertain derivation" with "**phoin**-ix," which is most certainly a **Phoen**ician word, for the phrase "**palm branches** of **palm trees**," ("baia tone phoinixone"), has the "palm *branch*," which is a symbol of the Phoenician Sun-god, "Baal."

It could be difficult to quickly climb a palm tree that has no lower branches, and cut a palm branch, - even deciduous "branches" were only just budding, so there couldn't be "boughs" of branches from such a "tree." The psalmist wrote of our Savior: "He that goes forth and weeps,* bearing precious seed, shall come again with rejoicing, bringing his sheaves *with him*" (Ps 126:6) (Lk 19:41).* This is foretelling His triumphal entry into Jerusalem on wave-sheaves, and will be repeated in the future kingdom as well, "bearing precious seed" as the saints of the ages, as His firstfruit sheaves are the 144,000 (1 Cor 15:23 – as this verse should read: "But every man in his own order; <u>anointed</u> firstfruits, afterward they that are <u>the</u> Christ's at His coming." see Rev 14:4) shouting hosannas and waving their *firstfruits* on the "Son of David." Remember the FF Omer is anointed.

The Phoenicians would always greet their King coming back victoriously from battle, waving the symbol of their sun-deity toward their king, and laying their garments in the way before him, in joyous celebration and homage to the sun-deity for their earthly salvation. The only other verse where "phoinix" is substituted, happens to be in one of John's other writings, in Rev 7:9, as the saints before the great white throne having "palms in their hands," yet actually "wave-sheaves in their hands." John's original compositions were in Hebrew, for all the idioms and sentence structure that comes thru in the Greek translation makes for proper Hebrew, but unnatural Greek. Remember, our Savior will be bringing His firstfruit sheaves with him (Ps 126:6).

The question remains: Would the Hebrews saints wave symbols of sun worship before a coming Messiah, or would they adhere to the terms in Leviticus 23, waving their firstfruit wave-sheaf offerings? Just as Aramaic words (customs) had been substituted in the Hebrew Torah, Phoenician words (customs) have been substituted into the Greek text. When altered leadership gets involved at both the religious and state levels, to make for complete political correctness, then the final filtration process is in place to get the last vestiges of hated "Jewishness" out of the NT by easily manipulated mistranslation.

Yet, we should not be dismayed, for YHVH had allowed these things to happen (Isa 29:10-14), that only those who search for Him with all their heart will find Him (Jer 29:13). He has promised that everything that is hidden will be revealed (Lk 12:2) to those who are willing to commit themselves to the dig (Mt 13:44), for the Spirit will guide us into all Truth (Jn 16:13) as long as we are willing to prove all things (1 Th 5:21).

These Firstfruits were considered the most honored of reapings, to be consecrated holy unto YHWH, as were all firstborn of man and beast (Exo 13:2). Green "karmel" grain is also the most nutritious stage of the fruit head, but does not fare well with long storage until it is fully ripe. Unless, of course, if you cut the stalk low and stand the bundle upright, like a tree, then the stalk will provide sustenance to the fruit head to be storable.

This is how the Firstfruits were cut and delivered to the Temple in Jerusalem, waved before the priest, and so arranged in the Temple courtyard in accordance to tribe on this 10th of the 1st month (Shabbos HaGadol -- Ex 12:3; Lev 23:10,12; Jos 4:19). This is that they might be waved before YHVH by the priests the next 7th day Sabbath morning, which is on the Firstfruit Omer day, the 17th of the 1st month (Lev 23:11). This is why our Savior cleansed the Temple, His Father's House, (of the leaven of the Pharisees) on the 10th, (yes, a Shabbat - not "palm" Sunday), to be so chosen as the long awaited "Lamb of God" on Passover the 14th, and the proper Firstfruits of the dead, that the great veil of the Temple would separate, to equate the work of the holy with the most holy.

"THE FIRST DAY OF THE WEEK" SCRIPTURE OR TRADITION?

At this veil separation, our Savior became the First Omer in the count on the 17th, and when the High priest waved that First Omer in the Temple early that morning, our Savior came before His Father as the heavenly Wave-sheaf offering, providing the free gift of salvation for all and redemption for Israel. This day of FF "sabbatone," just before our Savior first rose to His Father that day (Jn 20:17), before the ascension forty days later; the High Priest was in the dedicated field just outside Jerusalem ready to cut the ceremonial Firstfruit sheaf. On this particular 7th day Sabbath, this "third day" [i.e. since the "day with the preparation" (Passover/1st of UB)] was a special ceremony conducted by the High Priest, witnessed before the people for them to commence their count of "seven perfect Shabbats," called the Feast of Weeks (Lev 23:15 - IB), to the day of Pentecost Sabbath, the <u>Feast</u> of Firstfruits.

This is portrayed in a proper adaptation of Deut 16:9. The KJV translates this verse so that it would be compatible with their translation at Lev 23:11, making it appear that the individual Israelite is doing the work of cutting the first sheaf, beginning the Feast of Weeks on a day other than a 7th day Sabbath (like the "morrow after the Sabbath"[KJV]). Yet the Firstfruits (FF), now a "sabbatone" as a 7th day Sabbath, an Israelite would not cut a sheaf that day, but the priest only. The KJV is as follows:

> "Seven weeks shalt thou number unto thee: begin to number the seven weeks from *such time as* thou beginnest *to put* the sickle to the corn" Deut 16:9 KJV.

> If everyone did this back home, their return to Jerusalem, 50 days later, would be on different days. Now compare this to the same verse in the CVOT: *(Emphasis supplied)*

> "You shall count off seven weeks for your*self*. From *the* start of *the* scythe in *the* raised *grain*, shall you start to count off seven weeks." Deut 16:9

In the CVOT the count begins "From *the* start," without saying by whom. The "thou beginnest," in the KJV, has no "thou" in the script. Now look at the word "beginnest":

> H# 2490 חלל **chalal** - earlier Strong's - " ... **to** *begin* (as if by an "opening wedge"); denom. **(from 2485) to** *play* **(the flute)**: - **begin**, ... **pipe**, player on instruments, ..."

H#2485 חליל chaliyl – "**from 2490**; **a *flute*** (as *perforated*): - pipe."

Therefore, a proper rendering of this verse would be as follows:

"You shall count seven weeks for yourselves; from when the sickle **begins the flute** to the standing crop shall you begin to count seven weeks." (*lit.*) Deut 16:9

The High Priest, in a Firstfruits (FF) procession, went to a dedicated field just outside Jerusalem and on that special 7th day Sabbath morning (Lev 23:11), all Israel was there to witness (in the **midst** of the **week of UB**). With such a crowd of people in Jerusalem, not everyone could witness the cutting, but they would likely hear the flute, or the subsequent shouts of Hosanna, and know the sheaf was cut, and the very hour that the count of the seven weeks began. This becomes important in the "50" count (inclusive reckoning), to the very hour of spiritual out-pouring for "seven perfect Sabbaths" on Pentecost Sabbath.

This sheaf represented the Messiah, waved first, and then the Firstfruits (FF) sheaves in the Temple courtyard, which represents the 144,000, the anointed from the 12 tribes of Israel on that FF day. The Firstfruits ceremony was the annual representation of the weekly service with the exchange of the "sheaf" bread every 7th day Sabbath morning.

The children of Israel had prepared twice as much UB the day before (16th of the 1st), not unlike their forefathers, who in the midst of the Feast of Weeks' time (16th of the 2nd - Ex 16:1,7, like a 2nd month UB), started to pick manna in the wilderness; preparing twice as much on the preparation days, before each of the 7th day Sabbaths.

In the land of Judea, as the barley harvest was finishing midway into the 2nd month, the wheat harvest began, and even the highlands had adequate wheat ready in time for the Pentecost Sabbath (as the 6th of the 3rd month, Ex 19:1, 11). Back in the wilderness, once the children of Israel had agreed to the covenant of Torah, YHVH then instructed the people, through Moses, on the three-day preparation for that day.

The Stone Edition, The *Cumash*, has in commentary that preparations started on the "fourth of Sivan" (4th of the 3rd month), as the beginning of the three-day period, and continues to mention that the "third day would be the sixth of Sivan" (6th of the 3rd) (p.403), giving the nation two complete days to be ready for Pentecost Sabbath.

"The First Day of the Week" Scripture or Tradition?

The rabbis here, making reference to Ex 19:10-15, have the correct date, but the wrong day of the week elsewhere. The rabbis came up with this date knowing the 10th of the 1st was a Shabbat in Egypt before the Exodus (they call – *Shabbos HaGadol*), so Firstfruits was the following Sabbath, the 17th of the 1st (*A Family Guide to the Biblical Holidays*, p. 207), as 50 days from this date does bring you to the 6th of the 3rd month (no consecutive 30-day months with a lunar calendar). Using YHVH's properly intercalated calendar, this always brings you to FF Sabbath on the 17th of the 1st month, which is what is precisely stated in the Hebrew for the FF at Lev 23:11, ממהרת השבת "mee mohorawth ha Shabbat" or "from morrow the Shabbat," or morning of the 7th day Sabbath. Amazingly, in the Stone Edition, *The Chumash*, we find the following comment for Lev 23:11 (Ibid p. 685):

"Although the word שבת (Shabbat) ordinarily refers to the Sabbath, this cannot be the case here, because the verse does not specify which of the fifty-two Sabbaths is meant (*Rashi*; *Sifra*)."

Apparently rabbis' Rashi and Sifra need a specific 7th day Sabbath stated to satisfy them, (as though "from morrow the Shabbat" could not be the next morning Shabbat, or that Moses routinely specifies a given date for a Shabbat), but they are making inference here to the correct form of Sabbath, the 7th day Sabbaths, by citing the number "fifty-two." Ironically, there are consistently "fifty-two" 7th day Sabbaths in a 364-day calendar every year, and typically only 50 to 51 in a lunar calendar, or 54 to 55 in their 13 month year.

The law of averages for a lunar calendar to have only 52 Shabbats in any given year during their 19-year cycle is just under 8%. With the 364-day calendar, it is 100% (intercalation weeks, also "inseparable from their office," yet "not included" in the years En 75:1). In fact, according to the First Psalm Scroll of the DSS it says that king David composed 52 songs for the Shabbat offerings (one for each Shabbat in the 364-day year).

Another means to show that Pentecost was meant to be on a 7th day Sabbath is directly from Ex 19, the Sinai chapter. In verse 1 we are told that the children of Israel came into the wilderness of Sinai "in the third month" on "the same day," they had "gone forth out of the land of Egypt." Now it does not say the "self" same day, which would be the same date and day of the week, for we are told this is in the "third month." If Moses meant the 15th of the third month, he would have mentioned that number, but then we would be looking at a pattern that is much more than 50 days leading to Pentecost. Therefore, it can only mean the same day of the week, the same day they left Egypt, and from our previous calculations would have been the 5th day of the week (i.e. Thursday).

In verse 11, Moses is counseled by YHVH to tell the people to "be ready by the third day," to have their clothes washed, and "come not at your wives" on the "third day" (vs. 15), and then "on the third day" came YHVH upon the mount. If we count unto the third day, which would include that Thursday, we have – (1) Thursday, (2) Friday, (3) 7th day Sabbath. So the day of the week that YHVH came down upon Mount Sinai in "thunder and lightning" and "loud trumpet sounds" was on the 7th day Sabbath, as the people "shuddered" in fear for His Spirit was being poured out on this day.

To fast forward from here, when the company of Israel left the wilderness for the promised land by crossing the Jordan on the 10th on the 1st month (Jos 4:19), it was exactly 40 years from the date of the choosing of the lamb back in Egypt - the same day of the week, and the same date. Joshua, on this special 7th day Sabbath (the Shabbos HaGadol), had likely reaped a ceremonial first sheaf of grain from an open field before the chosen men from the twelve tribes (Jos 4:2); in order to fulfill the words of Moses in Lev 23:10, and keep the same appointments and time-intervals between.

Remember this is the ceremonial cut in coming into the promise land. Whether twelve sheaves were ceremoniously cut for each tribe that day as they had taken up twelve stones as a memorial, we cannot determine (Jos 4:3-9). For the miracle of the Jordan river parting before the Ark of the Covenant had occurred on this the "Dwelling Place of the Father's Miraculous Sign," Shabbat (Jos 4:19).

For the first time, from the next morning into the next few days, the Israelites themselves had occasion to find and bring their first cut-sheaves from open fields in the Gilgal area, to wave them before the priests, and prepare to the same day of the week, their male Passover lambs (Lev 23:12); "They kept the Passover on the fourteenth day of the month at even in the plains of Jericho" (Jos 5:10).

For numerous generations since, as all males of Israel came together in one place, later in Jerusalem during the days of the kings, to prepare for the Feast of Unleavened Bread (many traveling over a day's journey) in commemoration of the Passover preparation in Egypt, and the crossing into the promised land; they would enter the city of heavenly realms as a massive throng, a ceremonial parade on the 10th of the 1st month. Many would camp the day before in the hills of Jerusalem just off the main road, and awaken to the line-up activities before the grand procession of Israelites, organized by tribe, ready to be led by the high priest approaching the city, carrying their own first-sheaf, as an unleavened wave offering on their shoulders, and leading their lambs (a first born male yearling), ready to file into the Temple courtyard to relay their oblations on this 10th of the 1st (Shabbat).

If the lamb was counted worthy and blessed by the Levitical priest, the lamb would be taken to the extended family home, and given only water for the next 4 days. On the 14th (a Wednesday), the house was swept clean of any leaven, and unleavened cakes were prepared. The lamb's life was then taken, its blood applied to the doorposts and lintel, and its body prepared to be roasted whole in the late afternoon with the "purtenance" therein (Ex 12:9) now free of refuse. The bowels of the animal had to be cleansed by fasting, usually taking a minimum of three days, in order to roast the animal whole without the gut swelling from the heat with the flora overgrowth and blowing out the abdominal contents, making a sizable mess. Just as our Savior had fasted, as many days, His body skewered, saw no corruption and not a bone broken (Ex 12:46; Acts 2:31; Jhn 19:36).

As much as could be eaten that night was done so in haste on their feet, but when they entered the land of promise they could eat it in a reclined position, and what remained of the lamb's carcass was burned in the fire before dawn. The coming morning being the 15th, was a holy convocation, the 1st day of UB (Lev 23:6, 7). Therefore, the actual "passing-over" occurred at "midnight" (Ex 12:29). Many, after being up most the night, would "turn in the <u>morning</u> and go unto [their] tents." (Deut 16:7). This, along with the lamb consumed, is symbolic of our Savior being gone and "asleep" in the grave on the first day of UB. This Thursday – the day of sin redeemed; all Israel would rest in the early morning on this feast sabbath, before the holy convocation assembly that afternoon.

Then on the 16th (Friday) some barley harvesting was done in the vicinity of Jerusalem, everyone making double portions in preparation for FF as the start of the Feast of Weeks. Those who had traveled to Jerusalem from the highlands, could buy additional grain before that 7th day Sabbath if they hadn't enough near-ripe sheaves with them to make more UB with their families.

Remember, the Wave-sheaf Offerings were already presented before the priests in the Temple, before Passover, most of them having done so on that Shabbos HaGadol, on the 10th, but the priests may have gone to a dedicated field just outside Jerusalem and picked twice as much grain that preparation day before FF (surely that UB did not "stink" the next day). As the first-sheaves given the previous week on the 10th were lined upright in bundles in the Temple courtyard according to tribe, they continued to ripen over that week. These Firstfruits were holy, waved before the priests on the 10th, then waved by the priests before YHVH on the 17th (Lev 23:14,11), set-apart for the making of the showbread (sheavebread) for the Temple, to be done each and every preparation day (Friday) throughout the year.

As the 12 tribes typically contributed offerings for the morning and evening sacrifice (2 / day x 6 days / week = 12 tribes) each tribe had either a morning or an afternoon offering through the course of the work week. This is why the sheaves were bundled according to tribe, and why there were twelve loaves on the table of shewbread, more properly "sheavebread." (the bread in the <u>wilderness</u> was called the Bread of the Presence – made from Manna). The "sheavebread" would be made only of unleavened barley, each week of every year. So, on the Shabbat after Passover (the 17th) the priests would begin to wave the first of these first-sheaves in the morning, done tribe by tribe; may be in the order of their birth, Reuben through Benjamin; after the High Priest's cut sheaf was waved.

The "sheave" bread was exchanged every 7th day Sabbath morning in the holy place by the Levites; each loaf for each tribe arranged in two rows of six, so they each laid flat on the showbread table, again, likely in their order of their birth, for the course of the offerings in the week. When the morning of the 7th day Sabbath came, the Levitical family for that week, who had prepared the showbread the day before, would ceremoniously enter the holy place and exchange all the week-old showbread for the new; exemplifying the renewed Messiah, the Bread of Heaven, who presently resides as such in the Tabernacle made without hands, ministering and making intercession for us to this day (Heb 9:11; 8:2; 7:25).

Back to the feast of Unleavened Bread (UB), after the seventh and last day of UB, a holy convocation (shabbaton), the 21st of the 1st month (Wednesday) [Remember: day 4 means "redemption"], all of Israel returned back to their hometowns. They continued to "harvest" the barley during the Feast of Weeks bringing an Omer full of barley to the synagogue in their hometown each Shabbat, some in the lowlands may have started with the wheat. As the Israelites were reaping their fields back at home, they would bring an omer of grain before the priests each Shabbat for a count of seven Shabbats from the FF, and would observe Pentecost, as the "Feast of the Harvest of the Firstfruits" (Exo 23:16; 34:22) on that seventh Sabbath morning back in Jerusalem again, to the very hour of the Firstfruit wave-offering 50 days before (Deut 16:16) for "seven perfect sabbaths."

Pentecost was the culmination of the latter rain that had brought the grain to its final ripened harvest (the corners and gleanings left for others Lev 19:9, 10; 23:22). The offering of the two leavened loaves of the fully ripened grain on Pentecost (Lev 23:17) has several theories of symbolic meaning. One being that one leavened loaf was of barley, the other wheat, representing two special resurrections in the end of days; the barley one group of believers and the wheat another, both comprising the "great multitude" (Rev 4:9).

Blood Moon

Blood on anything is not good. In the body it represents life, but the shedding of it is for the remission of sins, to be placed on something as a sign of repentance of sin, or uncleanness, or an omen of judgment. Though YHVH is long suffering and slow to anger, He will again be "visiting the iniquity upon the children unto the 3rd and 4th generation." (Ex 20:5; 34:7; Nu 14:18; De 5:9). YHVH imputes iniquity, lays up iniquity, that one may bear his iniquity, yet YHVH can cover iniquity, and later purge iniquity, for those who sincerely and properly repent, but will "in no wise clear the guilty" (Ex34:7).

Ham begat Canaan, who was cursed for the sin of his father (Gen 9:22-27), who begat many sons, which included the Amorites, the Hittites, the Jebusites, and Sodom and Gomorrah (Gen 10:14-19). Ham also begat Cush, who begat Nimrod, out of which came Babylon, Ninevah, and the Philistines. Of course, a "generation" back then, by the length of a man's years was counted by the centuries instead of scores or decades. Much of this ancestry did not repent, neither in the days of Abraham, as we know that Babel was "visited" to its abandonment; the cities of Sodom and Gomorrah were "visited" to their destruction, but for others, their iniquity was "not yet full."

When Abraham received the covenant from YHVH, he was given a promise that his seed, though they will be afflicted by their captors 400 years, will "come out with great substance" and their oppressors, YHVH says, "I will judge" (Gen 15:13,14). Some of the nations that YHVH was to "visit" were spared destruction for another generation for the sake of some who had repented. "But in the fourth generation they shall come hither again: for the iniquity of the Amorites is not yet full" (vs.16). As a second witness, the city of Nineveh had repented, and that generation did not see its destruction; but the prophecy of Jonah against Nineveh was fulfilled many years later (Na 3:7).

Then there are those who "say they are Jews and are not," as our Savior says they are of "the synagogue of Satan" (Rev 2:9). And these will come and worship before the feet of the true congregation of Philadelphia and come "to know that I have loved thee" (Rev 3:9). At the mouth of 2 or 3 witnesses "shall a matter be established" (De 19:15). Modern Israel has recently completed another blood moon tetrad of lunar eclipse on their feasts marking impending judgment; yet for a remnant of believers among them, who have sighed and cried "for all the abominations … done in the midst thereof" (Eze 9:4), they have been spared thus far, yet as the prophets says:

> "I looked for a man among them who would build up the wall and stand before me in the gap on behalf of the land so I would not have to destroy it, but I found none." (Eze 22:30)

> "For three sins of Israel, even four, I will not turn back My wrath." (Am 2:6)

So, utilizing the moon, the Babylonian time-piece, with a blood moon tetrad (4 lunar eclipses on their lunar feasts - Passover, 1st of Tabernacles, Passover, 1st of Tabernacles) in Palestine starting in 1917 (with the British Mandate) and 1918; with another blood moon tetrad shortly after modern Israel's birth (1948) starting in 1949, then another blood moon tetrad starting in 1967 (Six-Day War)(their Jubilee) and again from 2014-2015 we have the 4 blood moons again, witnessed 4 times (1917,18; 1949,50; 1967,68; 2014,15) ("4" x "4" – Redemption for the Earth) denoting judgment that could come before 2019 [as the 42 months (1260 days)(Rev 11:2,3) starts no sooner than from the time of Passover in 2016]. Even with these apparent miraculous events for modern Israel, there has been nothing but "wars and rumors of war." From the day Israel became a nation, and a chartered member of the United Nations at its conception – up to this present time, she has suffered more strife and is responsible for more spilt blood than any other nation in modern times.

The Psalmist says, "When workers of iniquity do flourish: *it is* that they shall be destroyed for the age" (Ps 92:7). Today, Babylonian Israel is being protected by Babylonian Christianity. The last of the more recent blood moon tetrad, on their feasts, denotes the bringing of the next level of retribution to modern Israel, and may usher in the time of Jacob's Trouble, but not before the sealing of YHVH's servants. For "the stork in the heavens knows her seasons; ... But My people do not know the judgment of YHVH" (Jer 8:7).

These Blood Moon "symbols," or "omens," in the sky do not correlate with any true <u>Hebrew</u> feast day. Remember the Dark days were an omen before the death of the First born Egyptians that occurred at "midnight," with the only light and protection in the land of Goshen. So, when YHVH mentions that the lights in the sky are for "signs" (H#226 "owth" ... omen, prodigy, ..."), that can also mean coming destruction or plagues, but only upon the <u>un</u>righteousness, with protection and deliverance for His true people.

Blood moons followed by a darkened day (March, 2015) are harbingers of bad things to come on the lunar calendar, and that would not be on YHVH's time-piece for His true people. The Qumran community of Essenes by the Dead Sea had writings that delineated the phases of the moon for the sole purpose of anticipating the moves of their enemies! They even kept track of the priestly rotations in Jerusalem to determine which families were serving at any given week. In this way the community would be wise watchman on the wall, being especially diligent on the "Jews" lunar feast days, looking for stealth Zionistic forces that might try to take advantage, or strike on either side of the "Jews" "new" or "full moon."

The Essenes had seceded and were banished to the wilderness by the prevailing leadership in Jerusalem for a reason. "The author (of the DSS-4QMMT) states that disagreement on the (calendar and the feasts) caused the sect to secede from Israel" (*The History of Halakha and the Dead Sea Scrolls – Observations on 4QMMT*, p. 76). According to one translation of the oldest known writings of the Gospels dated to 70 CE, our Savior had said:

> "But immediately after the Great Persecution of the coming days, the sun religions will be darkened by confusion, the moon religions will be covered red with blood and cease to expand their light, revelations and messengers will fall from (heaven) and the ruling powers of the world of Shatan will be shaken." Mt 24:29 (OSE1 - *The Word of Yah, The King's Covenant*, p. 67)

Though this translation is considered controversial by some, these sun religions would include all Sunday worshippers that also venerate the solar days of Christmas and Easter. Moon religions would include all those that follow the moon and have their feasts at the fullness of the Harvest moons. The sun religions "will be darkened by confusion" as the Latter Rain Spirit of YHVH will be poured out in its fullness and an Awakening will come to cause a shaking out amongst its people, and the churches left to be ashamed. The two great moon venerators, the nations of Israel and Islam "will be covered red with blood" as the blood moon tetrad denotes and their war with each other will escalate.

On October 9th, 2009 (by the lunar calendar, Tishri 21, the Zionists Last Great Day) Mr. Barack Obama received the Nobel Peace Prize. 1260 days later (a time, times, and half a time = 1260 days – Dan7:25; Rev 11:3), on March 22nd, 2013 (Nisan 10, the day of the choosing of the lamb in preparation of Passover by that same lunar calendar), Mr. Obama receives a dignitary's welcome-parade into Jerusalem to receive another Peace Prize from the Israeli Kineset (a counterfeit to Zech 9:9). All of this before the blood moon tetrad warnings of 2014 - 2015. Will Mr. Obama, as the Zionists chosen lamb, somehow be tried as their sacrifice, only to become the savior of the new world order, through a soon-to-be-restructured United Nations?

Just as YHVH has His appointed times for the salvation of His people, all the miracles that happened to true Israel were before they were separated (not divorced) from YHVH, and taken into Babylon. The Adversary has his time-table as he has thought to "changed times and laws" Dan 7:25.

Today, the last of the latter rain is being poured out to ripen His remnant people of Ephraim and Judah (Hos 6:3; Jer 5:24; Eze 37:19) on His time-piece. Soon, all will be threshed and winnowed, that the chaff would be put to the wind of YHVH, for this Holy grain to receive His True Spirit, on Pentecost Sabbath, to be stored in preparation for the remainder of the harvest before the Feast of Ingathering, occurring right on time (2 Tim 3:1; Acts 2:17). A true pattern can be extracted from His Word for the people of the last days by prayerfully and carefully studying the books of the prophets, the book of Revelation; correlating the Gospels and the epistles in their previous language. The timetables for the end of days given to the prophets are in accordance to His "times appointed." This is in preparation for the anti-typical Feast of Ingathering that we might soon Tabernacle with Him.

May our heavenly Father, through the ministration of His Son, guide you dear Believer, as you further investigate these things, and other language studies, with the gifts He has given you - such as Bible resources, concordances, and other language references He has made available to all - by providing resources for purchase, access to church libraries, websites, or fellowship of Bible students who are able and willing to lend these; that we might share what has been revealed to us with those who have not, or have cared not.

"Till we all come in unity of the faith, and of the knowledge of the Son of God, unto a perfect man, unto the measure of the stature of the fullness of Messiah: That we *henceforth* be no more children, tossed to and fro, and carried about with every wind of doctrine, by the sleight of men, *and* cunning craftiness, whereby they lie in wait to deceive; but speaking the truth in love, may grow up into Him in all things, which is the head, *even* Messiah" (Eph 4:13-15 KJV).

Figure 1. – 364 Calendar as given back to Moses in Exodus 12.

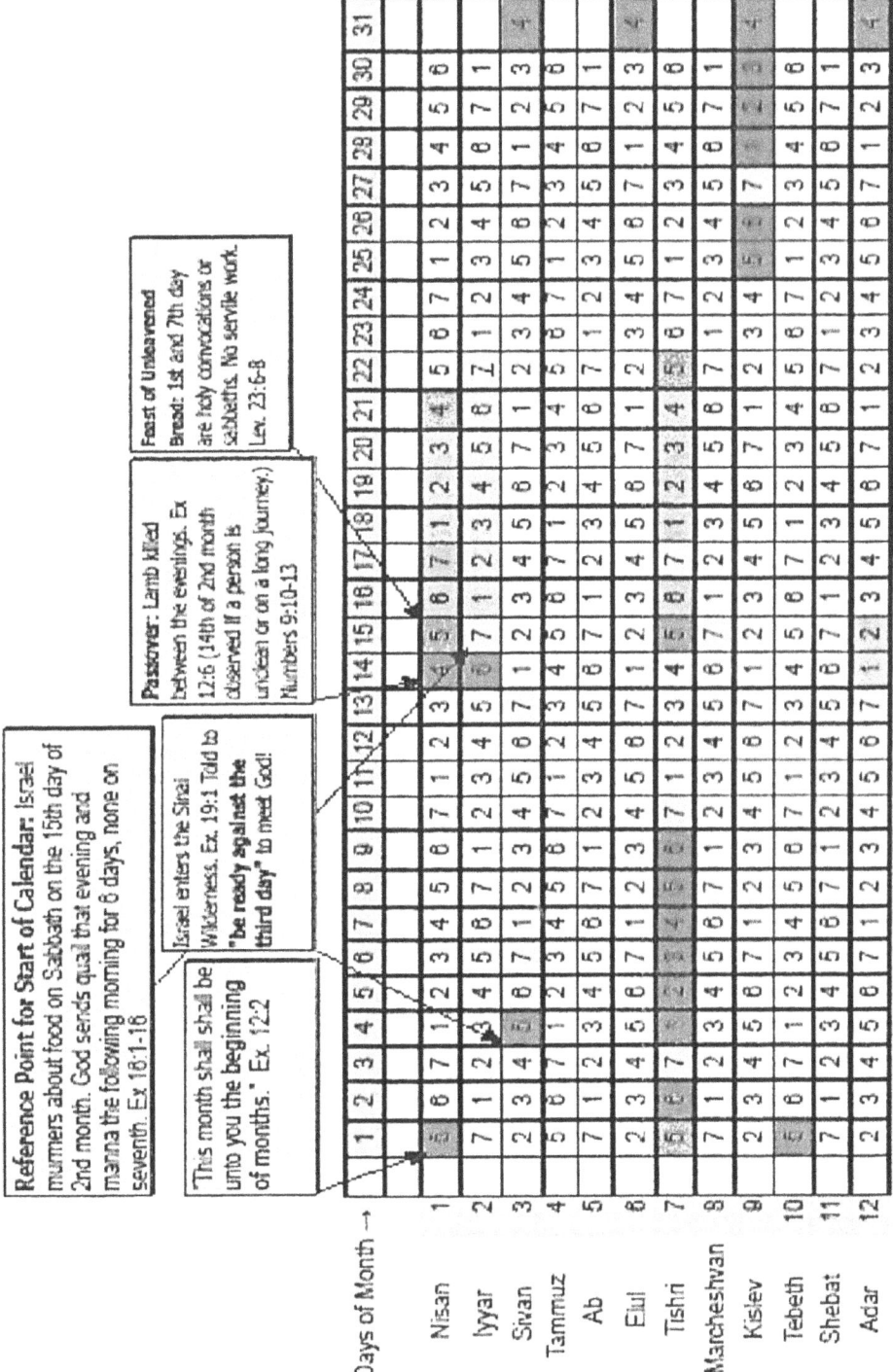

Figure 2 - The First Year Of Creation - The First Year and the Eighth Year on a 360-day Calendar share the same week day / date, as a 7 year pattern.

Day	1	2	3	4	5	6	7	8	9	10	11	12	13	14	15	16	17	18	19	20	21	22	23	24	25	26	27	28	29	30
Mon																														
1	Sun	Mon	Tue	Wed	Thu	Fri	SAB	Sun	Mon	Tue	Wed	Thu	Fri	SAB	Sun	Mon	Tue	Wed	Thu	Fri	SAB	Sun	Mon	Tue	Wed	Thu	Fri	SAB	Sun	Mon
2	Tue	Wed	Thu	Fri	SAB	Sun	Mon	Tue	Wed	Thu	Fri	SAB	Sun	Mon	Tue	Wed	Thu	Fri	SAB	Sun	Mon	Tue	Wed	Thu	Fri	SAB	Sun	Mon	Tue	Wed
3	Thu	Fri	SAB	Sun	Mon	Tue	Wed	Thu	Fri	SAB	Sun	Mon	Tue	Wed	Thu	Fri	SAB	Sun	Mon	Tue	Wed	Thu	Fri	SAB	Sun	Mon	Tue	Wed	Thu	Fri
4	SAB	Sun	Mon	Tue	Wed	Thu	Fri	SAB	Sun	Mon	Tue	Wed	Thu	Fri	SAB	Sun	Mon	Tue	Wed	Thu	Fri	SAB	Sun	Mon	Tue	Wed	Thu	Fri	SAB	Sun
5	Mon	Tue	Wed	Thu	Fri	SAB	Sun	Mon	Tue	Wed	Thu	Fri	SAB	Sun	Mon	Tue	Wed	Thu	Fri	SAB	Sun	Mon	Tue	Wed	Thu	Fri	SAB	Sun	Mon	Tue
6	Wed	Thu	Fri	SAB	Sun	Mon	Tue	Wed	Thu	Fri	SAB	Sun	Mon	Tue	Wed	Thu	Fri	SAB	Sun	Mon	Tue	Wed	Thu	Fri	SAB	Sun	Mon	Tue	Wed	Thu
7	Fri	SAB	Sun	Mon	Tue	Wed	Thu	Fri	SAB	Sun	Mon	Tue	Wed	Thu	Fri	SAB	Sun	Mon	Tue	Wed	Thu	Fri	SAB	Sun	Mon	Tue	Wed	Thu	Fri	SAB
8	Sun	Mon	Tue	Wed	Thu	Fri	SAB	Sun	Mon	Tue	Wed	Thu	Fri	SAB	Sun	Mon	Tue	Wed	Thu	Fri	SAB	Sun	Mon	Tue	Wed	Thu	Fri	SAB	Sun	Mon
9	Tue	Wed	Thu	Fri	SAB	Sun	Mon	Tue	Wed	Thu	Fri	SAB	Sun	Mon	Tue	Wed	Thu	Fri	SAB	Sun	Mon	Tue	Wed	Thu	Fri	SAB	Sun	Mon	Tue	Wed
10	Thu	Fri	SAB	Sun	Mon	Tue	Wed	Thu	Fri	SAB	Sun	Mon	Tue	Wed	Thu	Fri	SAB	Sun	Mon	Tue	Wed	Thu	Fri	SAB	Sun	Mon	Tue	Wed	Thu	Fri
11	SAB	Sun	Mon	Tue	Wed	Thu	Fri	SAB	Sun	Mon	Tue	Wed	Thu	Fri	SAB	Sun	Mon	Tue	Wed	Thu	Fri	SAB	Sun	Mon	Tue	Wed	Thu	Fri	SAB	Sun
12	Mon	Tue	Wed	Thu	Fri	SAB	Sun	Mon	Tue	Wed	Thu	Fri	SAB	Sun	Mon	Tue	Wed	Thu	Fri	SAB	Sun	Mon	Tue	Wed	Thu	Fri	SAB	Sun	Mon	Tue

Figure 3: The Seventh Year

Figure 3: The Seventh Year (Notice the 7th Year ends on a Sabbath)

Day	1	2	3	4	5	6	7	8	9	10	11	12	13	14	15	16	17	18	19	20	21	22	23	24	25	26	27	28	29	30
Mon 1	Thu	Fri	SAB	Sun	Mon	Tue	Wed	Thu	Fri	SAB	Sun	Mon	Tue	Wed	Thu	Fri	SAB	Sun	Mon	Tue	Wed	Thu	Fri	SAB	Sun	Mon	Tue	Wed	Thu	Fri
2	SAB	Sun	Mon	Tue	Wed	Thu	Fri	SAB	Sun	Mon	Tue	Wed	Thu	Fri	SAB	Sun	Mon	Tue	Wed	Thu	Fri	SAB	Sun	Mon	Tue	Wed	Thu	Fri	SAB	Sun
3	Mon	Tue	Wed	Thu	Fri	SAB	Sun	Mon	Tue	Wed	Thu	Fri	SAB	Sun	Mon	Tue	Wed	Thu	Fri	SAB	Sun	Mon	Tue	Wed	Thu	Fri	SAB	Sun	Mon	Tue
4	Wed	Thu	Fri	SAB	Sun	Mon	Tue	Wed	Thu	Fri	SAB	Sun	Mon	Tue	Wed	Thu	Fri	SAB	Sun	Mon	Tue	Wed	Thu	Fri	SAB	Sun	Mon	Tue	Wed	Thu
5	Fri	SAB	Sun	Mon	Tue	Wed	Thu	Fri	SAB	Sun	Mon	Tue	Wed	Thu	Fri	SAB	Sun	Mon	Tue	Wed	Thu	Fri	SAB	Sun	Mon	Tue	Wed	Thu	Fri	SAB
6	Sun	Mon	Tue	Wed	Thu	Fri	SAB	Sun	Mon	Tue	Wed	Thu	Fri	SAB	Sun	Mon	Tue	Wed	Thu	Fri	SAB	Sun	Mon	Tue	Wed	Thu	Fri	SAB	Sun	Mon
7	Tue	Wed	Thu	Fri	SAB	Sun	Mon	Tue	Wed	Thu	Fri	SAB	Sun	Mon	Tue	Wed	Thu	Fri	SAB	Sun	Mon	Tue	Wed	Thu	Fri	SAB	Sun	Mon	Tue	Wed
8	Thu	Fri	SAB	Sun	Mon	Tue	Wed	Thu	Fri	SAB	Sun	Mon	Tue	Wed	Thu	Fri	SAB	Sun	Mon	Tue	Wed	Thu	Fri	SAB	Sun	Mon	Tue	Wed	Thu	Fri
9	SAB	Sun	Mon	Tue	Wed	Thu	Fri	SAB	Sun	Mon	Tue	Wed	Thu	Fri	SAB	Sun	Mon	Tue	Wed	Thu	Fri	SAB	Sun	Mon	Tue	Wed	Thu	Fri	SAB	Sun
10	Mon	Tue	Wed	Thu	Fri	SAB	Sun	Mon	Tue	Wed	Thu	Fri	SAB	Sun	Mon	Tue	Wed	Thu	Fri	SAB	Sun	Mon	Tue	Wed	Thu	Fri	SAB	Sun	Mon	Tue
11	Wed	Thu	Fri	SAB	Sun	Mon	Tue	Wed	Thu	Fri	SAB	Sun	Mon	Tue	Wed	Thu	Fri	SAB	Sun	Mon	Tue	Wed	Thu	Fri	SAB	Sun	Mon	Tue	Wed	Thu
12	Fri	SAB	Sun	Mon	Tue	Wed	Thu	Fri	SAB	Sun	Mon	Tue	Wed	Thu	Fri	SAB	Sun	Mon	Tue	Wed	Thu	Fri	SAB	Sun	Mon	Tue	Wed	Thu	Fri	SAB

The Seventh Year (Notice the 7th Year ends on a Sabbath, so the 1st day of the 8th year is a sunday)

Appendices

APPENDIX A: EVALUATION OF THE TERM "New Moon"

OLD TESTAMENT (OT): Each instance of "new moon," in most translations, has been allocated by Strong's to be the Hebrew word:

H#2320 CHODESH - *(kho'-desh) [translated]* "new moon(s)" (20x's)

Yet this same Hebrew word is found to have an alternative meaning:

H#2320 CHODESH - (kho'-desh) "month(s), every month, monthly" **(256x's)**

Notice the predominant translation is relevant to "month," and that the Hebrew words "new" and "renew" are alphabetically very close to "*chodesh.*"

H#2318 CHADASH -*(khaw-dash')* renew (3), repair (3), renewed (2), renewest (2).

H#2319 CHADASH - *(khaw-dawsh)* new (52), fresh (1).

All three words have identical consonant sequencing, with slight differences in pronunciation, due to the varied vowel points between them making them distinct. A simple change in a vowel point could create a "new" or "renewed" month, as in "every month" or "monthly." But can the translation of "*chodesh*" ever really be "new moon?" Let us determine the Hebrew word for "moon" and see if there is any relation to "*chodesh.*"

MOON

H#3394 YAREACH - *(yaw-ray-akh)* moon (26).

This is the only <u>Hebrew</u> word for "moon" with no listed alternative meaning, and no traceable phonetic or root relation to any of our three previous words. To be sure there is no association we need to look at all the OT words related to "*yareach.*"

H#3391 YERACH - *(yeh'-rakh) uncertain orig.:* moon (2), month (11).

H#3392 YERACH - *(yeh'-rakh)* formal name of an <u>Arabian</u> patriarch (2).

H#3393 YeRAH - *(yeh-rakh)* Chaldean/Aramaic: month(s) (2).

Though these four words have no linguistic relevance to the previous three, we need to recognize the transgression from the Hebrew word for "moon" to the Aramaic word for "month." Here we have stumbled upon the apparent reason for the "new moon" confusion. Aramaic is a Hebrew dialect that developed during Israel's captivity in the region of Chaldea known as Babylon. During their seventy years of bondage, the Levites were compelled by the Babylonian priests to forsake their "times and laws" and scan the night sky every fourth week for the first visible lunar crescent to determine the beginning of the next month. Even to lighting a night fire on a hill, described as a signal for the surrounding villages of the new month, when the Babylonian priests did the same in veneration for the return of their moon god.

Because the cycle of the moon was the same as a month to the Babylonian, over time the Mosaic calendar was discarded and the Hebrew word "*yareach*" became associated with "month" to many of the captives. Thus the modulated Aramaic, "*yerah*," means both. Yet none of these words are related to "*chodesh*." Consequently, when Moses wrote "*chodesh*" he meant "season," "month," or "new month" depending upon the prefix and vowel points. There was no such dialect as Aramaic in Moses day. The reason why **#3391** is of "uncertain orig." is because it is found in three verses within the Torah, Exo. 2:2, Deut. 21:13, and 33:14, listed in your Bible margin as "an apparent Aramaic substitution." Yet if Moses meant for the Levites to calculate the month by the moon we would expect to find such instruction or example in his writings. Neither exist anywhere in the OT, but one word does allude to a lunar "crescent," but in each of the three instances, it refers to pagan moon jewelry:

H#7720 SAHaRON - (sah-har-one') ornaments (2), round tires like the moon (1), crescent-moon necklace:

The only scriptural reference to any literal phase of the moon, other than the one in contention, does not calculate time, delineate feasts, or evaluate any part of a month.

H#3842 LeBANAH - *(leb-aw-naw')* bright (full) moon; *[translated]* moon (3). *[contextually – full moon]*

Neither "*saharon*" nor "*lebanah*" share any traceable correlation to "*chodesh.*" Another point of consideration would be:

> "if 'chodesh' is also 'the moon,' why is 'chodesh' never used when it is obviously (meant to be) 'the moon' such as written in (*Emphasis supplied*)
>
> | | |
> |---|---|
> | Hab 3:11 | – 'the sun and the (moon) **yareach** stood still …' |
> | In 2 Kng 23:5 | – it is 'the sun and the **yareach**.' |
> | In Job 31:26 | – it is 'the sun and the **yareach**. |
> | In Ps 8:3 | – it is 'the **yareach** and the stars,' |
> | In Ps 72:5 | – 'the sun and the **yareach**,' |
> | In Ps 136:9 | – 'the **yareach** and the stars.' (etc.) |
>
> So why is 'chodesh' never used anywhere grouped to the sun, the stars, or the nighttime, all companions of the moon if it also means 'the moon'? Quite clearly, 'chodesh' is the Scriptural solar month." [Council of Elders, *The Word of YAH, The King's Covenant,* The Kingdom of YAH Publishers, Catoosa, OK. (2010) p.493]

It should be quite plain from this simple analysis of the Hebrew language that "*chodesh*" = **month** and "*yareach*" = **moon**. This leaves no justification to translate "*chodesh*" to anything relevant to "moon."

NEW TESTAMENT: (NT)

The phrase "new moon" only appears once in the NT, in Col 2:16, and the Greek index gives us the following word for it:

G#3561 NOUMENIA - (noo-may-nee'-ah) [translated] new moon (1).

This word can be broken down into three related Greek syllables found in Strong's NT index.

G#3501 NEOS - (*neh'-os*) <u>new</u> (12), younger (8), young (4).

G#3376 MEN - (*mane*) months (14), <u>month</u> (4).

G#3391 MIA - (*mee'-ah*) <u>single</u>: one (48).
        meaning: "**new month** " (*singular*)

You will notice that the word "mén" does not have an alternative translation of "moon," and we can see from this evaluation that "noumenia" really means "new month" singular. As confirmation, here are two other NT words using *#3376*, "mén," in a specific form, and one other related word found in a Greek dictionary.

G#*5150* **TRIMENOS** - (*trim'-ay-nos*) three months (1).

G#*5072* **TETRAMENOS** - (*tet-ram'-ay-nos*) four months (1).

Gk - **DIMENOS** - (*dim'-ay-nos*) two months
[*The Classic Greek Dict.*, Follet Pub., 1943]

By definition thus far, "**mén**" only means "month." Now let us find the Greek word for "moon" and determine if there is any correlation to the word "**mén**."

G#*4582* **SELENE** - (sel-ya'-nay) moon (9).

Gk - **SELENAIOS** - (*sel-ay'-nay-os*) of the moon.
[*The Classic Greek Dict.*, Follet Pub., 1943]

Gk - **PANSELENE** - (*pan-sel-ay'-nay*) full moon [Ibid]

Gk - **PARASELENE** - (*par-a-sel-ay'-nay*) moon halo
[*Funk & Wagnalls Stnd. Dict.*, F&W Pub., 1930]

From these sources, "seléné" is the Greek word for "moon," with no connection made to the word "mén." And if "panseléné" is "full moon," then a proper fabrication in the Greek for "new moon" would be closer to "neoseléné," but there is no such word in the NT. The only NT word related to *#4582* is:

G#*4583* **SELENIAZOMAI** - *(sel-ay-nee-ad'-zom-ahee)*
moon-struck; lunatick (2).

In conjunction, the ancient Greek word for our "Monday" (moon day) is:

Gk - **TES SELENES** - the moon's. [Jones, W. M., D.D., *A Chart of the Week*, Lang. #124, c. 1886]

Therefore, we can see, in evaluating the Greek, "new moon" should be "new month." The counterpart in the OT is more clearly delineated in Num. 10:10; 28:11, 14 as "the beginnings of your month(s)." Devout Jews, today, continue to evaluate the beginning of their month, and calculate certain feasts, based upon the observation of the first visible lunar crescent, just as their ancestors did in Babylon. This means the Jews did it in Messiah's time [as He said, beware the commandments of men and the leaven of the Pharisees, (Mt 15:9; 8:15)] and were doing it when King James commissioned his translation of the Scriptures. Maybe the English Bible scholars took it for granted that the Jewish practice of feast keeping in their day was as it was in the time of Moses. But, from our study, it seems apparent that Moses meant "new month," as in the beginning of a new month, and Paul meant the same in Col 2:16.

The calendar Moses used is so claimed in the books of Enoch and Jubilees and other scrolls found in Ethiopia and at the Dead Sea. Enoch and Jubilees were officially excluded from the OT by the established Jewish authorities back in 90AD, as these books denigrated the lunar calendar as having their seasons come in "ten days to soon," and "make an abominable day the day of testimony, and an unclean day a feast day" (Jub 6:36,37). Yet Enoch and Jubilees both account for a 364-day cycle that was reportedly used by both Abraham and Moses. (See Exo. 12:41).

Nevertheless, as the Babylonian Israelite tried to follow the Mosaic order of feasts, using the lunar calendar, the holy convocations wandered to different days of the week with each passing year. Some of these would periodically land on the 1st day of the week, construing veneration upon our Adversary. With the Mosaic calendar, (properly started) none of the holy feast convocations ever fell on the 1st day of the week.

The lunar calendar also requires a 13th month, about every three years, to keep pace with the seasons; but there is no mention of a 13th month (Adar II) anywhere in Scripture. And as Moses and the other prophets spoke of miraculous events that occurred for the children of Israel, recorded on certain numbered days in their month, we can find, by using the same 364-day template, that these special provisions happened on a 7th day Sabbath, the "Dwelling Place of The Father's Miraculous Sign."

The 3-day journey from Egypt into the wilderness ended on a Sabbath (not that first Sabbath – they hadn't left Egypt yet). Manna/quail promised, the Ten Commandments given, numbering of Israel per tribe, repeating the law, Moses last address to His people, crossing the Jordan, the Wave-sheaf offering (properly translated), Pentecost, Yom Kippur, even the deliverance from, and destruction of all their attacking enemies, including Pharaoh and Sennacherib, occurred on a 7th day Sabbath, establishing a prophetic pattern. Each nation mistakenly thought that the best day to overtake Israel would be on a day they were forbidden to raise the sword; and each time our Heavenly Father upheld His promise and delivered His children. In this, He typified His day of salvation for His people, judgment for those who were not, and perfect rest for a compliant people to culminate in a Sabbatical Millennium.

During their Babylonian enculturation, and for generations following, there were varying disputes among the Hebrews over the appointed times and laws. Yet the Judeans who prospered the most at the hand of the Babylonians were those who compromised the most, in an effort to escape sanctions and receive favor with their captors. The Talmudic writings, which genuinely account for the moon, are a melding of pagan rituals and Hebrew concepts that had their origins in Babylon, and they are not part of Scripture, Enoch, or Jubilees.

The Babylonian lunar calendar has been widely known and followed by the Jews since the time of Daniel, which is why Daniel is the one that says, the Adversary will "think to change times and laws" (Dan 7:25). But even Ezra, Nehemiah, leaders of the remnant believers, and the other prophets from that time forward, denote time-keeping elements in their writings that fit perfectly into the calendar spoken of in Enoch and Jubilees. So when Paul counseled the Colossians,

> "Therefore let no man call to question you in [kosher] meat [offering], or in [unfermented] drink [oblation], or in your obligations to feast days, or of the new 'month,' or in holy feast convocations, which are a shadow of things to come for the body of Messiah." (Col. 2:16,17 HTT).

He was encouraging them to hold to what he had taught them, when they were challenged by Babylonian-influenced feast keepers.

VERSE STUDIES

Many of the lunar constituents hold to five foundational passages to try and validate their claim. (**Gen 1:14**; **Ps 81:3**; **104:19**; **Jer 31:35, 36**; **Isa 66:23**). We will look at each one starting with:

> **Gen 1:14**:
> "And God said, 'Let there be lights in the firmament of the heaven to divide the day from the night; and let them be for signs, and for seasons, and for days and years.'"

The "days" were used to count by weeks, with the 7th day Sabbath as "seasons," or an "appointed time" (#4150 "moedim"), to mark each passing week. This "seasons" can also mean times of sowing or reaping in the garden and field, even at different times of the day, as before sin the weather was consistent for each day, all year; just as the Divine would meet with Adam in the "cool of the day" (Gen 2:15; 3:8-10). But this word "seasons" is inappropriately referred to by some to mean "appointed 'feast' time." Yet the feast days, as we understand them in Exodus and Leviticus, were prescribed as a remedy for sin in the plan of salvation. During the time in the garden prior to sin, Adam and Eve did not need these requirements, as they may have had other appointed times of Divine communion without restriction.

The word "them" in Gen 1:14 is specifically referring to day light and night light as two separate entities; the day "season," and the night "season." Remember there were no solemn assemblies to obtain deliverance or Divine protection; and there were no "seasons" such as winter, spring, summer, and fall until after the great flood.

> **Psalm 81:3**:
> "Blow up the trumpet in the new moon, at the full moon, on our feast day." (IB)

The KJV has: "Blow up the trumpet in the new moon, **in the time appointed**, on our solemn feast day." Some Lexicons have this term "full moon," but the single word for this is found only in the Aramaic manuscripts, used more with the new Bible versions, with the Aramaic word # 3677 "keceh." The Hebrew word for "full moon," as was mentioned earlier, is #3842 "lebanah," and is not there in the Hebrew text (the eastern manuscripts). Remember where the Aramaic dialect came from – that's right, from Babylon, the same place where the lunar time-keeping amongst Judaism got started. The inappropriate translation of "new moon" here again is the Hebrew word "chodesh" and should be "new month." So the verse should read: "Blow the shofar in the new month day, at the time appointed, on our solemn feast day." (*lit.*)

> **Psalm 104:19**:
> "He **appointed** the moon for **seasons**: the sun knows his going down." NKJV.

Contextually, the Psalmist is referring to the cycle of nature. An alternate translation is:

> "He **made** the moon **to mark** the seasons; the sun knows when to set" HCSB.

In every season the sun would be at a different angle in the sky, and set at different times and points on the horizon; just as the moon would be in a different point in the sky, through its cycles in any given season used in agrarian cultures for planting and harvesting, which includes Hebrew society.

> **Jer 31:35, 36**:
> "Thus says the LORD, who gives the sun for a light by day, *and* the **ordinances** of the moon and of the stars for a light by night, which divides the sea when the waves thereof roar; … 'If those **ordinances** depart from before Me,' says the LORD, '*then* the seed of Israel also shall cease from being a nation before Me forever.'" KJV

As opposed to the NAS version, for example, which has "the **fixed order** of the moon" in verse 35 and "If this **fixed order** departs from Me," in verse 36 actually representing a more accurate translation as the Hebrew word here #2706 "choq" and #2707 "chaqah" mean to "enact, bound, prescribe, law" and "delineate, intrench, portray." Neither word was meant to convey a feast concept. There is no "chodesh" (month) here, neither is it accompanied by a "moed," (appointment), a "hag" (solemn feast), nor a "yom" (day).

Notice, this supposed "ordinance" is "of the moon" (not Israel), as it does wax and wane and "divide the sea," cause the tide to come in, and make the "waves roar," which is not part of any feast. The "seed of Israel" includes the lost tribes of Israel that have dispersed into all the world (amongst the Gentiles), who will be grafted (Rom 11:17-25) into true Israel, in the new earth. So long as the sun, moon, and stars continue in their "fixed order," so too shall the earth, and subsequently His people.

And it was the greater light that was to determine the accounting of time, as the book of Jubilee states:

> "And God appointed the sun to be a great sign on the earth for days, and for Sabbaths, and for **months**, and for feasts, and for years, and for sabbath of years, and for jubilees, and for all seasons of the years." (Jub 2:9)

And written well before the flood, as a coming prophecy (En 10:2-4), Enoch relates here one conciliation to the inevitable:

> "And the sun and the stars bring in all the years exactly, so that they do not advance or delay their position by a single day unto eternity (the end of the age); but complete the years with perfect justice in 364 days." (En 74:12)

As any further intercalation is not rendered to change these 364 days in a year, just as the 364- days are not rendered to change the 360-day calendar, but to only be as an intercalated 360-day calendar:

> "And the leaders of the heads of the thousands, who are placed over the whole creation and over all the stars, have also to do with the four intercalary days, being inseparable from their office, according to the reckoning of the year, and these render service on the four days which are not reckoned in the reckoning of the year." (En 75:1; also 74:17 for the month)

So, to analyze all the imposed translations of "new moon," which are only found outside of Torah, we find they are all "chodesh." They are listed here besides the ones already addressed for you to investigate: 1 Sam 20: 5,18,24; 2 Kng 4:23; 1 Chr 23:31; 2 Chr 8:13; 31:3; Ezr 3:5,6; Eze 45:17; 46:1,3,6; Neh 10:33; Isa 1:13,14; 66:23; Hos 2:11; Am 8:5. (Feel free to utilize your resources to analyze each one of these in their context.)

In Jer. 8:1, 2, YHVH is saying there will be those who will bring out the bones of the kings of Judah, her princes, priests, prophets, and the inhabitants of Jerusalem and spread them before the sun, moon and stars, "whom they have loved," "served, and after whom they have walked, and whom they have sought, and whom they have worshipped: they shall not be gathered, nor buried; they shall be for dung." The lunar calendar comes from those nations who worshipped the host of heaven (see also Deut 17:2-5).

Isa 66:23

"And it shall come to pass, *that* from one new moon to another, and from one Sabbath to another, shall all flesh come to worship before Me, saith the LORD" (KJV).

Isaiah, in his last chapter, refers to New Jerusalem, and again the inappropriate word given here as "new moon" is "chodesh," yet in this same Bible version we find toward the end of the book of Revelation, John also describes New Jerusalem and the Temple therein and writes that "the city had no need of the sun, neither of the moon" (Rev 21:23). This is just as the prophet also says regarding the New Jerusalem in:

Isaiah 60:19, 20

"The sun shall be no more thy light by day; neither for brightness shall the moon give light unto thee; but (YHVH) shall be unto thee an everlasting light, and thy God thy glory. Thy sun shall no more go down; neither shall thy moon withdraw itself: for (YHVH) shall be thine everlasting light, and the days of thy mourning shall be ended." (KJV)

The Enoch intercalated 360-day calendar will no longer need to be intercalated in the new earth; we will be back to just the 360-day calendar that was, and is, perfect in the parameter of the Sabbatical Year (360 x 7 = 2520).

"The four *perfect* numbers, 3, 7, 10, and 12, have for their product the remarkable number 2,520. It is the Least Common Multiple of the ten digits governing all numeration; and can therefore, be divided by each of the nine (single) digits (1-9) without a remainder. It is the number of chronological perfection (7 x 360)"
[E.W. Bullinger, *the Companion Bible*, Appendix #10].

The perfect numbers 3 (structural perfection), 7 (spiritual perfection), 10 (ordinal perfection), and 12 (governmental perfection) are the four "perfect" numbers ("4" – Redemption, to redeem perfection). In this present dispensation, the 364-day calendar is considered by many scholars and chronologists to be the most accurate **and** consistent calendar known to man; reconciled using the Torah, Enoch and Jubilees, confirmed by the dates given by the other books in both the OT and NT.

Appendix B: SABBASI / SABBASIN = FEAST OF WEEKS

Mt 12:1   Our Savior, on the "sabbasi," went through grain fields with His disciples.
12:2   Pharisees accuse Him of not keeping "sabbato" (*See footnote*).
12:3,4   Savior explains how David entered the house of "God" and he and his men ate the shewbread, which was not lawful for them to eat.
12:5   Savior rebukes Pharisees on the "sabbasin" stating that the priests in the Temple profane the "sabbaton" and are guiltless.
12:8   And then informs the Pharisees that He is the "Lord of the 'sabbatou,'" also.
12:10   Later in their synagogue there was a man with a withered hand, and they asked Him if it was lawful to heal on the "sabbasi."
12:11   Our Savior asked "What man among you if he had a sheep fall into a pit on the 'sabbasin' would not lift it out"
12:12   [Is not] man better than sheep. Wherefore it is lawful to do well on the "sabbasi."
Mk 2:23   Our Savior in the grain fields, on the "sabbasi," with His disciples.
2:24   Pharisees ask why the disciples do not fully keep "sabbasin"
2:25,26   Savior explains the same story of David and the shewbread,
2:27   Our Savior said that the "'sabbaton' (*feast sabbath*) was for the sake of man, not man for the sake of the sabbaton' (*feast sabbath*)" and
2:28   that the Son of Man is "Lord of the sabbatou'" (*feast* and *7th day Sabbath*), also.
3:2   Man with a withering right hand in the synagogue on "sabbasi."
3:4   Our Savior asks whether it is lawful to do good on the "sabbasin" or evil
Lk 6:1   Our Savior, on the 2nd "sabbato" after the 1st, went through the same fields.
6:2   Pharisees ask the Savior why He does not follow the law for the "sabbasi."
6:3, 4   The Savior tells the same story of David and the shewbread.
6:5   And proclaims that He is the "Lord of the 'sabbatou.'"
6:6   Another "sabbato" (possibly the 3rd "sabbato") He enters the synagogue.
6:7   There was a man with a withered right hand on the "sabbato."
6:9   And the Savior asks if it is lawful to do good or evil on the "sabbasin"

All are of the same stories - in summary: "sabba<u>si</u>"(singular) and "sabba<u>sin</u>"(plural) are "sabba<u>to</u>"(s) that occur only during the Feast of Weeks, and these are related to "sabba<u>tou</u>" in the fact that they are 7th day Sabbaths during a feast time, ["sabbatou's" are both feast and weekly Sabbaths]. Two other vss., Mk 1:21 and Lk 4:31 have "sabbasin" and "sabbasi" respectfully, each record our Savior delivering a man of an unclean spirit;

and Lk 13:10 accounts our Savior teaching in a synagogue on a "sabbasi," healing a woman who was bent over.

The synagogue ruler was angry saying there are <u>6 days</u> to work, and to be healed, but not on (the) "sabbatou" (Lk 13:14) (a "sabbato" during the feast of weeks). There are seven "sabbasi," 2 or more of these are "sabbasin," [FF is a "sabbatone," the first "sabbasi" in the count of Feast of Weeks]. These are all the "sabbasi" and "sabbasin" in the NT, and none of these stories are in John. Notice in Lk 6:1 it was "the 2nd 'sabbato' after the 1st."

According to the **earlier Strong's** the extra word here at Lk 6:1 is G#*1207* "deuteroprotos"(*second-first*), "the second (after the first)… of the seven Sabbaths … before Pentecost." This fifty-day period is counted by 7th day Sabbaths, with each week being part of this feast.

Appendix C: AS TO THE FIRST ADAM, SO TO THE LAST

Though Adam had received the pristine "breath of life," sin ultimately gained dominion over him and the world. The One who "made" Adam, came back to this world to abolish sin. Offering up His sinless flesh to be renewed to life by the same "breath" of His Father, that He might be the hallowed "last Adam," as Paul quotes for us:

> "So also it has been written, 'The first man, Adam, became a living soul, the last Adam a life-giving Spirit.'" 1 Cor 15:45 (IB)

In the KJV, there are the italicized words *"was made"* before "a quickening spirit"(last Adam) giving the impression that what Paul was quoting was written after the resurrection, yet Bible footnotes refer the reader back to Gen.2:7 as the only known verse that has any relevance, and only to the first portion of this statement for it is not even a partial quote. What was "written" was the entire sentence, in Emphasis to the previous verse (vs.44), but this phrase is not found in any conventionally known book of the Testaments, old or new, as you might expect as Paul says: "it has been written …." So, if 1 Cor 15:45 and Gen 2:7 are properly transcribed, the only logical explanation would be that this quoted passage is missing from Scripture, or in some extra-biblical book.

It is well known by theologians that in both the OT and NT there are references made back to particular events not previously written, quotes made that aren't found, and even entire books mentioned in the OT that are not listed in the front page of our Bibles. Apparently, either these writings have not been discovered, not been authenticated, or were found well after Protestant standardization and have been classed into other writings (i.e. DSS). The scrolls mentioned in the OT that are not included in our Bibles today are the books of Nathan, Gad, Jasher, Shemaiah, Jehu, the Wars of YHWH (which could be Jasher), the prophecies of Ahijah and Oded, and the visions of Iddo the prophet, the grandfather of the prophet Zechariah, whose writings are still part of the Scriptures today (The listing of these books are found in the following: Nu 21:14, Jos 10:13, 18:9, 2Sa 1:18, 1Ki 11:41, 1Ch 29:29, 2Ch 9:29, 12:15, 13:22, 15:8, 20:3,4).

Many historians, and some learned scholars do state that there should be more books than those traditionally accepted in the Old Testament. Though there are over 200 different ancient mid-eastern scrolls and tablets found in Hebrew, Aramaic, and Greek, relating in some way to ancient Israel, many of these have been deemed either compromised

(Gnostic), incompatible (Apocrypha), or as promotional commentaries with dubious authorship (Pseudepigrapha), but not all pseudepigrapha are questionable. The book of Jubilees is classed as pseudepigrapha and shown to be congruent with the established books of the OT, as a narrative review on the books of Genesis and Exodus that could be the most important commentary on the Torah available for Truth-seekers today.

In many places Jubilees expands concepts, supplies details, solves questions and removes doubt. Extending from the Creation of the world to the written Law at Sinai, this book emphasizes the everlasting validity of the law, while repudiating paganisers, apostates, and a growing Hellenistic spirit that also arose at the time it was compiled into 50 chapters (c. 135 BCE), which the author states would threaten the very existence of the nation of Israel.

There are details on the 364-day calendar originating with Noah, prophesied of by Enoch, with warnings of coming leaders that would walk after the times and feasts of the Gentiles; specifically denigrating the ordained 364-day calendar with the impending use of a lunar calendar that will lose the heavenly order:

> "For there will be those who will assuredly make observations of the moon –how (it) disturbs the seasons and comes in from year to year ten days too soon. … and make an abominable day the day of testimony, and an unclean day a feast day, and they will confound all the days, the holy with the unclean, and the unclean day with the holy, for they will go wrong as to the months, and sabbaths and feasts and jubilees" (Jub 6:36, 37).

The book of Jubilees also gives many rational details as to **why** many ordinances and feasts were to be kept on certain days of the month.

There are at least three claims as to why Jubilees may have been dropped from the OT by the prevailing leaders of Judean Israel back in the days of the Council of Jamnia (90 AD). The very age when the early disciples were gaining momentum in proselytizing both Jew and Gentile [exponentially since the destruction of Jerusalem (70 AD / CE)], disseminating the miraculous testimonies of the long-awaited Messiah, who despised the traditions of men.

Most are unaware that Peter had quoted the book of Jubilees in 2 Ptr 3:8, "But, beloved, be not ignorant of this one thing, that one day *is* with the Lord as a thousand years, and a thousand years as one day."(quoted from Jub 4:30), and Paul made evident his use of another calendar other than that of the Pharisees (Acts 20:6; Col 2:16; 1 Thes. 5:1). Today, there are leading linguists and professors from prominent universities that have actually included Jubilees in the Torah. Not to intentionally infer a lost book of Moses, but merely a composition of teachings attributed to Moses (possibly edited out of Genesis and/or Exodus or even Deuteronomy during the Babylonian captivity) that was compiled and re-organized, and faithfully scribed during a period of reawakening shortly after the time of the Maccabees (c. 200-150 BC); that the coming last-day believers would ultimately have all of Moses once again.

So, we might ask ourselves: Should these unbelieving, compromising, self-appointed Jews determine for the true believer, the embodiment of the Word of YHWH? Prior to this council meeting in Jamnia, it is believed that Jubilees was among the scrolls in the synagogues. As these Jews had announced the decision to purge the synagogues, the Essenes, out in the wilderness, got word of the decision to eliminate Enoch and Jubilees from the teachings and they went about collecting these scrolls from as many synagogues as they could before the official decree arrived ordering them to be burned. There were many more complete scrolls of Jubilees found at Qumran (DSS) than any other scroll (15), and (7) complete scrolls of Enoch.

And even though Moses and John of Revelation wrote that no one was to add or detract from the "statutes" and "judgments," or the words of the end-time "prophecy" (De 4:2,12:32, Rev 22:18,19), we have to keep in mind that Enoch and the material found in Jubilees were likely part of the Word back then. If John actually passed down to us a Table of Contents of YHVH's Word, with page or scroll numbers, we would very likely find these two works in the list. In fact, the *SDA Bible Dictionary* states, "No historical account of the formation of the OT has been preserved, either in the Scriptures themselves or in other reliable historical documents" (p. 179). (See References).

The "mother church" ratified the more recent Jewish canon (90 AD / CE) with the present day NT Gospels and Letters and included many Apocryphal writings. The Protestants rejected these Apocrypha, but no declaration was made regarding any other Pseudepigraphal works. Yet Jubilees is to the books of Genesis and Exodus, as the Chronicles are to the books of Samuel and Kings. It should be pointed out here that the books of Chronicles 1 & 2 are classified as Pseudepigrapha. Therefore, it would seem reasonable to include such a harmonious book as Jubilees into the Scriptures; and Enoch, though there are some difficult passages, they are not unlike those in a few other sacred books. With all this in consideration, let us take the liberty to compare the Genesis account of Adam's beginning with that of Jubilees, line upon line, and consider these two with a third dependable source, a Greek translation of Josephus, and see if we have enough witnesses to establish what might be termed an unconventional doctrinal position.

Observation was made at Gen 2:2, in the KJV, that "<u>on</u> the seventh day God ended his work." Most other English translations say the same, some say "'in' the seventh day," essentially conveying the idea that it was during the Sabbath hours that "God ended his work." Going to Gen 2:2 in the Hebrew IB we find that the word "day," of the seventh day, is the *bet* form of #3117: "ביום" which is "in daylight the seventh" or "by daybreak," referring to the early morning hours of the "day" as "yom" refers to "light."

A few English translations do have the rendering "by the seventh day," essentially implying "up to" the seventh morning, but the *bet* preceding is a prefix that actually means "in." So, if we entertain the idea that YHVH had ended His work in the early morning hours of the Sabbath, and confirm this with other witnesses in proper English translation, let us see if we can determine what might have been the last work He did that week, and what precedent this may have on Sabbath worship.

The book of Jubilees gives a few more details on certain days of the Creation week in chapter 2:

> On the first day, "the Lord God" created "seven great works," the heavens, earth, waters, the spirits, abysses, darkness, and light (Jub 2:2).

Jubilees continues by mentioning that the spirits (in the middle of the seven), were seven angel groups created on this first day, each given various responsibilities in the future of YHVH's plan. It is of interest here that YHVH creates a group of seven in the center of the seven on the first day. There are no added insights to the Genesis record on the second, third, and fifth days, a couple of inconsequential, but compatible points on the fourth day, and a particular point on day six relevant to man. Day six starts in verse 13:

> "He created all the animals, and cattle, and everything that moves on the earth" vs.14 "And <u>after all this</u> He created man, …"

> vs.16 "He finished all His work on the sixth day – all that is in the heavens and on the earth, and in the seas and in the abysses, and in the light and in the darkness, and in everything."

After all things were made into the sixth day, "He" then creates man (vs.14). Yet, keep in mind, in Genesis 1:26 the Word states "Let us make man," and will be addressed shortly. But take notice that Jubilees 2 gives the quantifier in vs. 16 of what was "all His work" that He "finished" into the sixth day. The remainder of Jubilees 2, vs. 17 to 33, then gives details, specifics and emphasis regarding the importance of the Sabbath day.

Chapter 3 of Jubilees expands on points in Genesis 2 with details that continue to be compatible with our present rendering. Jubilees 3:1 begins, "And on the six days of the second week" the angels brought the animals before Adam for him to name, the:

> "**beasts** on the **1ˢᵗ day**; the **cattle** on the **2ⁿᵈ day**; the **birds** on the **3ʳᵈ day**; and all that which **moves on the earth** on the **4ᵗʰ day**; and that which **moves in the water** on the **5th day**." Jub 3:1 (Emphasis supplied)

Jubilees 3:1-4 equates to Genesis 2:18-20, only we see Adam naming all the animals through the second week, not on the sixth day of the first week as virtually all of us have assumed and were taught in church school, yet there is no indication in Genesis 2 as to when this was done. The presumption has always been just before that first Sabbath, but you will notice that this "seventh" day was already blessed and sanctified much earlier in the chapter back at Gen 2:3.

Our concept of Adam and all the land animals being created on the sixth day, then Adam naming all the animals in creation, seeing he was alone, then put to sleep, a rib taken from his side to form his helpmeet, and then being awakened to receive her to become one complete flesh - all this happening on that first 6th day makes for a pretty intense schedule when you think about it.

But even if Adam had all 12 hours of day-light on the 6ᵗʰ day to name "every living creature" (Gen 2:19); by conservative estimates that would average out (with about 10,000 "kinds" of animals back then, compared to hundreds of thousands of "species" today) to 833 animals / hour, or nearly 14 animals / minute (double that if he had only 6 hours).

Though Adam was vastly more superior than his "prodigy" today, would YHVH expect that kind of performance from such a green-eared human, even though he was made in His image? If indeed, he did have 5 days to name them that would be about 167 animals / hour, or just under 3 animals / minute.

In order for YHVH to approve of Adam's names for the animals (Gen 2:19), it would make sense that Adam had to spend some time getting familiar and appreciating them. According to Jubilees, on the <u>fifth</u> day of the <u>second</u> week, after naming the last grouping of animals, Adam is put to sleep, a rib (a curve) was taken from his flesh, then was awoken on the <u>second sixth</u> day, and the womb-man was brought to him, and Adam named his last creature and called her "my wife" as she was taken from her husband (Jub 3:5-7). Interestingly, though "Elohim saw everything that He had made" and called it "very good" (Gen1:31) on the first 6th day, Creation was fully completed and documented by the second 6th day; and Adam would have had all of that day to be with his wife to show her all the marvelous wonders, and then prepare for their first Sabbath together.

The confusion comes in at Gen.1:26-28 with the use of the word "them." Giving us the idea that Eve was already on the scene, as the chapter ends with "the evening and the morning were the sixth day."(vs.31). Yet in Genesis 2, after "God" blessed and sanctified the Sabbath day, and gave life to Adam;

> In verse **8**, God "planted a garden … and there He put the <u>man</u> He had formed," **not** "**them**."
>
> In verse **15**, YHVH "took the <u>man</u> and put him in the Garden of Eden to dress it and keep it," **not** "**them**."
>
> In verse **16**, YHVH "commanded the <u>man</u>, saying, Of every tree of the garden thou (man) may freely eat: …", **not** "**them**."
>
> In verse **17**, YHVH continues with the man, "of the tree of the knowledge of good and evil, <u>you</u> (man) shall not eat of it: for in the day that <u>you</u> eat of it <u>you</u> shall die." Though later implied to Eve, as part of Adam, this was directed to the man, **not** "**them**."
>
> In verse **18**, YHVH said, "*It is* not good that <u>man</u> should be alone," **not** "**them**."

In verse **19**, He "brought" all the animals to "<u>Adam</u> to see what he would call them," **not** to "**them**."

In verse **20**, "<u>Adam</u> gave names to all" the animals, **not** "**them**," because "for Adam there was not found a help meet" yet.

Seven times in Genesis 2 directives are given specifically just to Adam before he is put to sleep (Gen 2:8, 15, 16, 17, 18, 19, 20) (*Emphasis supplied*).

In Jubilees 2:14, it says that Adam was given dominion over all the animals, not "them;" which makes sense since Adam named all the animals, not "them" (Gen 2:20). Therefore, in consequence, the English translation of the Hebrew would logically make Gen.1:26-28 a <u>synoptic</u> <u>conclusion</u> to the Creation, as Eve was in the "rib" [curve] of Adam (a Hebrew idiom, - just as Levi was in the loins of Abraham, Heb 7:5, even three generations out); which brings us back to Genesis 2:2, and what it was that "God" finished "in the seventh day."

We are ready now to call on our third source; a Greek manuscript of the writings of Josephus. In *The Antiquities of the Jews*, Book 1, Ch. 1, Sec.1 and 2, Josephus has translated into Greek (with a direct Greek-to-English equivalent) [St. Edmundsbury Press Ltd., Suffolk, England.(1991) pp.16,17. ISBN: 0-674-99267-9]:

> "The sixth day He (Elohim) created the race of four-footed creatures, making them male and female: on this day He also formed man."

On this first 6th day there were only male and female **creatures**, and the word "formed" of "man" is found in Strong's G#*1085* "genos" (related to "gene") meaning "assembled structure, being made, or wrought." Comparable to the Hebrew #3335 "yatsar - to frame, to mould" at Gen 2:7 - Josephus continues:

> "Thus, so Moses tells us, the world and everything in it was made in six days in all; and on the seventh God rested and had respite from His labors, for which reason we also pass this day in repose from toil and call it the sabbath, a word which in the Hebrew language means 'His rest'."

It says "everything ... was <u>made</u>," and Gen 1:31 corroborates "everything that he had <u>made</u>;" the Hebrew for "made" in Gen 1:31 is:

6213 עשה "asah- to *do* or *make* (broad definition) … gather, provide, fashion, prepare …"

Hence, "God" was done fashioning and preparing "everything" on the sixth day; - as Josephus continues into Sec. 2 of Ch. 1, of Book 1. (*Emphasis supplied*)

"And here, unto this **seventh day**, Moses begins to interpret nature, writing on the formation of man in these terms: 'God fashioned man by taking dust from the earth and **instilled into him spirit and soul**.'" (1.1.2)

Previously we had read how that on the sixth day man was "formed," or assembled, then, according to the Greek, "in" or "by" the seventh day (yom – light), the body was given a "spirit and soul!" The words in Genesis 2 seem to match; **after** the "Elohim" had blessed and sanctified the Sabbath day (vs.3), Adam is then mentioned for the first and only time of having received the "breath of life" into his nostrils directly from "YHWH" (vs.7).

From Gen 1:1 to Gen 2:3, "God" is "Elohim," from the creation of heaven and earth to the blessing and sanctifying of the seventh day. Scholars tell us that "Elohim" can be either singular or plural. Certainly when "Elohim said 'Let us make man in our image….'" Elohim is plural, and when "Elohim saw all that He has made" on the 6th day, this was singular, for Jn 1:3 refers to our Savior as "All things were made by Him; and without Him was not anything made that was made." In addition, Job 33:4 seems to shed light on how this was done:

"The Spirit of God (El) made me, and the Breath of the Almighty (El Shaddai) gives me life." (*lit.*) (*Emphasis supplied*)

As Job continues, "I also was formed from the clay"(vs.6), we see a collaborative effort on the part of the Father and Son. Could this "Breath of the Almighty" been the last "work" on the seventh day? It would parallel the timing of what the "last Adam" accomplished, as Paul may have been trying to convey in 1 Cor 15:45, and we are told that it was the Father that placed the breath back into His Son in the resurrection (Gal 1:1; 1 Ptr 1:3; Rom 6:4). In contrast, the more widely accepted English translation of Josephus is vastly different from its Greek counterpart here:

"Moreover, Moses, **after** the seventh day was over, begins to talk **philosophically**; and concerning the formation of man, says thus:

'That God took dust from the ground, and formed man, and inserted in him a spirit and a soul.'" (1.1.2)

Before we revisit the Greek, the observation should be made that this sentence makes no correlation to the previous sentence made at the end of Section 1, and has Moses "talk"ing "philosophically," contrived to be on the first day of the week. Though most Christians understand Adam to be fully alive on that first 6th day, this translator has Moses making a post-creation summary on the origins of man, attempting to give some spiritual relevance to Sunday, as if he is addressing an assembly on that day. Of course, this inference would only reinforce the false honor given to Sunday in many English *versions* of the OT and NT, while neglecting still another Sabbath truth.

This Whiston rendition of Josephus, touted the best English translation ever, was supposedly composed from the Greek by a Cambridge theologian named William Whiston in 1737. Though Mr. Whiston has been highly esteemed for his efforts, he may have relied heavily upon either of the two earlier English translations before him; one completed by Roger L'Estrange in 1702, and/or the other by Thomas Lodge in 1602, neither of which are published today, and the few existing copies are inaccessible.

The direct Greek-to-English construct of this sentence is getting to the source of the problem, and is in contention with Wm. Whiston's version; the primary issue being "after" vs. "unto." The Greek word here is *meta* again, unconjugated, the definition of which can be found in the Strong's G#*3326* (see "On The Time Appointed," p.109 for a more complete evaluation). Another "Whiston" word improperly translated, and placed incorrectly, is his word "over," which in the Greek is "*peri*" *#4012*; more closely related to "around," or "about," and via syntax should be connected to the word "writing," as in "writing *about* the formation of man." Just replacing the proper "about" for his "over" in his translation creates a nonsensical term for Mr. Whiston.

So, if these texts of Jubilees and the Greek Josephus are compatible with our English version of Genesis 1 and 2, then let us consider another witness. In Jub 3:17 we are told that Adam had completed "seven years exactly" in the garden of Eden when the serpent came "in the second (2) month, on the seventeenth (17) day" to successfully tempt Eve. In Jub 3:9, we are given the date when Adam was "brought," or "put" (Gen 2:8), into the garden:

> "And **after** Adam had completed **forty days** in the land where he had been created, we (from the angels perspective) brought him into the garden of Eden to till and keep it, but his wife they brought in on the eightieth day, …"

The next few verses give rationale to Levitical laws of uncleanness and purification for the woman bearing a male or female child (Lev 12), about which we all have wondered. The interesting concept here is that "after" "forty days," Adam is brought into the garden, which would be day 41. If Adam was fully created on the sixth day, and each month was as they were when Noah was building the ark (each of 30 days), then the 41st day Adam entered the garden would have been the 16th day of the 2nd month, counting his first day as day 6 of the week, but this is not what the text says. Jub.3:17, has the 17th day of the 2nd month, as "seven years exactly" (See also Gen 7:11; Jub 5:22, 23).

Doing the math; since a week is composed of the same number of days (7), as the years mentioned here (7), then regardless of where in the numbered days of the month you may be, exactly (7) years earlier, to the same numbered day of the month, would always be the same day of the week, because both are divisible by seven (see Figures 2-3). Counting the 41 days back from the 17th day of the 2nd month has Adam receiving his first breath, coming forth in full physical and mental capacity on the 7th day of the 1st month, the seventh day of the creation week! Early that first Sabbath morning, Adam awoke for the first time, likely to begin an incredible angel-guided tour to view the creative works of the Mighty God (El), (based on the "blue prints" of El Shaddai, the Almighty God) on the very day that is called "the Dwelling Place of the Father's Miraculous Sign" (see "Multinational Transliterations," p. 56 for the analysis on the word "Sabbath").

This lends the greatest significance of YHVH blessing and sanctifying the seventh day for the face-to-face Breath of Life given to His very own image, as the greatest miracle of creation. It was not "because" He rested (Gen 2:3 - KJV) that He blessed and sanctified the 7th day Sabbath, but "**when** on it He rested"(*lit.*):

> H#3588 כי "kiy":- "indicating *causal* relations of all kinds … and, for, how, yea, [because, in, so, than] that, since, then, **when, while**, + [forasmuch, inasmuch, where) as, assured[-ly]], …"

If you evaluate multiple "kiy" throughout the Hebrew OT, you will find this word with all the same vowel points as that at Gen 2:3, where it is actually translated "when" or "while;" so at Gen 2:3 it would be best "when on it He rested." It was not <u>because</u> He rested that He blessed and sanctified the 7th day, but because He had placed His Spirit into the image of His likeness, making man a living soul on that day! Otherwise, the "rest" would be more honorable than the labor He was resting from, which does not make sense. Remember that YHVH had said:

> "Verily My Sabbaths you shall keep: for it *is* a **sign** between Me and you throughout your generations; that *you* may know that I *am* YHVH that does sanctify you" (Ex 31:13; Eze 20:12).

All of a sudden, this verse has more meaning now. That word "sign" is in Strong's with the following definitions:

> #226 אות "owth – a *signal* (lit. or fig.), as a *flag, beacon, monument, omen, prodigy, evidence,* etc.:- mark, **miracle**, (en-) **sign**, token."

But it gets better. In the (IB), for Ex 31:13, this word "owth" has a three letter suffix that is not translated, that is spelled ה וא , identical to:

> #1933 ה וא "havah – a prim. root [comp. 183, 1961] supposed to mean prop. to **breathe**; to *be* (in the sense of existence)" (as a verb *Bold supplied*)

Appearing as אות ה וא , so Ex 31:13 should read: (*Emphasis supplied*)

> "Verily My Sabbaths you shall keep: for it *is* a **breathing miracle** between Me and you throughout your generations; that *you* <u>may</u> <u>know</u> that I *am* YHVH that does sanctify you."

It seems rather evident at this point that His Sabbaths are meant to be a covenant renewal for the "miracle of breath" given by YHVH to each one of us; because He brought us to life in the first Adam on Shabbat morning, and bought us eternal spiritual life in the last Adam on Shabbat morning, quickening our spirit (1 Cor 15:45).

If "His rest" is a type of dwelling place of repose, what greater miraculous sign is there than being the living image of the Divine Creator, intimately brought to life on the day He asks us to "dwell" with Him (Isa 58:13,14; 66:23)? This completes the meaning why the number seven means "spiritual perfection," because we were fashioned after

His image, and given a measure of His Life "by the seventh day." Everything He made was "good" by the sixth day, but His "finished" work was worthy of sanctification on the seventh day.

If YHVH wanted to bless and sanctify a day simply for our reflection of His marvelously created world, He would have blessed the sixth day (Gen.1:31). If it was for the sake of the angels He created, for them to oversee His coming creation, He would have blessed the first day, for on this day He created "all the spirits which serve before Him - ..." (Jub.2:2), which may explain why the Adversary has always wanted it blessed.

As Adam, "man" was "prepared" on the sixth day ("6" – means "man" and "preparation"), the "showbread" (sheavebread) was prepared fresh that same day of the week, to be blessed and sanctified as the new spiritual bread early Sabbath morning in the holy place of the Temple (Lev.24:8). The week-old shewbread was eaten by the priests that Sabbath morning, in the holy place, as the new showbread, "most holy" of "offerings"(vs.9), was anointed on the table, meant to be symbolic of the first and last Adam coming to life that same hour of the week. The eating of the week-old bread in the holy place could be symbolic of the marriage covenant between Adam and Eve (Jub.3:6,7), that Shabbat morning; the two becoming "one in unity" [#259 echad – untied in similarity (Gen 2:24)], as a pattern of the marriage of the "last Adam" and His Bride (Jn 6:31-51; Rev 19:7).

Each one of us is meant to be a living Temple made to embody the sanctuary service just as the priest blessed and exchanged the showbread every Sabbath morning; representing both the living body of Adam and the spiritual being of our Savior. So if the Sabbath, as a "dwelling place," is actually a marriage covenant, and the "Father's miracle" is that of man and woman as the living image of YHVH, then the Sabbath is a type of weekly betrothal of the coming marriage ceremony between the Lamb and His bride. Every individual has the breath of the living YHVH, meant to be renewed as an indwelling place for the Father on this day; that by fully accepting His Son, He might do His good pleasure in us, to be part of the Bride on that great day – unified in the tangible Spirit of the Father with Him. Herein are hid all the treasures of wisdom and knowledge (Jer 3:14; Mt 25:10; Rev 19:9; 1 Cor 2:7; Eph 1:5,13; Col 2:3).

Now for the "Rest" of the Story

A forensic analysis of the word "rested" in the 4th commandment (Ex 20:11).

> #5117 - נוח - **nuwach** - "*rest*, i.e. *settle* down; **used in a great variety of applications**, **lit. and fig.**, intrans., trans. and causat. (action word – verb) (*to dwell, stay, let fall, place, let alone, withdraw, give comfort,* etc.) [Strongest Strongs: 'to lament, wail, to leave, allow']: - cease, be confederate (allied), lay, let down, (be) quiet, remain, (cause to, be at, give, have, make to) rest, set down." (apparent discrepancies)

As each Hebrew letter has a meaning; to put them in a particular order to create a word, the letter combination should give you a sentence definition of that word.

> נ – **seed, beginning of "new" life, sprout, offspring, to continue, this letter can also mean son or heir as the next generation**
> (as the seed refers to the **continuation of life** to the next generation)
>
> ו – **tent peg or nail, to tie together, to add, to support, to secure in place**
> (to **add**, tie meanings of letters or words **together**)
>
> ח – **derivative of a tent wall, wall of separation, creating two separate halves,** (i.e. *secular* – outside; *spiritual* – inside)
> (divides, separating **two divisions** in the tent)

[Heb. letter definitions. - Benner, J.A., *The Ancient Hebrew Language And Alphabet*, pp. 54, 55, 59, 74, 76, 82

A similar Hebrew word is also called "rest," but the letter meanings in their sequence should give the true definition, and so, by a "multitude of counselors let a thing be established" (Pro 15:22). [Notice each word has a נ (nün – "n" sound) followed by a ח (chet – *ch* or hard "h" sound) with the occasional ו (vav – "oo" or "oh" sound) read from right to left.]

נח	5146 – **Noach** –	(Noah) "rest"	**(new life before point of division)**
נחור	5152 – **Nachor** –	(Nahor) "snore" (action)	**(loud deep-breathing)**
נחר	5170 – **nachar** –	"nostril, snorting, to snore"	(to **breath-in**)

נחיר	5156 – **nachiyr** –	"nostrils" (for **breathing**)
נחם	5162 – **nacham** –	"to sigh, breath strongly," (**many** or **large breath**)
נחש	5175 – **nachash** –	"to hiss, to whisper" (**breath-out** through **teeth**)
נפח	5301 – **naphach** –	"to blow hard, to puff, expire" (**breath-out** through **open mouth**)
חי	[2416 – **chay** –	fresh, strong, <u>alive</u>, life, living (two sides of the hand)]
רוח	[7307 – **ruwach** –	wind, by resemblance <u>breath</u>, (strong) exhalation, blast, spirit] (**head** or chief **spirit-breath**)
נוח	5117 – **nuwach** –	**New-life Spirit-breath** (<u>separation</u>: breath <u>in</u> and <u>out</u> spiritual- in, physical- out)

When a nün precedes a chet we see a strong correlation to the act of breathing.

Even this same **new seed**-image of YHVH (#5117), that came to **life** by the **spiritual breath** (YHVH is Spirit) in the form of Adam, as the last addition to the creation; that Adam might be the **physical** representation of YHVH brought to life on a **separate** day from the animals, and have consequent dominion (a **separation**) over it. YHVH had Moses speak His covenant to the people (Ex 31:13), and placed it in stone for a memorial.

> "For *in* six days YHVH made heaven and earth, the sea, and all which *is* in them, and He **New-life Spirit-breathed** (#5117 - נח) (creating a separation) on the seventh day. <u>Because of this</u> YHVH blessed (honored) the Sabbath day and sanctified it (set it apart)."   Ex 20:11 (*lit.*) (*Emphasis supplied*)

If YHVH had simply "rested" (the usual translation here for #5117) on the Sabbath, would this have been a legitimate reason for Him to bless <u>and</u> sanctify the day? YHVH wants us to reason things through (Isa 1:18), He wants things to make sense to His people (Isa 1:3), His very own image. There had to have been some significant event on that day for YHVH to both bless and sanctify it.

If we replaced "rest" in every #5117 location (46X) with "renewed life-breath," this would lend a whole new dimension to many passages. As the ox and ass and other working creatures received "renewed life-breath" on the 7th day Sabbath (as man gave them a day free from labor)(Ex 23:12; De 5:14; Isa 7:19), YHVH's presences gives the same (Ex 33:14; De 3:20; Jos 1:13,15), YHVH "life-breathed" on the waters of the Jordan (Jos 3:13), His people received "renewed life-breath" from their enemies (De 12:10; 25:19; Jos 21:44; 2 Sam 7:1,11; 1 Kng 5:4; 1 Chr 22:9,18; 2 Chr 14:6,7; 20:30; Ne 9:28;

Job 3:13; Ps 125:3; Isa 14:3,7; 23:12; Da 12:13; Hab 3:16), YHVH receives "renewed life-breath" after expending His wrath (Exe 5:13; 16:42; 21:17; 24:13), in keeping the commandments your brethren received "renewed life-breath" as promised (Jos 22:4; 23:1; Isa 28:12; 57:2), neither birds nor wild animals were to receive "renewed life-breath" in the harvest (2 Sam 21:10), the Spirit of Elijah "life-breathed" on Elisha (2 Kng 2:15), the Spirit of YHVH "life-breathed" on the branch from the root of Jesse (Isa 11:2), on Mount Zion (Isa 25:10), and YHVH has given "renewed life-breath" to His people (1 Chr 23:25; 2 Chr 15:15; Job 3:17; Pro 29:17; Isa 63:14; La 5:5; Eze 44:30).

Understand that the new-life breath (nuwach) for physical life was from the set-apart or holy Spirit (ruwach). The difference between the two is the meaning of the first letters. ר ("r") is the letter "reysh," which means "Top, Beginning, First, Chief, Head" and נ ("n"), the letter "nün," means "Continue, Perpetuate, Offspring, Heir" (*The Ancient Hebrew Language And Alphabet*, pp. 59, 64), as the head Spirit-breath gives a measure of His Spirit-breath to continue and perpetuate new life.

So, Noah (נח) certainly did not represent "rest" as we understand the word today, but a new way of life on the "other side," of a global cleansing flood that brought reduced vitality and a shorter life span. Noah exemplified the opposite of "rest" in building a colossal ship, attempting to evangelize the anti-deluvians, then over-seeing the spawning of new life in a devastated world. After Noah was born:

> "And he (Lamech) called his name נח (Noach – new life at the point of division), saying, 'This *one* shall נחם [(nacham - #5162) **large breath** - like a 'blast' (#7307 – ruwach) from YHVH's nostrils - Ex 15:8] us because *of* our deeds, and because *of the* grief of our hands *resulting* from the ground that YHVH has cursed." (CVOT), Gen 5:29

Would it make sense that YHVH would give us "rest" because of our "deeds" and consequent "grief?" As "the carnal mind *is* enmity against God" (Rom 8:7), this "rest" would not be consistent with Scripture, as YHVH has said:

> "Wherefore 'I am disgusted with this generation,' and said, 'They do always stray *in* heart, and they have not known My ways. So, *do* I swear in My wrath, they shall <u>not</u> enter into My rest.'" Heb 3:10, 11 (18) (*lit.*)

Here, talking of the generation in the wilderness, was YHVH not disgusted with the anti-deluvians as well? (see Gen 6:5-7) When you think about it, there was no "rest" for Noah or his family at all, before or after the flood. The only "rest" he may have had after the flood was from the obligation to evangelize outside his family. Any meaning to "rest" here would be like the pause or "breath" in reading poetry or singing a song.

The other "rest" problem is the generalized definition of Sabbath. Several times in the OT the word Shabbat (#7676)(sabbath), considered to be "rest," is preceded by a shabbaton (#7677)(sabbath, rest), and is typically translated "rest." This would then technically give you, "rest rest," which would be a bit redundant lacking description. If we break these words down to their individual letters we have the following:

    שבת - Shabbat   שבתון - shabbaton

ש – shin – to eat, to break down, ruminate, begin digestion
          [fig. – to meditate, to cogitate (to learn)]
ב – bet – layout of a tent, with men's and women's quarters
ת – tav – signature, identification mark, to identify people, places, or
          things, i.e. a room, desert, son, dwelling, etc.

ש – two front teeth, sharp, to cut, press down, to devour, to digest
ב – tent, covering for the family, dwelling
ת – sign, mark, target to shoot for
ו – (vav) - to tie together, to add, to support
נ – (nün) - seed, "new" life, offspring, to continue

    שבת – to **learn** of the **dwelling place** of YHVH's **sign**
        (For He was the One who blessed it and sanctified it)

The difference in letter analysis between the two words is that "sabbatone" (#7677) has the ו נ (add + new life = **added renewal of life continued**); as in rehearsing each of these "shabbaton/e" (feasts, a type of rest) for renewed spiritual life through the year - year in, and year out continually.

Some may ask, "Why would YHVH allow such adulteration of His Word." Yet His Words have not changed, only man's interpretation of them. It is within His Divine purpose to allow the truth to be hidden (Pr 25:2) that we might search for Him with all our heart (Jer29:13). Just as the U.S. Supreme Court has been changing definitions of words in legal terms to affect certain laws to their favor; theocracies in centuries past have done the same to incline certain doctrine to their traditions (Jude 4,15; 2 Thes 2:9,10). This is another reason why Paul says we should "rightly divide (each) word" (2 Tim 2:15), that we might "contend for the faith which was once delivered unto the saints" (Jude 3). As YHVH gives each person the opportunity, should we not utilize the tools (Bibles, Concordances, Dictionaries, Hebrew Language and DSS studies) He has made available?

מנוח - 4494 - manowach – home, settlement (**blood, continues life**, with a **separtation** of kind, as in <u>blood line</u>.)

For all who choose (ח) to follow YHVH are of the seed (נ) of Abraham (Rom 4).

Appendix D: Preparation/ Sabbaton/ Preparation/ 7th day Sabbatone

(day 3)	(day 4) PREPARATION Passover–Pascha				(day 5) FEAST / SABBATON Passover-Pascha / 1st day UB		(day 6) PREPARATION 2nd day of UB		(day 7) 7TH DAY/SABBATONE 3rd day of UB	
	LAST SUPPER									
	GATHSEMANE									
	JUDGMENT HALL									
	CRUCIFIXION	9 AM								
	LAMB OF YAH SLAIN	3 PM			LAMB CONSUMMED		PRIESTS HIRE ROMAN GUARDS		WAVE SHEAF OFFERING	
									RESURRECTION	
TUESDAY 13TH ABIB	NIGHT	WEDNESDAY DAY 1 14TH ABIB			1 NIGHT	THURSDAY DAY 2 15TH ABIB	2 NIGHT	FRIDAY DAY 3 16TH ABIB	3 NIGHT	SABBATH 17TH ABIB
		Mt 27:57-61 Mk 15:42-47 Lk 23:50-55 Jn 19:32-42 *Early Morn Texts* Mt 27:1; Mk 15:1; Lk 22:66; Jn 18:28				Lk 23:56 Jn 19; (31)		Mt 27:62-66 Mk 16:1		Mt 28:1 Mt 28:11-15 Mk 28:1 Mk 16:9-13 Lk 24:1 Lk 24:13-21 Jn 20:1 Jn 20:19-25

LITERAL TRANSLATIONS - in Mt, Mk, Lk, and Jn (*Corrections* **_Bolded_**)

Mt 27:62-63 Then on the **day following that which belongs with the preparation**, the chief priests and the Pharisees came together unto Pilate, Saying, Sir, we remember that that deceiver said, while he was yet alive, '**unto** three days I will **arise**.' …

Mt 28:1 *In the* **twilight, then a seventh-day feast**, as it *was* dawning into **that one seventh-day feast**, Mary Magdalene and the other Mary came to view the grave.

Mk 15:42 And *it* **becoming** evening **already**, since it was *the* preparation, that is, *the* day before the **feast** sabbath, …

Mk 16:1-2 And the **feast days coming to pass**, Mary Magdalene, and Mary the *mother* of James, and Salome, bought spices, **so** that **coming** they might anoint Him. And very early *on* **that one seventh-day Sabbath**, at the rising of the sun, they came unto the tomb.

Mk 16:9 And rising early on the first **Seventh-day Sabbath of the feast**, He appeared first to Mary Magdalene, out of whom He cast seven devils.

Lk 23:54 And that day was the preparation, and the **feast** sabbath drew on. …

Lk 23:56-24:1 And returning, they prepared spices and ointment, and **ceased their labor** *on* the **feast** sabbath according to the **precept**. Then upon the **seventh-day feast Sabbath**, while still very early, they came to the tomb . . .

Jn 19:31 Therefore the Jews, because it was preparation time, **to the intent** that the bodies should not remain on the cross **unto** the **7th day** Sabbath, (for **many are** the day**s** of that **feast time**), asked Pilate that their legs might be broken, and they be taken away.

Jn 20:1 And on the **seventh-day feast Sabbath**, Mary Magdalene came early to the tomb, yet still dark**ness** on the tomb, . . .

Jn 20:19 Then it being **late afternoon** on that day, the **seventh-day feast sabbath**, and the doors having been **locked** where the disciples were assembled, . .

In light of this analysis, consider the very scholarly work at the following location: www.12hoursabbath.com

Appendix E: The Time & Season of Our Savior's Birth to Secure the Sabbatical Year

In Mt 24:20 our Savior says, "But pray ye that your flight be not in the winter, neither 'εν σαββατω'" or "in Shabbat" understood to be a 7th day Sabbath (the word "day" found in most translations is supplied, not being in the Greek, and is not *italicized* as it should be). With respect to the usage in the original language, the Sabbatical year was also referred to simply as "Shabbat." There was no derivation or reconfiguration. In Lev 25:2, 4, 6, and 8, each making referrence to the Sabbatical year, and each time it was referred to simply as "Shabbat." Consequently, since the Greek here has "in" Sabbath, not "on," and the context deals with a series of days, "winter," the time of "great tribulation" (day$\underline{s}$ plural), "And except those day$\underline{s}$ should be shortened . . ."(Mt 24:22), this must be referring to a series of consecutive days, which in this case, "in sabbath" can only mean a Sabbatical year.

The Hebrews had received extra provisions from YHVH in the sixth year, and had them stored away to last through the resting of the land on the seventh, and the planting in the eighth, up to the ninth year (Lev 25:21, 22); which is good reason to pray that you won't have to flee in the sabbatical year, and leave your food as enemy "spoil." And since the word "Shabbat" means "Dwelling Place of the Father's Sign," and has been shown to be a day of miraculous deliverance for the children of Israel; then could it not be also a "year" of miraculous deliverance for his people as well.

As the 7th day Sabbath is important to follow and keep, is blessed and sanctified, so too the sabbatical year should be important to maintain; that we might be made ready in the "preparation," the sixth year, to receive the double portion, that it might carry us through the year of flight or "blight," and thru the next season (Lev 25:22). So, let us determine the Sabbatical year as best we can.

Recalling our brief description in scripturally determining the year of creation, we can calculate the Sabbaticals and see how this pattern may fall in respect to our Saviors physical time on earth (see "Thy Word is Truth," p. 137). If indeed our Savoir was conceived, fashioned in the womb and born, all in a sabbatical year, and the official commencement of His earthly ministry at a Sabbatical years end to announce the seven year count-down to the next Jubilee, as He entered his 30th year (from conception),* then the following could be: (**bold** and underlined are likely the sabbatical years)

```
                    * Birth        BC CE
        BC  7  6  5  4  3  2  1  1  2  3  4  5  6  7  8  9  10  11  12  13  14
                                            ‡              Passion      Jubilee
        15  16  17  18  19  20  21  22  23  24  25  26  27  28  29  30  31  32
                                           Fall       3½      Spring  3½   Fall
                                              |—————————— 7 years ——————|
```

(* - Our Savior's Conception; - ‡ Our Savior's ministry commences) Notice there is no zero BC or CE; and this timeline brings the only Wednesday (full moon) crucifixion date in the Passover month at the right point between sabbatical years (28 CE)(the counterfeit - Dan 9:27; Rev 11:2; 13:5, etc.). This is compatible with the concept of Sabbaticals since Adam's creation, bringing our Savior's conception to a Sabbatical year.

Between the years 27 and 34 CE is when the vast majority of denominations declare the year of our Savior's Passion. Most have 30 CE as the Passover month that year, in accordance with the lunar calendar, as the full moon that month was on a Friday; arbitrarily chosen to retain the Sunday discovery of an empty tomb or resurrection. Between these same years, 27 and 34 CE, besides 28 CE, there is one other year that has a Wednesday Pesach (Passover) full moon; and interestingly enough that happened to be the Jubilee year (31 CE). Not to validate the use of a lunar time-piece, but this became an omen to the Pharisees to awake the attention of the majority, as the minority points these things out to them.

As the Sabbatical years were pronounced in the latter half of the Hebrew calendar year on the Day of Atonement, the same pattern exists in the counting of the 7 "sabbasi," (7 Sabbath's) leading to Pentecost. With all the activity, it commenced about mid-morning on FF when the High Priest ceremoniously takes the Firstfruits in the dedicated field.

The Fall of 24 CE was the ending of the sixth sabbatical week of years and the beginning of the seventh, when our Savoir proclaimed the "acceptable" (favorable) year, in the beginning of the last week of years leading to the Jubilee [This is the same pattern for the millenial week, as the end of the sixth millenium would usher in the seventh, and the seventh is the beginning of the 1000 (millenium) kingdom (Rev 20:4); and halfway into the "seventh day" of that millenial week would be a completion of the services for that week (2 Ptr 3:8)]. So, from the commencement of our Savior's ministry to the Gospel formally going to the Gentiles, possibly with the Jews stoning of Stephen that year, was the seven year trial fulfilling the seven woes pronounced on them by our Savior in the midst of the week (of years).

Therefore, if the fall of 31 CE is the beginning of the Sabbatical Jubilee, then we can add multiples of 49's to that year to determine our present day Jubilee. This would make 1991 our last Jubilee, with the next one in 2040. Yet an interesting aspect is, with several other seemingly valid scriptural studies that presently seem to point to the time-period in the middle of 2017-2019; the first half of the year 2019 happens to be the latter half of the mid-point Sabbatical in the Jubilee cycle, leaving 3-½ weeks of years before 2040. This could be accomplished early in the 7th millenium with the restoration of the earth, since 6000 years of sin is accomplished by 2019 (see p. 138, 139). At present, this is only interesting speculation and requires more study. May the reader be inspired by these teachings to so prayerfully investigate, with consideration of the following table.

Age	**Approx. Years**	**Gematria**
Adam - to - Noah	1000	(1) unity / commencement
Noah - to - Abraham	1000	(2) agree / disagree
Abraham - to - David	1000	(3) to resurrect / to complete
David - to - Savior	1000	(4) earth / redemption
Savior - to - Reform	1000	(5) tabernacles / Divine favor
Reform - to - Present	1000	(6) man / preparation
Present - to - End of MK*	1000	(7) spiritual perfection / life

* (Millenial Kingdom)

Appendix F: Seven forms of the Greek "Sabbaton" - G#*4521* [G#*4315*]

Seven forms of the Greek "Sabbaton" in the NT — Strong's Greek Index – G#*4521* [G#*4315*]

7th Day Sabbaths			Feast Sabbaths – Feast of Weeks		Feast Sabbaths	All Convocations
Plural	Singular	Singular	Plural	mid-week *feast sabbath*	7th day *feast Sabbath*	*feast* and 7th day
SABBATA	**SABBATO**	**SABBASI**	**SABBASIN**	**SABBATON**	**SABBATONE**	**SABBATOU**
Acts 17:2	Mt 12:2	Mt 12:1	Mt 12:5	Mt 12:5	Mt 28:1	Mt 12:8
	Mt 24:20	Mt 12:10	Mt 12:11	Mk 2:27 (2)	Lk 4:16	Mk 2:28
	Lk 6:1	Mt 12:12	Mk 1:21	Mk 15:42 [pro-]	Acts 13:14	Mk 6:2
	Lk 6:6	Mk 2:23	Mk 2:24	Lk 23:54	Acts 16:13	Mk 16:1
	Lk 6:7	Mk 3:2	Lk 6:9	Lk 23:56	Col 2:16	Lk 6:5
	Lk 13:14	Lk 4:31		Jn 5:9	(Mt 28:1)	Lk 13:14
	Lk 13:15	Lk 6:2		Jn 5:10	(Mk 16:2)	Lk 13:16
	Lk 14:1	Lk 13:10		Jn 5:18	(Lk 24:1)	Lk 14:5
	Lk 14:3			Jn 9:14	(Jn 20:1)	Jn 19:31
	Jn 5:16			Jn 9:16	(Jn 20:19)	Acts 1:12
	Jn 7:22			Acts 13:27	(Acts 20:7)	(Mk 16:9)
	Jn 7:23 (2)			Acts 13:42	(1 Cor 16:2)	(Lk 18:12)
	Jn 19:31			Acts 15:21		
	Acts 13:44			Acts 18:4		
1	15	8	6	14 [1]	5 (7)	10 (2)

59 – "sabbath(s)" **1 – ["day before (feast) sabbath"]** **9 – "week"** **(8 – "first *day* of the 'week'")**

Dan 7:25 – "And he shall ... wear out the saints of the Most High, / and intend to change religious festivals and laws." IB / HCSB
Changing: feast *sabbath* to "sabbath" – Sabbath to "sabbath" – Sabbath to "first *day* of the 'week'" - and their timing.

Sabbata / Sabbato, as a transliteration from the Hebrew #7676, correlate contextually here with the 7th day Sabbath. The accounts of "sabbasi" are the Feast of Weeks as delineated in Appendix B; for during those weeks an omer of grain was offered on each of the seven Sabbaths. This is why our Savior was in the grain field with His disciples. The priests can profane the *feast* day in service at the Temple (Mt 12:5), and "the *feast* sabbaths were made for man, not man for the *feast* sabbaths" (Mk 2:27), as the 7th day Sabbath belongs to YHVH (Ex 20:10; De 5:14). The Day of Atonement was always a 7th day Sabbath (Lev 23:32; 16:31; Lk 4:16) by the 364-day calendar. The two Mary's prepared spices after the mid-week holy convocation, the 1st day of UB (Lk 23:54,56). Our Savior teaching over the "sabbatou" in the synagogue (Mk 6:2), and telling the infirm man of 38 years to take up his bed and walk on a *feast* day makes a lot more sense (Jn 5:9,10); as well as the feast day of Hanukkah, the feast of lights, for He placed clay on the eyes of a blind man and made him to wash (Jn 9:14-16). Having a way to travel for all feast and weekly Sabbaths (Acts 1:12), reading of the prophets on the feast sabbaths (Acts 13:27), as the Gentiles so inquired on these days (vs. 42); Moses and the law, so read on the feasts (Acts 15:21; 18:4).

Appendix G: IS KING JAMES YOUR KING?

King James the 1st had taken the throne after a long and spiritually progressive reign of Elizabeth I, who successfully kept the Catholic church at bay, as they attempted to take her life several times and raised up military and naval forces in an attempt to fracture her ever expanding providentially Protestant empire that grew to where the sun never set on her territories. With their tactics apparently restricted by God, the Roman church continued to hone its next prince in line to that throne.

It is not the intent of this writer to diminish ones confidence in the Bible, or incite antagonism without a legitimate cause. But it seems that a remarkably high percentage of Bible believers have come to accept the KJV as the infallible Word of God; and admittedly, the vast majority of it is accurate and prose-worthy, except where it relates to certain fundamental doctrine and times and laws. Regarding the many accolades for this Bible over the years, it seems we have swallowed the Protestant propaganda pill.

Do you ever remember a time when the majority was right on any political issue? With the broad diversity of denominationalism, why wouldn't the same be true in religious circles? This is why we need to be wise as serpents in our analysis of the Word, and harmless as doves in dealing with our Christian neighbors and fellow brethren.

All kings throughout the once Roman Empire were descendants of the governors of their respected regions in the age of the Caesars. When the Empire was breaking up and dissembling (as an orchestrated plan), these governors were required to take a particular coronal ordination to become independent monarchies on the condition to never dissolute the Holy Roman Church from their respective borders; or they would have their royal position abdicated, usually from within. Down through the ages most sovereigns complied with Rome. Those who came to challenge Rome, suffered the consequences because they were bound by a vow.

So, all European monarchies were essentially governorships entitled in Rome. Is it any wonder that all the royal families were intermingled amongst themselves? This royal heritage could not afford any uncontrolled Reformation, regardless of the clamor from the people, and had to sanction counter-reformation measures determined from Rome. Consider the following summary of English religious history:

The formal beginnings of a Reformation from within the only "Christian" church at the time began in England with the influence of John Wycliffe; that was reinforced after his death by the testimony abroad of John Hus, and Jerome, for whose cause Wycliffe's own bones were exhumed and burned. Wycliffe had produced the first English version of the NT, and the Proverbs and Psalms, all from the Latin; some of which later escaped detection to retain enough embers of life through the years to inspire several scholars; the most notable and prolific being William Tyndale. Tyndale, also spurred on by the reform movements in Germany, had completed an English translation of the NT from Greek manuscripts, and his work was published in 1526 and disseminated to key literates throughout the British Isle in a successful, but somewhat clandestine manner.

Soon Tyndale had to cross the English Channel for the elusive printing to continue in several locations on the continent, with the works being smuggled back into England. This had frustrated Henry VIII, for the wave of anti-papistry swelling throughout his realm. Despite the threats and persecutions posed upon his subjects, his only reasonable tactic was an act of counter-reformation, declaring a new church for England (Anglican Church) with the public excuse to allow a process of divorce so he could marry Anne Boelyn, and legitimize matrimony amongst the clergy. Most of the history books twist this point. The Pope had actually annulled Henry's previous marriage, and declared his office, "Defender of the Faith," of which Henry was delighted [A.T. Jones, *The Two Republics,* p. 580], a title still used by English monarchs today.

Interestingly, soon after Tyndale's eventual martyrdom, Henry appointed a Tyndale associate to edit Tyndale's NT, and his several OT works, and sanctioned these scriptures just a few years later, calling it the Great Bible (Coverdale Bible) in 1539. In the very next year, the formal organization of the society of Loyola was established within the Roman church, for the church now needed "secret service" men under oath in many places to police the counter-reformation movement.

Shortly thereafter came the brief reign of Bloody Mary, who, in an attempt to bring a reformed Catholicism back by force, martyred some 300 preachers and scholars, including Bishops Latimer and Ridley, which caused a near-exodus of remnant groups, and severely crippled the theology schools at both Oxford and Cambridge. Some of the scholars that escaped converged on neutral ground in the city of Geneva, Switzerland, from where the Bible by the same name originated.

Then Elizabeth, though resolutely declared Protestant (likely for all the evil she had witnessed with her sister), her hands tied because of her coronation vow, could not dispel all papal practices from the Anglican church, nor all Catholics from the land. In addition, she had to keep the Puritans in check in order that they might not gain ascendancy over the counter-reformation efforts within the state-recognized church. She may have allowed more for the Puritans if they had not imposed "nothing less than utter subversion of the State" to enforce religious precepts [Ibid. p.594], or so the story goes.

Because Elizabeth had marginalized her vow before the Roman church, her life was threatened many times, and wars were raised against her at sea by the Catholic Spanish Armada, as her territories across the globe continued to providentially expand that these new (quasi) Protestant regions might balance out soon-to-be neighboring Catholic lands.

Because the Catholic cause lost Mary Queen of Scots, Elizabeth's cousin, partly to the influence of John Knox in Scotland, she was ousted from her position when her son James was just one year old; of whom James never saw again, and was forced to acquiesce to her execution when he was 21 years of age. James was baptized a Catholic, raised by Presbyterian governors, and as a boy king "had been a trophy in the hands of rival noble factions in Scotland, kidnapped, held, threatened, and imprisoned.

"James retreated from the brutality and anarchy. He became chronically vulnerable to the allure of beautiful, elegant, and rather Frenchified men. He loved hunting, excessively, an escape from the realities, at one point killing every deer in the royal park at Falkland in Fife, which had to be restocked from England. It has been calculated that he spent half his waking life on the hunting field." [A. Nicholson, *God's Secretaries*, *The Making of the King James Bible*, p. 7 (multi-source book (129)] Yet to his credit "when he attended to business he could do more in an hour than others could do in a day" [Ibid. p.8].

When James received the news that Elizabeth had died, a grand procession had already begun to form in Edinburgh Scotland on April 6th, 1603 to congratulate him on the new expanded kingdom. Scotland now became part of England to become Great Britain. He would become the reigning king of England, Scotland, Ireland, and France. Preparations for the formal ceremony were in the works during his trip south to the palace complex in London England.

Throughout that first summer in 1603 "any questioning of the doctrine of the church of England was politically subversive," as "anti-Puritan propaganda flooded the country."

[Ibid. p.39] Catholic priests were released from the Tower, but there is no mention of any Puritans being released from the dungeons, and "a flood of English Roman Catholics started to return from the European continent" that summer of his coronation. [Ibid. p.84]

During his celebration parade toward London, coming from Scotland, the famed "Millenary Petition" was brought to his attention and was officially presented to him at the outset of his reign, for it received its name from the signatures it had, from "a thousand ministers, asking for a reformation of the English church, to rid it of the last vestiges of Roman Catholicism and bring to a conclusion the long lumbering agony of the English Reformation…. This Millenary Petition, was the seed from which the new translation of the Bible would grow." [Ibid. p.34]

Now, by this time in history, there were already several English Bibles, and/or NT, not all of them accessible, - the Wycliffe, and Tyndale were taboo, (all the known ones in publics hands were burned), the Coverdale, and Matthews were state-sanctioned, the Geneva was created outside the country and was undermined by the Whitchurch, and Bishop's Bibles, printed during Elizabeth's reign, which were heavily laden with Latin philosophies. The Bishop's Bible, named after the bishops who translated it in 1568, was a royalist and anti-Puritan document to answer the Geneva Bible completed in the previous decade.

The Geneva was the most regarded by the sincere Christian reader, if he could afford one, yet these were generally shared amongst mostly home groups that James was trying to discourage. James himself "violently disliked" the Geneva, mostly because of the margin notes, as he refused to have anything but just the words of the Bible itself. Yet the Geneva Bible would be found to have thousands of differences with the King James Bible. In the Geneva Bible, "the word 'tyrant', for example, which is not to be found in the King James Bible, occurs over 400 times." [Ibid. p.58]

The first meeting of religious leaders of the opposing sides in January of 1604, intending to determine what measures would be taken for English Christendom, looked "like a cartoon of Jacobean England. This included the grand theatre of the royal Presence Chamber, derisive courtiers, satin-lined prelates, a self-indulgent king, and a pitiable line-up of put-upon and ascetic Puritans, [who were] sitting on their bench like the accused at a trial [rather than as] equal partners in a negotiation for the future of the church" [Ibid. p.44, 45]. The two sides were deeply opposed on critical points of doctrine.

At the first Parliamentary address with the new king in March of 1604, "most of its members were sympathetic to the Puritan cause" and James had to lecture the constituents on "the nature of kingship, on his own nearness to God, and how all positions were not independent from the crown 'but derived from him.'"[Ibid. p.63]

James became vehemently opposed to any Puritans involvement in the translation even though they were the ones who had legally garnered and presented their petition that instigated the whole translation process. Yet in order to appear fair that the Puritans would be without legitimate complaint, the king did allow two veteran scholars, one from Oxford, the other from Cambridge, that were declared "Puritans," who were devout kings-feet kissers. However, there may have been some legitimacy to the king's decision if what the Puritans were looking for was something short of grammatical flow, even though the Geneva, which they greatly valued, was very readable.

The king soon afterwards declared that there should be "one uniform translation … done by the best learned of both universities … reviewed by the bishops, and the chief learned of the church …presented to the Privy Council … to be ratified by his Royal authority; to be read in the whole church, and no other." [Ibid. p59] "This ferociously Episcopal and monarchist Bible was to be the only (sanctioned) translation … The treasured Geneva Bible would be forced to retreat into the privacy of people's homes and could no longer be used for public preaching." [Ibid. p.60]

In the summer of 1604 those who would not subscribe to the use of the surplice, the cross, confirmation, the use of wedding rings and other symbolic gestures and practices were expelled from the Anglican church, "about 80 ministers from a body of about 8000. (dissented) …Among this one percent were those who in time became the leaders of the Pilgrim Fathers." [Ibid. p.86] Not trusting the king, with Bloody Mary in their past, is there any wonder why several Puritan and eventual Separatist groups would wind up leaving England? Even many of these could not stand the debauchery in the Netherlands, and were willing to brave their lives across the Atlantic for the new world.

Regarding the Puritans requests for a "non-episcopal" work, just the plain word of God, "truly transmitted – to that request James had said, in effect, 'Yes; I will give you the very opposite of what you ask,'" for the state-recognized institutions had sent to the king "long and high-flowing refutations of every point in the Puritans Millenary Petition" [Ibid. p.60]. Yet we are also told that "the men at the core of this Oxford group were deeply engaged with the realities of money and power." [Ibid. p.155]

"James would not tolerate any suggestion of his own royal authority being questioned. The royal supremacy over church and state was the foundation of his position as King." [Ibid. p.38] A favorite line use by James in various communications and occasionally in his presentations was a quote from Tacitus: "Those who do not know how to dissimulate, know not how to rule" [Ibid. p.6]. "Accordingly he issued a proclamation commanding all Puritans to conform or suffer the full extremity of the laws, ... Meanwhile, some of the Puritans seeing the same prospects from old, ... drew off from the Puritan party, as well as from the church of England, and advocated a complete separation from both systems ... that each assembly of worship is entirely independent of all others, and self-governing; that all points of doctrine or discipline are to be submitted to the congregation ... and each congregation should elect its own pastor, (these became known as) *Congregationalists*, and nicknamed *Separatists*." [*The Two Republics*, p.598, 599]

The scholars chosen for the actual translation process were university students and professors that relied upon the "writings of Jerome, St. John Chrysostom, Augustine, and Origen." [*God's Secrataries*, p.76] James was not so concerned with the clarity of the word, as were those of the Geneva, or straightforwardness like that of Tyndale, but for its "richness, suggestiveness, and harmonic resonance," [Ibid. p.78] using "Hebrew, Greek, and even Aramaic scripts." [Ibid. p.73]

"Circumlocution" [round-about-ness] was a word in common usage amongst the translators to describe their approach to certain passages. Many of the translators were decidedly anti-Puritan and became anti-Separatist, constantly spewing derogatory one-liners when the topic was brought up in conversation; neither did they lend a hand, give resources to the poor; but literally avoided the occasional plagues of London by resorting to the safety of the universities and the palace complexes.

To read the accounts of many of those who officiated the translation process, these could best be described as a pack of pathological hypocrites and proverbial deceivers that would put many a Pharisee to shame. The rules and instructions that the translators adhered to had no intimation of piety, no directive for prayer, or the spirit of inspiration, no concept that the translators were involved in a sanctified work.

The king in his rhetoric and haughty language was not unlike the Pharaoh of Egypt, for he was quoted of saying before Parliament that it is the king's word over God and rebuked the assembly for not prioritizing his position, sounding like the Pope himself. In his approach to his subjects, he was much like Herod, as the only thing to be tolerated was his position. There were even discussions during the years of the translation process, not unlike today, about Papal and Protestant reunification. Attempts at imposing unity stimulated anarchy, violence and revolt, for James said, "the (Anglican) church should take the initiative and mould the new Bible to its own purposes" [Ibid. p.65].

The King's interpretation of Romans 13 is much different than that of the Puritans or Separatists; when the text says: "Let every soul be subject to the higher powers:" (v.1) because King James had equated his position to that of God, he had no one to answer to but himself. A more literal translation of vs 1: (*Emphasis supplied*)

> "Let <u>every</u> soul (including judge, priest, and king) be subject unto higher authorities; as there is **no authority greater than YHVH**, but the existing authorities were so **arranged of YHVH**" (*lit.* Rom 13:1).

The KJV has "there is no power but of God," and that these are "ordained of God." The next verse regarding authority states they should be the "instrument of YHVH" not an "ordinance" (vs.2); a little further at vs. 4 it should read that the ruler is a "servant of YHVH" not a "minister of God" as King James calls himself (Rom 13:4, 6).

By the end of 1604, public confidence was beginning to wane regarding James true affiliation, and the direction he intended to take the Church of England with a pending new translation overseen by a pre-judicious staff. And now, with Separatists groups beginning to form and crop-up in various locations across the land, this threatened to overwhelm their "homeland security" agents, so further measures needed to be taken.

On November 5, 1605, with the king and his queen, his princes, peers and other members of the legislative assembly present for the commencement of the joint session of Parliament at its opening, came the event that would define Jacobean England. There was a supposed failed attempt to blow-up Parliament, the king and all the leaders of the monarchy, by a group, we are told, of renegade Catholics bent on returning England to the auspices of Rome. They reported that multiple barrels of gunpowder were found on the ground floor, underneath the chamber of the House of Lords where they were gathering. This is known today as the "Gunpowder Plot."

It is the conclusion of some, that the ultimate design was that the schemers were to be caught, a conspiracy averted to effect and sway the mind of the people for the Catholic influx, and pro-Catholic decisions made earlier in the king's reign. This was largely a successful false flag operation that was foist upon the unsuspecting public to prove the kings loyalty to the cause of Protestantism; though some, including many Puritans, saw right through it.

The idea surfaced that the Spanish were poised to invade, yet they were already welcome to the isle and a peace treaty had been signed between them in the summer of 1604 and trade and custom revenues had soared. If indeed Spain was behind this, why was there no further investigation recorded? It was only after pressure from the growing popular suspicion of foul play that James, sometime later, reneged at least in a public document, his treaty with Spain. Even so this event raised the anxiety index enough to usher in the long sought for deification of the office of king that James wanted and needed for state-sanctioned acceptance of the new bible amongst the populace in this age of Reformation momentum.

There was quite a royal celebration shortly after the Gunpowder incident that involved the queen and all her ladies, the king and his closest courtiers, some of the translators, and a few royal relatives that came from the allied nations in Europe for one of the most extravagant and overt drunken stupors of the kings reign. There were royal staged performances given to make pretense to the royal couple as Solomon and the queen of Sheba. "Parliament, which had been dominated by a suspicion of Stuart (James' Surname) profligacy, crypto-Catholicism, and Scottishness, now fell over itself to provide money, loyalty, and support for the king." [Ibid. p.106]

The translators that were in the House of Lords on the fateful day would generate sermons that came to be printed, became wildly popular, even best sellers and distributed all across England. The Jesuits who were placed on trial and ultimately executed were knowingly, willingly sacrificed for the sake and intent of the order. Knowing the conditions of England and its place in history with territories across the globe, and its potential influence worldwide, the English language was bound to go into virtually every continent. They had to make it appear with certainty that King James was indeed a confirmed Protestant with this staged, highly publicized event, as the KJV was contrived to eventually be the flagship English Bible for the next several centuries, and come to be the standard by which others would be measured.

The question remains, however, that at the last moment while all the dignitaries were present in the House of Lords, that the plot was exposed for such sensational publicity. There is no record of anyone being caught in the act to either guard it, or ignite it and with no comment ever given in the history books regarding the continuity of the barrels, the powder, or any viable point of detonation. How did such a great amount of gunpowder get where it was without detection? And why were there not enough previous safeguards to bring this to light before? How did this masterminded crew prevent anyone from finding it for the several weeks that it was supposedly there until just before the fuse was to receive the flame? The rumors of a long dark tunnel to transport their gunpowder never emerged into any evidence. Alternatively, was that rumor a cover for their breach of security on the building? This supposed breach seems no different from the presumed penetration of the complex intelligence network designed to protect the people of the United States in 2001.

The way that the accused Jesuit priest Henry Garnet (who gained knowledge of the pending act through the confessional without reporting it), and the leader of the conspirators, Guy Fawkes, were supposedly tortured and killed was the same way Catholics would do to declared Heretics; when there is no room for such cruel treatment according to the Scriptures, but only present in amongst cultic belief systems. These types of tactics are used to play on the emotions and fears of the people.

It is the reasonable suspicion of many that the one who exposed the scheme was also a Jesuit; just as there were Jesuits in the royal court. A Jesuit will defraud and expose another Jesuit for the sake of the order; in this case to make it appear that king James was not Catholic at all. "Indeed, the Jesuit is always speculating on the vocations for martyrdom ... even to die as a victorious martyr." [P.D. Stuart, *Codeword Barbêlôn*, p.133] "even their conduct towards each other is one of continuous act of deceit and spying .. to respond with dissembling and equivocation" [Ibid. p.136].

One could ask, "Now how can a man confess a sin he has yet to commit?" Yet the French philosopher Voltaire states, "'whenever a Prince of Orange, or a King of France was to be assassinated the Jesuit assassin always prepares himself by the sacrament of confession.'... Guy Fawkes and his conspirators all took secret oaths and received the Sacrament of the Eucharist of the Church in preparation." [Ibid. p.49]

There was a lot of social and religious unrest in those days. "Shakespeare's great tragedies and the King James Bible are each other's mirror-twin." [A. Nicolson, *God's Secretaries*, p.239] Even so this Gunpowder Plot was a brilliant false flag operation by the crown, knowing ahead of time that a minority would not accept it, they were assured that the historical account for future generations would be recorded as a genuine Jesuit attempt to subvert the British to Catholicism. For this date is still celebrated every year in Britain as Guy Fawkes day, played as a day of victory for Protestantism over the Roman church; while the Catholic hierarchy exults in the same celebration for its stealthy work over the centuries to accomplish her counter-reformation goals, where today, all major Protestant religions have fundamental doctrines in common with her. Whether the Catholic Church is castigated is of little consequence to her, so long as people are unaware that they themselves are Catholic.

Interestingly enough, after the first printing of the KJV in 1611, the appetite for the Geneva Bible became overwhelming, until finally king James put a hold on its printing in 1616, and the KJV, from that point forward, was referred to as the "Authorized Version." "Robert Barker, printer to the king, a chaotic man who would end up in debtor's prison, bought up the Dutch Geneva editions, added a title page with the fraudulent date 1599 clearly stamped on it, and flogged them to a ready market. ... By the 1620's, within a decade from the release of the KJV, the illiteracy rate among the gentry went from 30% to effectively Ø and public libraries were first commissioned then." Meanwhile, "presses in Amsterdam and Dort started to roll, producing Geneva Bibles for the English market well into the 1630's." [Ibid. p.228]

"Even more strangely, given the sanctity with which the text of the King James Bible has been regarded in later ages, the very people who might have championed it continued to use the Geneva Bible. (The lead Translator, called the Interpreter General) Lancelot Andrewes nearly always took his sermon texts from the Geneva (even though the only Bible sanctioned for public readings was the KJV). Even William Laud (staunchly anti-Puritan, and Andrewes right-hand man), the most anti-Calvinist bishop in the church, quoted from the Geneva. Most extraordinary of all, Miles Smith in the Preface to the new KJV translation, quotes from the very Geneva Bible, which it was, in part, intended to replace. And in the Separatist congregations in Amsterdam, Leiden and eventually on the *Mayflower*, it was of course the Geneva Bible they took with them" [Ibid. p. 229].

Yet James was able to keep the state and various factions appeased with expulsion and conformity measures, with issue volleys persisting until they grew into unforgiving tensions sometime after 1625, during the more severe reign of James' son, Charles I. This ultimately culminated in the English Civil War by 1639, where "a higher proportion of the British population was killed than in any war before or since." [Ibid. p.62].

In the wake of the war many documents were uncovered that proved the intent of many key figures, in the days of the translation, "had been leading the Church of England on the path to Rome." [Ibid. p.188] It was much later that the public came to find that "all the documents of the Privy Council between 1600 and 1613 were destroyed in a Whitehall fire" [Ibid. p.150] (Whitehall was one of several royal palaces). And it was actually during the restoration of England, after the civil war and the great London fires in the 1660s that the KJV came into its own in England as a "national text and the symbol of England as God's country." [Ibid. p.229]

In the mid 1800's, "Dr. F. Scrivener, a scholar working to modern standards, attempted to collate all the editions of the King James Bible then in circulation, he found more than 24,000 variations between them."[Ibid. p.226]. Subsequently, what does "Authorized Version" mean? The "Jacobean Englishmen consistently called their church, not Roman, but catholic [in order to embrace all]." [Ibid. p.241].

So, who is your King? Moses and John the Revelator say we should not add or detract from the statutes or the prophecies (Dt. 12:32; Rev 22:18). Remember that the King of Kings, who is the same yesterday, today and forever, who does not change, states that the only thing he will take away is your sins, and the only thing He will add is your salvation, if we abide by <u>His</u> Word.

Appendix H: EMBRIOLOGICAL CELEBRATION

Scripture refers to the human frame as the Temple of God bought with a price (1 Cor 16:3; 6:20) to be of reasonable service to our fellow man as a living sacrifice (Rom 12:1). And as we have come to appreciate the extent of YHVH's perfection in the sanctuary (Ps 18:30; 77:13), the following study will show how His perfection is literally intertwined in every soul born of women; each made in His image from their very beginning. Everyone who comes into this sinful world fulfills a complete year of feast days in their development, as the perfect commencement in His plan of salvation (Ps 139:13,14; Isa 49:5). Redemption and atonement have been ascribed for each one of us from birth. Could this be why it is that we are referred to as the Temple of the living God (2 Cor 6:16)?

The Cycle of Gestational Salvation

Feast Day	Day & Month	Commission	Stage of Development
1. Choosing the Passover Lamb	10th of the 1st	A Yearling is Selected without spot or wrinkle Begins purging for Passover	**Mature Follicle:** is chosen, LH & FSH begin to surge for ovulation
2. Passover (preparation for the week of Unleavened Bread)	14th of the 1st	Slaying of the Lamb by the Family and Eaten Blood on the Doorposts	**Ovulation:** Egg Release Graafian Follicle Slain Reabsorbed by Ovary Blood spot released on Fimbriae, Lintel and posts of Fallopian tubes
3. 1st Day of Unleavened Bread	15th of the 1st	Partaking of Unleavened Bread First Ceremonial Holy Convocation No Yeast in the House	**Conception:** Holy Convocation "assembly" i.e. "Sperm & Egg" If Yeast in Tube/Uterus - then No Conception
4. Wave Sheaf (Firstfruits) First Omer	17th of the 1st (Beginning Feast of Weeks)	First Heads of Barley grain Reaped Priest Waves it in the House of Yah, the Sanctuary	**Embyo** becomes a Blastocyst Waved thru Fallopian tube by Cillia cells Enter the – Uterine House

"The First Day of the Week" Scripture or Tradition?

5. 7th Day of Unleavened Bread	21st of the 1st	Holy Convocation No Yeast in the House	**Implantation** complete in Uterus sanctuary Holy "Assembly" If Yeast in Uterus – then No Implantation
6. Pentecost (Holy Spirit outpouring)	6th of the 3rd (Feast of FirstFruits)	All Men, made in Yah's image, required to appear before Yah - Yah's Spirit poured out	**Fetus:** by this day, all ext./int. structures now present to have full Human appearance – the image of Yah
7. Trumpets (the Loud Cry)	1st of the 7th	Blowing of Shofars Blown each of the next Nine Days leading to Day of Atonement	**Auditory** structures: Anvil, Hammer, Stapes Ossify – Now able to hear Loud Sounds
8. Day of Atonement	10th of the 7th	Israel's sins Removed Blood Cleansing of the Most Holy Place -Reconciling to Yah	**Marrow Blood:** Begins this day to make Own Blood cells - now Needs Atonement
9. 1st Day of Tabernacles (Holy Convocation)	15th of 7th (Beginning Feast of Ingathering	Celebrating the Grain, Olive, & Grape Harvest Booths of branches made to Commemorate Dwelling in Wilderness Experiential time	**Brain** network, and all organs established Begins Sensoral Input; (eyes open) Experiences begin
10. 8th Day of Tabernacles (Holy Convocation)	22nd of the 7th (End of Feast of Ingathering)	Called Last Great Day Solemn Assembly Booths are disassembled	**Lungs** are mature Hyaline Membrane complete – If born this day can "Tabernacle" out of the womb

APPENDICES

11. 1st Day of Hanukkah (Dedication)	25th of the 9th (Beginning Feast of Lights)	Celebration of Temple Rededication Eight day Cleansing begins with one day of Oil	**Birth:** First day of average birth; Celebration - Child brought to Light Body Temple delivered [skin fat (oil) increases]
12. 8th Day of Hanukkah	1st of the 10th (Last day Feast of Lights)	All 8 Lamps on the Hanukkah Menorah are lit - Rededication complete Israel is restored	**Circumcision:** on the 8th day - Symbol of -putting away of the flesh the Body Temple is Accepted - set-apart
13. Purim	14th and 15th of the 12th	Gallows for Mordecai used on Haman – All Israel Raises their Heads High - days of Feasting and Gladness	**Raising Head** full 90° smiles spontaneously and can Laugh out-loud, Squeal, and Clap

"Now may the God of peace, who brought up from the dead our Master Messiah – the great Shepherd of the sheep – with the blood of the everlasting covenant, equip you with all that is good to do His will, working in us what is pleasing in His sight, through our Savior Messiah, to whom be the glory forever and ever. Amen." Heb 13:20,21 HCSB

References

Bibles:

Bullinger, E. W., (1999). *The Companion Bible*, Facsimile product of (1922). Authorized Version of 1611, (KJV). Grand Rapids, MI: Kregel Publication, Republished. ISBN: 0-8254-2099-7

Green, J. P., Sr., (1986). *The Interlinear Bible, Hebrew-Greek-English*, (IB), Sovereign Grace Publishers, Lafayette, IN.: ISBN: 1-878442-82-1.

Heston, M.R., (2007). *The Law of YHVH in the New Testament*, Featuring the Honest Truth Translation, (HTT), Weaverville, CA: Examine-All-Things Ministries.

Holman Bible Publishers, (2004). *Holman Christian Standard Bible*, (HCSB), Nashville, TN: Holman Bible Publishers.

Jones, A., Ed., (1968). *The Jerusalem Bible*, Reader's Edition, (JB). Garden City, NY: Doubleday & Co., Inc..

Knoch, A.E., (1983). *Concordant Literal New Testament*, (CLNT), Canyon Country, CA: Concordant Publishing Concern.

Knoch (family), (2012). *Concordant Version of the Old Testament*, (CVOT), Almont, MI: Concordant Publishing Concern.

Lamsa, Geo. M., (1985). *The Holy Bible from the Ancient Eastern Text*: (LAP) G.M. Lamsa's translation from the Aramaic of the Peshitta. San Francisco, CA: Harper & Row.

Lockman, F. N., *et al*, Editors (1973). *New American Standard Bible*, (NAS). Carol Stream, IL: Creation House, Inc..

McDonald, Curtis, (2001). *New Race of People Translation*, (NRP) Selected Bible Books and Passages, Sacramento, CA: McDonald Publishing.

Young, R., (1976). *Young's Literal Translation*, (YLT). Guardian Press, ISBN: 9780890860199.

Concordances:

Brown, F., Driver, S., & Briggs, C., (1997). *The Brown-Driver-Briggs Hebrew and English Lexicon*, Peabody, MA: Hendrickson Publishers,.

Strong, James, *The Exhaustive Concordance of the Bible*, Peabody, MA: Hendrickson Publishers, ISBN: 0-917006-01-1

Strong, James, (2001). *The Strongest Strong's Exhaustive Concordance of the Bible*, Fully Revised and Corrected by Kohlenberger & Swanson, Grand Rapids, MI: Zondervan Publishers.

Young, R., (1981). *Young's Analytical Concordance to the Bible*, Nashville, TN: Thomas Nelson Publishers.

Dictionaries & Commentaries:

Berube, M.S., (1982). *The American Heritage Dictionary*, Second Collegiate Edition, Boston, MA: Houghton Mifflin Company.

Cassell's *Latin Dictionary*, Revised by Marchant & Charles, New York, NY: Funk & Wagnalls, Co.,

Council of Elders, (2010). *The Word of YAH, The King's Covenant*. (OSE1) Catoosa, OK: The Kingdom of YAH Publishers

Horn, S. H., et al., (1979). *Seventh-day Adventist Bible Dictionary*. Revised Edition. Washington DC: Review and Herald Publishing, LCCN: 60-12204

Knoch, A.E., (1968). *Concordant Commentary on the New Testament*. Santa Clara, CA., Concordant Publishing Concern.

Nichols, F. D., et al., (1953). *The Seventh-day Adventist Bible Commentary*, Washington DC: Review and Herald Publishing, vol. 1, 5, 6.

Scherman, N. & Zlotowitz, M., (2000). *The Chumash*, Stone Edition, Brooklyn, NY: Mesorah Pub., Ltd. ISBN 10: 0-89906-014-5

Smith, W. A., (1975). *Dictionary of the Bible*, Revised Edition, by F.N and M. A. Peloubet, Grand Rapids, MI: Zondervan, LCCN: 88014-0410

Vine, W. E., (1966). *An Expository Dictionary of New Testament Words*, Old Tappan, NJ: Fleming H. Revell Co.

Watts, N., (2007). *Oxford Greek Mini Dictionary*, Second Edition, Oxford UK: Oxford University Press,

Webster, N., (1996). *American Dictionary of the English Language*, Facsimile Production of First Edition, 1828, by the Foundation for the American Christian Education, San Francisco, CA. New York, NY: Original Publication: S. Converse.

Other References:

Abegg, Flint & Ulrich, (1999). *The Dead Sea Scrolls Bible*, San Francisco, CA: Harper Collins Pub.

Arrabito, J., (1988). *History of the Sabbath*, Angwin, CA: LLT Prod.

Benner, J.A., (2004). *The Ancient Hebrew Language And Alphabet*, College Station, TX: Virtual Bookworm.

Charles, R. H., (1913). *The Apocrypha and Pseudepigrapha of the Old Testament, The Book of Jubilees, and The Book of Enoch.* Oxford, UK: Clarendon Press.

Compton, C. B., (1999). *The Difference Between the Enoch and Lunar Calendars: A Time Study of the Dead Sea Scrolls*, Meadow Vista, CA: Lighthouse Publications.

Eisenberg, A., Murkoff, H.E., Hathaway, S.E., (1989). *What to Expect the First Year*, New York, Workman Publications.

Eisenman, R. & Wise, M. (1992). *The Dead Sea Scrolls Uncovered.* Boston, MA: Element Books, Inc.

Good, J., (1991). *Rosh HaShanah and the Messianic Kingdom to Come.* Hatikva Ministries, Port Arthur, Texas

Hole, J., (1990). *Human Anatomy and Physiology*, 5th Ed., Dubuque, W.C. Brown Publishing

Jones, A.T., (1891). *The Two Republics.* Battle Creek, MI: Review and Herald Publishing.

Levitt, Z., *A Child is Born*, (video), Dalas, Berg Productions, Zola Levitt Ministries

McDonald, C., (2000). *Enmity: A Critical Review*, Sacramento, CA: McDonald Publishing's.

McDonald, C., (2001). *What Day Was It?*, 2nd ed., Sacramento, CA: McDonald Publishing's

Moore, K.L., (1988). *The Developing Human, Clinically Oriented Embryology*, 4th ed., Philadelphia, W.B. Sauders Co.

Nicolson, A., (2003). *God's Secretaries: The Making of the King James Bible*, New York, NY: Perennial of Harper Collins Publishers,

Sampson, R. & Pierce, L., (1999). *A Family Guide to the Biblical Holidays.* Shelbyville, TN: Heart of Wisdom Publishers, ISBN: 9780970181602

Stuart, P. D. (2009). *Codeword Barbêlôn*, Enfield, London, UK: Lux-Verbi Books.

Sussman, Y., (1990). *The History of Halakha and the Dead Sea Scrolls – Observations on 4QMMT*, (in Hebrew) Tarbiz 59.

Taber, C.W., (1993). *Cyclopedic Medical Dictionary*, 17 ed., Philadelphia, F.A. Davis Co.

Telushkin, J., (1991). *Jewish Literacy, The Hebrew Calendar and Jewish Holidays*, New York, Wm. Morrow Co.

Trimm, J., (2005). *The Books of Enoch*, Hurst, TX, The Institute for Nazarene Jewish Studies

White, L. (2008). *Fossilized Customs*. Louisville, KY: Torah Zone Publishing, ISBN 0-9584353-6-7

Wise, Abegg & Cook, (1996) . *The Dead Sea Scrolls: A New Translation*. San Francisco, CA: Harper Collins Pub. ISBN 0-06-069200-6.

Wooten, B. R. (2002). *Israel's Feast and Their Fullness*, St. Cloud, FL: Key of David Publishing. ISBN: 1-886987-02-5

Index

A

Abel 94

Abib 83, 84, 85, 91, 93, 94, 139

Abihu 87

Abraham 1, 11, 30, 31, 94, 125, 138, 154, 169, 183, 193

Adam 27, 29, 94, 140, 141, 171, 177, 180, 181, 182, 183, 184, 185, 186, 187, 188, 190, 197

Appointment(s) 1, XIII, 25, 26, 30, 87, 133, 137, 142, 172

Ancient V, VII, IX, XV, 4, 5, 9, 18, 26, 37, 55, 56, 57, 74, 77, 83, 90, 91, 137, 144, 168, 177, 189, 191, 215, 217

Aramaic XI, 91, 147, 166, 171, 177, 205, 215

Ascension 8, 60, 80, 148

Atonement 8, 15, 32, 33, 35, 36, 38, 86, 88, 89, 90, 112, 113, 114, 117, 139, 197, 211, 212

Authority 10, 16, 71, 90, 142, 204, 205, 206

B

Babylon 18, 29, 30, 60, 77, 79, 83, 90, 91, 93, 94, 104, 113, 114, 124, 125, 132, 137, 138, 143, 154, 155, 157, 166, 169, 170, 171, 179

Baptism 8, 15, 86, 88, 89, 90, 129

Barley 93, 117, 128, 144, 149, 152, 153, 154, 211

Beat 145, 146

Benjamin 153

Benjamite 78

Birth 14, 83, 84, 85, 86, 89, 90, 129, 140, 153, 155, 196, 197, 211, 213

Blood V, 7, 15, 39, 40, 41, 74, 100, 152, 154, 155, 156, 157, 193, 201, 204, 211, 212, 213

Boris 80

Branches 84, 145, 146, 212

C

Cain 94

Calendar I, II, VI, VII, VIII, 18, 20, 25, 26, 27, 28, 29, 30, 31, 32, 33, 34, 35, 37, 39, 41, 73, 91, 92, 93, 94, 104, 112, 113, 114, 115, 123, 124, 125, 126, 128, 130, 131, 137, 138, 139, 140, 141, 142, 143, 144, 150, 156, 157, 159, 166, 169, 170, 173, 174, 178, 179, 197, 217

Camp 84, 151

Canon 27, 138, 179

Chodesh 31, 137, 142, 165, 166, 167, 172, 173, 174

Christian(s) I, II, V, XI, 10, 14, 27, 30, 45, 46, 56, 57, 63, 75, 80, 83, 92, 97, 155, 185, 200, 201, 203, 215, 216

Chronology 108, 140

Codex 49

Colossians 16, 124, 170

Commandment(s) XIV, 14, 17, 18, 38, 46, 57, 63, 85, 107, 108, 114, 125, 127, 169, 190, 191

Concordance X, XIV, 3, 4, 5, 6, 7, 19, 37, 49, 71, 193, 216

Constantine 41, 94

Convocation 5, 7, 15, 16, 19, 26, 32, 34, 39, 40, 60, 62, 75, 78, 84, 100, 101, 106, 108, 117, 123, 130, 152, 153, 169, 170, 211, 212

Courtyard 93, 101, 147, 149, 152, 153

Covenant 7, 25, 28, 38, 40, 63, 64, 88, 113, 125, 127, 129, 132, 141, 151, 154, 156, 167, 187, 188, 213, 216

Creation 29, 45, 64, 139, 140, 141, 160, 173, 178, 180, 182, 183, 184, 185, 186, 188, 190, 196, 197, 215

Crescent 34, 112, 144, 166, 169

Critical 17, 18, 35, 79, 98, 203, 217

Crucifixion V, 7, 39, 63, 72, 74, 76, 77, 80, 83, 86, 90, 91, 92, 93, 101, 105, 197

Cycle(s) 15, 25, 27, 28, 30, 34, 35, 86, 89, 93, 112, 126, 139, 140, 141, 142, 144, 150, 166, 169, 172, 198, 211 211

D

Damascus 123, 124

Daniel 25, 27, 56, 90, 94, 130, 137, 141, 170

Dead V, VII, XI, 20, 26, 28, 29, 30, 31, 33, 36, 47, 51, 56, 60, 63, 64, 72, 76, 79, 85, 91, 105, 116, 124, 129, 138, 148, 150, 156, 169, 213, 217, 218

Death 30, 63, 64, 74, 80, 83, 88, 94, 105, 113, 123, 125, 127, 130, 132, 156, 201

Definition 4, 6, 16, 18, 20, 37, 45, 49, 50, 64, 71, 86, 87, 98, 99, 100, 103, 109, 115, 121, 122, 123, 168, 184, 185, 187, 189, 192, 193

Dictionary 4, 6, 9, 37, 45, 46, 49, 50, 56, 67, 100, 122, 168, 179, 216, 217

Disciple(s) I, V, VII, XIII, XIV, 8, 10, 13, 15, 18, 39, 40, 49, 59, 60, 64, 72, 73, 74, 77, 86, 87, 103, 110, 112, 114, 116, 124, 128, 129, 142, 145, 175, 178, 195

Doctrine XIII, 6, 57, 97, 158, 193, 200, 202, 203, 205, 209

Dwell 83, , 104, 125, 187, 189

E

Elizabeth 84, 200, 202, 203

Emmanuel 84

English IX, 4, 7, 9, 16, 19, 20, 37, 38, 41, 46, 48, 49, 50, 51, 57, 58, 72, 76, 89, 97, 98, 100, 104, 106, 115, 138, 169, 180, 183, 184, 185, 200, 201, 203, 207, 209, 210, 215, 216

Enoch II, 26, 28, 29, 31, 125, 127, 138, 139, 140, 141, 169, 170, 173, 74, 178, 79, 180, 217

Equinox 84, 86, 139, 140, 141

Eutychus 116, 117

F

Faith III, VI, VII, VIII, XIV, 6, 15, 46, 63, 97, 158, 193, 201

False II, III, V, 8, 114, 117, 185, 207, 208

Father I, III, VI, VIII, IX, XIII, XIV, 6, 7, 9, 14, 18, 25, 29, 31, 36, 39, 40, 56, 57, 59, 60, 64, 71, 72, 75, 76, 85, 87, 88, 91, 93, 94, 103, 123, 125, 129, 132, 133, 140, 141, 147, 148, 149, 151, 154, 157, 169, 170, 177, 184, 186, 188, 196, 204

Feast of Weeks 19, 38, 85, 109, 123, 148, 149, 152, 153, 175, 176, 211

Festival 30, 123, 124, 125, 127, 128, 142

Firmament 171

Firstfruit(s) 8, 16, 19, 36, 38, 39, 50, 60, 62, 74, 92, 94, 109, 117, 123, 129, 146, 147, 148, 149, 150, 153, 154, 197, 211, 212, this

Flood 27, 28, 30, 94, 112, 123, 126, 138, 141, 171, 173, 191, 192, 202, 203

Flute 148, 149

Forefathers 149

Forty 60, 78, 80, 85, 88, 89, 148, 186

Fountains 125

Friday V, 34, 51, 63, 72, 74, 75, 80, 91, 92, 97, 101, 106, 113, 114, 132, 151, 152, 153, 197

G

Galilee 84, 88, 107

Gematria 26, 28, 40, 112, 113, 139

Generation(s) 17, 28, 32, 36, 57, 64, 74, 90, 91, 126, 144, 151, 154, 155, 170, 183, 187, 189, 191, 192, 209

Geneva 41, 203, 204, 205, 209

Gentile(s) 8, 13, 15, 57, 62, 124, 127, 143, 172, 178, 197

Gethsemane V, 74, 103

Gilgal 151

God I, II, IX, XIII, XIV, XV, 6, 7, 8, 13, 16, 17, 18, 25, 26, 27, 45, 46, 52, 55, 56, 57, 59, 63, 64, 71, 79, 84, 85, 87, 88, 90, 92, 97, 106, 117, 132, 143, 146, 148, 149, 158, 166, 171, 173, 174, 175, 180, 182, 183, 184, 185, 186, 191, 200, 202, 204, 205, 206, 208, 210, 211, 213, 217

Gospel(s) IX, 13, 19, 25, 36, 49, 52, 58, 73, 74, 75, 79, 84, 86, 106, 108, 109, 110, 156, 157, 179, 197

Grammatical X, 4, 50, 51, 106, 204

Green's 20

H

Hag 20, 31, 123, 137, 172

Heis 3, 48, 108, 109

Henry 201, 208

Hezekiah 45, 74

High Priest 7, 8, 83, 92, 140, 148, 149, 152, 153, 197

Holiday(s) 18, 32, 89, 123, 124, 217

Holy Day(s) 4, 123

I

Ignorance 127

Inclusive Reckoning 38, 62, 74, 76, 78, 79, 85, 92, 149

Index XI, XII, 3, 4, 5, 6, 7, 19, 20, 31, 46, 48, 51, 98, 103, 109, 122, 167, 183, 207

Ingathering 14, 144,, 212

Iniquity 143, 154, 155

Instruction 16, 30, 32, 118, 137, 138, 139, 144, 166, 205

Intercalary 27, 29, 125, 126, 138, 144, 173

Intercalation 28, 29, 112, 125, 139, 140, 173

Interlinear X, XI, 5, 13, 20, 37, 48, 51, 62, 64, 65, 67, 71, 86, 89, 98, 114, 215

Interpretation XIV, 3, 10, 30, 31, 45, 47, 64, 65, 71, 100, 101, 107, 110, 117, 137, 142, 192, 206

Israel 25, 30, 33, 36, 39, 40, 55, 60, 61, 74, 77, 78, 83, 87, 88, 90, 91, 92, 93, 94, 101, 113, 124, 125, 127, 130, 131, 143, 144, 145, 146, 148, 149, 150, 151, 152, 153, 155, 156, 157, 166, 169, 170, 172, 173, 177, 178, 196, 212, 213, 218

J

Jacob II, 30, 125, 156, 203, 206, 210

Jamnima 138, 142

Jericho 151

Jerusalem XI, 8, 13, 14, 15, 60, 62, 77, 78, 79, 84, 85, 90, 92, 93, 101, 117, 118, 124, 128, 129, 130, 131, 132, 145, 146, 147, 148, 149, 151, 152, 154, 156, 157, 173, 174, 178, 215

Jew(s) I, III, V, 13, 18, 29, 30, 35, 45, 76, 77, 83, 91, 102, 104, 113, 121, 124, 128, 132, 138, 155, 156, 169, 170, 178, 179, 183, 195, 197

John I, 8, 13, 14, 52, 56, 63, 73, 83, 85, 86, 87, 88, 128, 146, 147, 174, 176, 179, 201, 202, 205, 210

Joshua 151

Jubilee(s) II, 26, 28, 31, 35, 38, 89, 125, 126, 127, 139, 141, 142, 143, 155, 169, 170, 173, 174, 178, 179, 180, 181, 182, 183, 185, 196, 197, 198, 217

Judah 77, 78, 104, 131, 173

Jupiter 83, 84

K

Kai 13, 105, 107, 108, 146

Karmel 144, 145

King II, XI, 3, 4, 7, 10, 15, 18, 28, 36, 37, 67, 71, 72, 77, 78, 79, 80, 87, 89, 90, 92, 94, 115, 117, 121, 129, 131, 140, 146, 150, 151, 156, 167, 169, 173, 179, 200, 202, 203, 204, 205, 206, 207, 208, 209, 210, 216, 217

Kuria 56

Kuriachi 58

L

Lamb 40, 74, 84, 85, 90, 92, 93, 94, 100, 123, 129, 145, 148, 151, 152, 157, 188, 211

Law III, XIII, 6, 7, 8, 9, 10, 15, 16, 17, 18, 20, 30, 32, 38, 46, 60, 63, 94, 97

Learned XIV, 20, 56, 71, 129, 177, 204

Leaven 39, 78, 93, 128, 147, 152, 154, 169

Levi 39, 84, 153, 166, 183

Levite(s)

Lunar III, 18, 29, 30, 34, 35, 39, 83, 90, 91, 93, 94, 104, 112, 114, 124, 126, 128, 137, 142, 143, 144, 150, 155, 156, 157, 166, 169, 170, 171, 172, 174, 178, 197, 213, 217

Luther 80

M

Magdalene 49, 59, 105, 106, 109, 110, 195

Magnify 10

Mainstream VI, 6, 9, 50, 97, 122

Manna 33, 60, 149, 153, 169

Manuscript(s) IX, XII, 3, 7, 20, 29, 50, 51, 71, 138, 171, 183, 201

Mars 83, 84

Mary 41, 49, 59, 64, 84, 85, 92, 93, 105, 106, 109, 110, 195, 201, 202, 204

Mazzaroth 138

Messiah IX, XIII, XIV, 10, 18, 61, 63, 83, 84, 90, 91, 97, 114, 123, 147, 149, 153, 158, 169, 170, 178, 213

Meta 9, 99, 100, 110, 111, 185

Methusela 31

Meton 143

Moed 31, 126, 137, 171, 172

Month 6, 15, 18, 25, 26, 27, 28, 30, 31, 32, 33, 34, 35, 40, 41, 77, 78, 79, 83, 85, 88, 89, 91, 92, 93, 94, 100, 112, 113, 114, 123, 124, 125, 126, 127, 130, 131, 132, 137, 139, 142, 143, 144, 145, 147, 149, 150, 151, 153, 155, 160, 165, 166, 167, 168, 169, 170, 172, 173, 178, 185, 186, 197, 211

Moon 30, 31, 83, 90, 91, 93, 124, 126, 127, 137, 138, 142, 144, 154, 155, 156, 157, 165, 166, 167, 168, 169, 170, 171, 172, 173, 174, 178, 197

Morrow 36, 37, 38, 88, 92, 98, 114, 115, 116, 148, 150, 217

Moses II, 8, 13, 15, 25, 28, 30, 31, 33, 36, 46, 61, 78, 85, 86, 88, 91, 94, 100, 101, 107, 113, 123, 124, 125, 130, 137, 142, 144, 149, 150, 151, 159, 166, 169, 170, 179, 183, 184, 185, 210

N

Nadab 87

Nazareth 88, 89

Nebuchadnezzar 77, 79, 91, 94, 130 131

New month 123, 124, 126, 127, 137, 144, 166, 167, 168, 169, 172

New moon 31, 126, 137, 144, 165, 166, 167, 168, 169, 171, 172, 173, 174

New year 84, 89, 138

Nicholas 80

O

Old Testament II, VI, XI, 4, 100, 165, 177, 215, 217

Ordinances 7, 8, 17, 121, 125, 127, 130, 131, 172, 178

Oxford 37, 49, 50, 122, 201, 204, 216, 217

P

Pagan(s) II, III, IX, 40, 46, 57, 63, 64, 79, 86, 87, 94, 124, 132, 142, 166, 170, 178

Palm 84, 92, 146, 147

Passion II, VII, 74, 75, 93, 97, 128, 197

Passover 8, 14, 36, 39, 40, 73, 74, 77, 79, 83, 90, 91, 92, 93, 94, 100, 101, 102, 106, 107, 113, 123, 128, 129, 148, 151, 152, 153, 155, 157, 197, 211

Path(s) 124, 127, 141, 210

Pattern II, 7, 18, 19, 25, 26, 27, 31, 33, 34, 35, 39, 62, 78, 85, 113, 126, 139, 140, 141, 150, 157, 170, 188, 196, 197

Paul II, XIV, 8, 10, 13, 14, 18, 62, 72, 110, 112, 114, 115, 116, 117, 118, 121, 122, 123, 124, 143, 169, 170, 177, 179, 184, 193

Pentecost 8, 14, 19, 35, 38, 39, 58, 78, 79, 84, 85, 86, 87, 88, 90, 109, 117, 123, 125, 129, 148, 149, 150, 154, 157, 170, 176, 197, 212

Pharisee(s) V, 14, 59, 60, 61, 74, 75, 88, 90, 91, 93, 98, 100, 101, 104, 112, 123, 127, 128, 129, 144, 147, 169, 175, 179, 195, 197, 205

Pope 80, 201, 206

Preparation VI, 15, 27, 32, 34, 40, 60, 61, 62, 72, 73, 74, 75, 77, 86, 93, 97, 98, 100, 101, 102, 104, 106, 107, 113, 117, 132, 148, 149, 151, 152, 153, 157, 188, 194, 195, 196, 202, 208, 211

Priest(s) XV, 7, 8, 13, 14, 15, 28, 32, 36, 39, 40, 58, 60, 62, 73, 74, 80, 83, 90, 91, 92, 93, 98, 100, 101, 114, 140, 142, 144, 147, 148, 149, 151, 152, 153, 154, 156, 166, 173, 175, 188, 195, 197, 203, 206, 208, 211

Protestant 46, 71, 177, 179, 200, 202, 206, 207, 209

Protos 4, 48, 51, 58, 109, 176

Pseudepigrapha 125, 178, 179, 217

Q

Queen 41, 202, 206, 207

R

Rabbis 10, 28, 29, 31, 57, 89, 91, 104, 113, 114, 126, 139, 142, 150

Redeem 29,, 113, 152, 174

Redemption 29, 40, 139, 148, 153, 155, 174, 211

Religion 63, 64, 114, 156, 157, 209

Remember 10, 14, 16, 19, 59, 61, 64, 67, 71, 88, 90, 91, 94, 107, 110, 112, 113, 137, 146, 147, 151, 152, 153, 156, 171, 187, 195, 200, 210

Remnant II, VIII, XIV, 90, 94, 113, 114, 138, 141, 155, 157, 170, 201

Reuben 153

Revelation 25, 27, 86, 141, 156, 157, 174, 79

Resurrection V, 13, 18, 25, 27, 33, 36, 39, 41, 45, 47, 56, 58, 59, 63, 64, 72, 74, 77, 80, 86, 108, 154, 177, 184, 197

Righteousness 112, 141, 142, 156

Ripen 143, 144, 153, 154, 157

S

Sabbatical 15, 20, 28, 29, 35, 86, 89, 90, 114, 139, 140, 141, 170, 174, 196, 197, 198

Sacrifice XIV, 7, 14, 15, 16, 39, 74, 87, 92, 93, 94, 101, 123, 129, 153, 207, 211

Sadducee(s) 61, 88, 90, 91, 93, 104

Saint(s) XIV, 19, 20, 27, 122, 123, 146, 147, 193

Salvation XIII, 16, 25, 26, 57, 60, 132, 147, 148, 157, 170, 171, 210, 211

Salvific 123

Saturn 55, 83, 84

Season(s) 93, 112, 113, 124, 126, 127, 128, 144, 156, 166, 169, 171, 172, 173, 178, 196

Sheave(s) 8, 60, 93, 145, 146, 147, 148, 149, 151, 152, 153, 188

Sinai 30, 33, 49, 64, 86, 88, 123, 131, 150, 151, 178

Singular 16, 20, 51, 67, 109, 111, 167, 168, 175, 184

Sivan 149

Standard V, XI, XII, 76, 93, 100, 129, 137, 143, 177, 207, 210, 215

Star(s) 29, 55, 56, 83, 90, 138, 167, 172, 173

Sun 15, 17, 19, 21, 26, 27, 28, 29, 30, 51, 56, 57, 63, 76, 86, 100, 108, 109, 138, 141, 146, 147, 156, 157, 167, 172, 173, 174, 195, 200

Sunday II, V, 18, 19, 30, 34, 38, 41, 45, 46, 47, 48, 56, 63, 74, 75, 80, 86, 92, 97, 108, 114, 117, 127, 132, 138, 147, 157, 185, 197

Symbol 39, 40, 64, 85, 113, 139, 146, 147, 152, 154, 156, 188, 204, 210, 213

Symbology 26

T

Tabernacle(s) 5, 7, 14, 19, 27, 29, 32, 39, 40, 78, 83, 84, 85, 90, 113, 117, 131, 132, 139, 144, 153, 157, 212

Talmud III, 14, 32, 60, 85, 113, 137, 138, 170

Temple 6, 7, 15, 25, 35, 58, 72, 74, 75, 79, 85, 92, 93, 101, 114, 128, 129, 130, 131, 132, 140, 147, 148, 149, 152, 153, 174, 175, 188, 211, 213

Theos 57

Thessalonians XII, 124, 143

Thirty 30, 78, 79, 89, 90.

Thursday 32, 40, 101, 112, 113, 114, 115, 130, 131, 132, 139, 140, 150, 151, 152

Time III, VI, XII, XV, 3, 6, 7, 13, 14, 15, 18, 19, 25, 26, 27, 28, 29, 30, 31, 32, 36, 37, 38, 39, 46, 49, 55, 57, 64, 71, 72, 73, 74, 77, 78, 79, 80, 83, 84, 85, 86, 88, 89, 90, 91, 93, 94, 97, 100, 101, 103, 104, 105, 106, 108, 110, 111, 112, 115, 116, 117, 118, 121, 122, 124, 125, 126, 127, 128, 129, 132, 137, 138, 139, 141, 143, 145, 148, 149, 151, 155, 156, 157, 166, 167, 169, 170, 171, 172, 173, 175, 178, 179, 182, 183, 184, 185, 186, 192, 195, 196, 197, 198, 200, 201, 202, 203, 204, 209, 212, 213, 217

Torah 14, 15, 31, 60, 89, 125, 137, 142, 144, 147, 149, 166, 173, 174, 178, 179, 218

Tradition I, II, IX, XIII, XIV, 3, 4, 6, 7, 8, 9, 10, 14, 16, 18, 30, 32, 40, 41, 45, 46, 47, 52, 57, 62, 67, 71, 80, 83, 84, 87, 89, 110, 121, 122, 124, 125, 137, 144, 177, 178, 193

Translation II, VI, XI, XIII, XIV, 3, 4, 6, 7, 8, 9, 17, 18, 19, 20, 30, 31, 32, 37, 38, 41, 45, 46, 47, 49, 50, 56, 57, 58, 60, 61, 64, 67, 71, 72, 87, 97, 98, 99, 100, 103, 105, 106, 108, 109, 110, 111, 114, 115, 117, 126, 137, 138, 139, 142, 143, 144, 147, 148, 156, 157, 165, 168, 169, 172, 173, 180, 183, 184, 185, 190, 195, 196, 201, 203, 204, 205, 206, 209, 210, 215, 218

Translator III, 3, 4, 7, 18, 20, 37, 40, 66, 71, 86, 107, 117, 121, 185, 205, 207, 209

Transliterated IX, 19, 20, 47, 55, 58, 123,

Transliteration IX, 5, 14, 16, 19, 20, 47, 49, 55, 57, 67, 110, 122, 186

Tribes 40, 91, 149, 151, 153, 172

Troas 110, 112, 114, 115, 116

Truth I, II, VI, VII, XI, XIII, XIV, 6, 30, 37, 40, 67, 71, 72, 86, 94, 97, 99, 113, 117, 121, 122, 124, 127, 137, 138, 143, 147, 158, 178, 185, 190, 192, 196, 215

Tyndale 41, 201, 203, 205

U

Unleavened XI, XIV, 8, 13, 16, 29, 39, 49, 73, 74, 78, 93, 100, 101, 106, 110, 114, 116, 123, 128, 129, 131, 139, 149, 151, 152, 153, 211, 212

US Naval XI, 83, 91, 93

V

Vine 40, 216

Visible 34, 112, 125, 166, 169

W

Walk XIII, 56, 59, 60, 61, 62, 87, 108, 121, 127, 129, 173, 178

Wave-sheaf 147, 148, 152, 170

Wave-sheaves 146, 147

Way I, XIII, 10, 15, 18, 25, 26, 27, 32, 35, 39, 40, 57, 58, 60, 62, 71, 77, 80, 84, 94, 97, 100, 105, 116, 122, 123, 124, 125, 127, 142, 144, 145, 146, 147, 156, 177, 191

Wednesday V, 28, 34, 40, 76, 80, 83, 86, 91, 92, 93, 94, 101, 113, 115, 132, 152, 153, 197

Week I, V, VI, VII, 3, 4, 5, 13, 15, 18, 19, 20, 21, 25, 26, 27, 28, 29, 30, 31, 32, 33, 34, 35, 36, 37, 38, 39, 40, 45, 46, 47, 48, 49, 51, 52, 55, 56, 58, 59, 61, 62, 63, 64, 65, 66, 67, 71, 72, 73, 74, 75, 76, 78, 79, 80, 85, 86, 87, 88, 89, 94, 97, 98, 102, 104, 107, 108, 109, 110, 112, 113, 114, 116, 117, 123, 127, 129, 131, 132, 139, 140, 141, 144, 145, 148, 149, 150, 151, 152, 153, 156, 160, 166, 168, 169, 171, 175, 176, 180, 181, 182, 185, 186, 188, 197, 198, 208, 211

Wilderness 26, 33, 45, 84, 86, 88, 91, 113, 123, 149, 150, 151, 153, 156, 169, 179, 192, 212

Women 59, 60, 76, 77, 106, 107, 192, 211

Wycliff 41, 201, 203

X, Y

Yereach 165, 166

Yom 31, 39, 137, 170, 172, 180, 184

YHVH III, IX, 30, 31, 33, 34, 46, 52, 56, 60, 63, 64, 67, 78, 79, 84, 86, 89, 90, 91, 92, 94, 104, 112, 113, 114, 115, 117, 122, 123, 124, 125, 126, 129, 130, 132, 133, 137, 138, 140, 142, 143, 144, 147, 150, 151, 153, 154, 156, 157, 173, 174, 179, 180, 182, 186, 187, 188, 190, 191, 192, 193, 196, 206, 211, 215

Young's XI, 5, 6, 20, 215, 216

Z

Zachariah 85

Zedekiah 77, 79

Personal Notes

Milton Keynes UK
Ingram Content Group UK Ltd.
UKHW031814110124
435868UK00007B/555